For the first time in history tank was to encounter tank.

Page 189.

TANK WARFARE

THE STORY OF THE TANKS
IN THE GREAT WAR

By
F. Mitchell, M.C.

With many Illustrations from photographs, maps, etc.
and from original drawings by
Reginald Cleaver
and
Captain R. L. Phillips

THOMAS NELSON AND SONS LTD
LONDON EDINBURGH NEW YORK TORONTO PARIS

All rights reserved
THOMAS NELSON AND SONS, LTD.
London :
35-36 Paternoster Row, E.C.4
Edinburgh :
Parkside Works, Dalkeith Road
Paris :
25 rue Denfert-Rochereau
Toronto :
91-93 Wellington Street West
New York :
381-385 Fourth Avenue

First published September 1933
Reprinted October 1934 ; October 1935

CONTENTS

1. The origin of tanks—Undaunted pioneers—Little Willie and Big Willie—The camp of mystery 1

2. A chapter about machinery, which can be skipped by those who prefer to go straight on with the story in Chapter 3—What a tank is—How it goes—What it is capable of doing 15

3. The curtain goes up on the Somme—Amazement and terror of the Boche—What the Tommies thought 25

4. The all-conquering "female"—Mud—Through snow and ice at Beaumont-Hamel 39

5. Mark II.—The tank loses its tail—Bellying and ditching —The struggle for existence 44

6. Smashing through at Arras—The cruise of the *Lusitania* —In the snow at Bullecourt—The lone fight at Monchy — Armour - piercing bullets — Undaunted crews 49

7. Training at home—Strenuous times at the Cadet School —The depot at Wool—Thrills of the first tank ride 68

8. Improvements—The Mark IV. tank—Blowing up the Boche—The unditching beam—The "hush-hush" scheme 88

9. The dreaded salient—Treachery—Ugly rumours—How to empty a "pill-box"—Fighting for sixty-two hours—*Fray Bentos* holds up the Boche . . . 99

10. Swallowed up in the mud—Captain Robertson wins the V.C., and establishes a tradition—The Poelcapelle disaster—Whitehall loses faith—Salvage . . . 117

11. *The Only Way* at Cambrai—The general leads his land fleet—Triumph of the tanks—Captain Wain achieves the impossible—The lone gunner—A tank commander at bay 131

CONTENTS

12. The extra hand—A gearsman sees red—Desperate fighting at Fontaine—A tank to the rescue—Shaking off the Boche—How Private Smith died . . . 152

13. The Great Retreat—Repairing a breakdown—Attacked by aeroplanes—A rearguard action—The mad sergeant—Holding the gap—A bold raider . . . 164

14. Villers-Bretonneux—Tank meets tank—Whippets in full cry—The turning of the tide 184

15. The Mark V. arrives—The German tanks—With the "Aussies" at Hamel—Brave Americans—A brilliant show—With the French at Moreuil . . . 199

16. How a battle is planned—Mark V. star tanks—Bluff—Detraining at night—Spying out the land—Battle orders—The approach march—The hi-hi bird . 212

17. The exploded dump—Zero hour—A receipt for a village—Tiny and Co.—The great cruise of *Musical Box*—Thrilling raid of armoured cars—Flotsam . . 231

18. The faithful servant—The man of peace—"Slippery" in a tight corner—The perfect little gentleman—Buried alive—Fruits of victory 248

19. Tank crews sorely tried—A lame tank—A one-man tank—Never say die! 257

20. Crossing the Canal du Nord—The attack of the wooden tanks—Peace at last—The flag reaches Cologne . 267

21. Tanks in Egypt—The French *chars d'assaut*—The U.S.A. Tank Corps 273

22. What the tanks accomplished—The infantry's battering-ram—How they affected the Germans—A civilian force 282

23. Post-war machines—Mechanized warfare—Cross-country lorries—The amphibious tank—The pole-jumping tank—The four-track tank—The Halger-Ultra bullet—Tanks in the future—Destruction or peace? 291

GLOSSARY OF TANK TERMS 306

INDEX 309

LIST OF ILLUSTRATIONS

"For the first time in history tank was to encounter tank" . . . . *Frontispiece*	
Approach March	1
A Mark I. tank in action on the Somme . . .	24
"A tank is walking up the High Street at Flers, with the British Army cheering behind" . .	32
Diagram showing position of crew and guns in Mark IV. tank	89
Daily Tank Log	103
"They swarmed over the machine" . . .	160
A Whippet tank	166
After the heavy fighting at Fontaine-Notre-Dame .	196
A captured German tank, the *Elfriede* . . .	196
Section of Mark V. tank	200
"Suddenly swerved, crushing both guns and gunners into the ground"	206
An aerial photograph of the German front near Dodo Wood	216
O.P. Chart	220–221
Secret Barrage Map	224–225
The Carden-Loyd amphibian tank coming ashore .	296

ACKNOWLEDGMENTS

THANKS are due to the authors for kindly allowing me to quote from the following volumes : *Tanks, 1914-1918*, by Sir Albert G. Stern ; *Tanks in the Great War*, by Major-General J. F. C. Fuller ; *The Tank Corps*, by Major Clough Williams-Ellis ; and to the Editor of *The Spectator* for permission to reprint an article by me from this periodical, which appears as part of Chapter 12 ; to Messrs. J. M. Dent and Sons, Ltd., for permission to use the story of my tank duel, which was published in *Everyman at War* ; to Mr. D. G. Browne for permission to use material from his book, *The Tank in Action*, and one of his photographs ; to *The Tank Corps Book of Honour*, edited by Major R. F. G. Maurice, used for reference while writing this book ; and to Captain R. L. Phillips, R.A.S.C. (T.A.), for his valuable help with sketches.

Thanks are due also to the War Office and H.M. Stationery Office for permission to reproduce part of the 1/20,000 War Map produced by the First Survey Battalion, Royal Engineers, which appears on pages 224 and 225 ; the Imperial War Museum for permission to use a photograph of the Mark V. tank for guidance in making the sectional drawing on page 200 ; the Air Ministry for the aerial photograph on page 216 ; and *The Illustrated London News* for permission to base the frontispiece and wrapper upon a drawing which appeared in that periodical.

F. M.

TANK WARFARE

CHAPTER 1

The origin of tanks—Undaunted pioneers—Little Willie and Big Willie—The camp of mystery.

WAR brings out the worst and the best in men, and under its murderous pressure things are accomplished which in times of peace would be called incredible. But in the Great War, 1914-18, the British were the only nation to produce an entirely new weapon. British inventive brains, combined with the solidity of British engineering ability, brought forth the Tank, that strange monster of iron which has revolutionized the art of warfare.

It was constructed with the object of assisting and protecting the infantry when they were advancing under fire, and was the first machine which really succeeded in its object, though many attempts had been made in the past, ranging from the war-chariots of the ancient Assyrians and Britons and the Chinese war-cart of 1200 B.C. to the sailing-ship on wheels which is said to have been made for the Prince of Orange in 1599.

Probably the first mechanically propelled machine of the kind was that invented in 1769 by a Frenchman named Cugnot, who constructed a steam-engine on a wagon body. It managed to reach a speed of two and a half miles an hour, but had to stop every twenty minutes to get up steam, and when the inventor displayed its prowess to representatives of the French Government by knocking down a wall, he was put in prison. The first real step towards the development of the tank, however, was the invention by an American, in 1888, of a steam-wagon running on an endless caterpillar track, the caterpillar system having originated in the device of an Englishman, Richard Lovell Edgeworth, which was patented as far back as 1770.

Batter's tractor anticipates the tank in many details, especially in the steering gear. With the coming of the high-speed internal-combustion engine the way was made clear, for it was a combination of this engine and the caterpillar track that enabled a vehicle to cross soft ground by means of a track or endless belt, in such a manner that the weight was distributed over a large area of ground.

Several experiments in motor-driven caterpillar tractors were made before the war by the War Office, though not for fighting purposes, and in 1903 Mr. H. G. Wells, who has foretold many things, wrote a prophetic story vividly describing monstrous war machines somewhat akin to tanks.

More strange than this is the story of Mr. L. E. Mole, an Australian, who in 1912 actually submitted to the War Office a design for a climbing, fighting, track-driven machine. In its pivoted ends and flexible chain tracks for steering a curved course it seems to have been superior to the tank. Such a startling proposal was immediately put out of sight by the authorities, and the design had no influence at all on the actual invention of the tank, because the War Office took no action concerning it, and the plans were not generally known until the war was over.

EARLY EFFORTS

There is also a story of a Nottingham plumber who submitted a design for an armoured cross-country machine to the War Office some years before the war. The plumber received the usual letter of acknowledgment, but heard nothing more. After the war had been over some time the plan was discovered in a dusty pigeon-hole marked, " The man is mad."

Germany can also claim a tank inventor, for in 1913 Herr Goebel designed an armoured land cruiser, a terrific affair bristling with guns, which he drove up and over an obstacle in the shape of a ninety-foot pyramid at Pinne in Posen. In 1914 he tried to repeat the demonstration before a huge crowd at the Berlin Stadium. The machine began to climb up a short slope of thirty degrees, but came suddenly to a standstill, and in spite of his frantic efforts Herr Goebel could not start it again. The crowd became tired of waiting and held a meeting of protest, at which they indignantly demanded their money back, and so many insults were hurled at the unfortunate inventor that he never dared again to submit his invention to the public gaze.

All these preliminary attempts came to nothing, because they lacked the terrible impetus of war-time necessities, but the Great War made the coming of the tank almost inevitable.

Two months after the outbreak of the war a state of deadlock existed along the whole western front, from the Belgian coast to the Swiss frontier. It was almost possible to walk from end to end of this great line of trenches, which were protected by thick belts of barbed wire, machine guns, and quick-firing artillery. It was impossible for either side to break through, and all attacks resulted in heavy losses, the attacking troops being held up by uncut wire, and slaughtered by the sweeping fire of machine guns.

TANK WARFARE

In 1915 the Germans almost succeeded in smashing through the line at Ypres by using poison gas, but this foul method of warfare, which was in direct opposition to the Hague Convention, recoiled on their own heads, for the Allies used it against them, and as the prevailing winds on the French front were westerly, the enemy received much more than he ever gave. An antidote, too, was soon found in the gas mask.

Poison gas could never break the deadlock. Some entirely new weapon had to be found.

In October 1914 Lieut.-Colonel E. D. Swinton, a man of great foresight and imagination, who was then acting as Official Military Correspondent with the British Expeditionary Force, under the name of "Eyewitness," came to the conclusion that some sort of armoured machine was necessary, which could force its way through barbed wire, climb across trenches, and destroy or crush machine guns.

Before the war his keen mind had studied deeply the art of outwitting the enemy. I remember as a boy reading with great delight his thrilling tales of warfare called the *Green Curve*, which he wrote under the name of "Ole Luke Oie." Little did I realize then that I should one day be in the corps which his powerful imagination had brought into being, and of which he was the original commander.

A friend had written to him telling him about a Holt caterpillar, "a Yankee tractor which could climb like the devil." "Ah, here is the very thing to cross trenches!" thought Colonel Swinton, and he sent forward a scheme to the War Office, on October 20, 1914, for the construction of caterpillar machine-gun destroyers. They were to be heavily armoured, equipped with guns and machine guns, and capable of crossing trenches, and either cutting or flattening out barbed wire.

COLONEL SWINTON'S PLAN

Thus was the idea of the tank born!

Its history, until that idea took shape and became a real solid tank fifteen months later, is of one long fight against officialdom.

The War Office, as perhaps was only natural, did not take kindly to any original suggestions. Some of the higher officials pointed out that such fantastic machines would take over a year to build, and by that time the war would be over, so for the time being the scheme was turned down.

But Colonel Swinton was not easily daunted; he returned to the charge in January 1915, and again urged the War Office to consider his proposals. This time something was done. In February 1915 experiments were made with an adapted Holt tractor. It was tried out over obstacles, which it was not designed to negotiate, and consequently failed. A Foster-Daimler wheeled tractor of 155 h.p., which had been fitted with a novel trench-bridging device, was also tested in May, but it was not successful in crossing trenches, and so the idea of a land-cruiser was abandoned as impracticable.

In the meantime, unknown to the War Office, other forces had been experimenting and planning. Colonel Swinton's proposals had been seen by Mr. Winston Churchill, the First Lord of the Admiralty, and his restless, intelligent imagination grasped at once the tremendous possibilities of the idea. He had had experience with armoured cars in Belgium, and the R.N.A.S. (Royal Naval Air Service), now that warfare was stationary in France, was idly kicking its heels in England. He was therefore anxious that they should be employed in naval fighting on land, and the very name of land-cruisers appealed to him instantly.

In January 1915 he wrote to Mr. Asquith, then Prime Minister, suggesting that some form of trench-crossing machine should be made. He also proposed the use of large armoured shields on wheels, and the fitting up of steam-tractors with armoured shelters. His idea was not so much the construction of a weapon of offence as an armoured vehicle for carrying troops forward under fire. He was also turning over in his mind a plan, made by Major Hetherington, R.N.A.S., for the construction of a huge landship with three big wheels.

This was to consist of a platform, mounted on three wheels, and armed with three turrets, each containing two 4-inch guns, and propelled by an 800-h.p. Sunbeam Diesel set.

The diameter of the wheels was to be 40 feet, the length of the machine 100 feet, the height 46 feet, clearance 17 feet, and top speed 8 miles per hour !

It was reckoned that this tremendous machine would be able to pass over water obstacles having good banks, and from 20 feet to 30 feet width of waterway. Also, owing to its clearance, it would ford rivers with good beds where the water was not more than 15 feet deep. Small obstacles, such as banks, ditches, bridges, trenches, and wire entanglements it could easily roll over. Such was the optimism of 1914 that it was hoped that these machines would be used in crossing the Rhine.

The Landship Committee was formed in February 1915 to study the question under Mr. D'Eyncourt, who came to the conclusion that the weight of such a vast machine would be at least 1,000 tons, and that it would offer too great a target to artillery.

It was therefore decided to build some on a smaller scale, and six 16-feet big-wheel landships were ordered, while experiments were also made with steam-rollers joined together, creeping-grip caterpillars, and pedrail tractors.

In June 1915 the War Office, which had definitely

abandoned its idea of land-cruisers in May, suddenly heard for the first time of the activities of the Admiralty Landship Committee. The result was that a joint Naval and Military Committee was formed.

The big landships had now been abandoned, for the wooden models, or "mock-ups," as they were called, showed the design to be too fantastic, and in August this struggling band of enthusiasts received another set back. The whole of the Armoured Car Division was disbanded, and Squadron 20, R.N.A.S., which had carried out all the experimental work, was threatened with an immediate transfer to the Army.

As the Army refused to give a single man for this newfangled landship fleet, in despair the committee appealed to Mrs. Pankhurst for suffragettes, and although no details of the work could be given, sixty women immediately volunteered. But they were not required. The Admiralty was at last persuaded by Mr. D'Eyncourt to hand over Squadron 20 of the Armoured Car Reserve, and to increase the strength of this unit from 50 to 600 men.

About this time Colonel Swinton, the man who had first suggested the use of tanks, returned from France to a post at the War Office. He was delighted to hear of the existence of the Landship Committee, and immediately arranged an interview with the secretary.

"Lieutenant Stern," he said, "this is the most extraordinary thing I have ever seen. The Director of Naval Construction appears to be making land battleships for the Army, who have never asked for them and are doing nothing to help. You have nothing but naval ratings doing all your work. What on earth are you? Are you a mechanic or a chauffeur?"

"A banker," replied Lieutenant Stern, most truthfully.

TANK WARFARE

After this meeting Colonel Swinton did everything in his power to help the tank idea forward.

Mr. Tritton and Lieutenant Wilson, two brilliant engineers, working day and night, evolved the design of "Tritton" or "Little Willie," after the nickname given to the German Crown Prince by our troops. Colonel Swinton saw the full-sized model at Lincoln, and described it to General Headquarters as follows :

"The naval people are pressing on with the first sample caterpillar. They have succeeded in making an animal that will cross 4 feet 6 inches, and turn on its own axis like a dog with a flea in its tail."

But when eventually constructed and tried out, "Little Willie" developed certain faults. He had a defective balance. His centre of gravity had somehow slipped.

The War Office was now asking for a machine that could cross a trench 5 feet wide with a parapet 4 feet 6 inches high. For this "Little Willie" was too short, and so the undaunted pair, Lieutenant Wilson and Mr. Tritton, set to work again on a new design. They reckoned it would require a wheel with a diameter of 15 feet. They pondered and sketched, they sketched and pondered, when suddenly a brilliant thought occurred to them: "Why not have the tracks passing completely round the body of the machine ? "

Then, with great excitement, they gradually worked out the peculiar shape of the first tank, which was based on the big-wheel idea. The underside is really the segment of a wheel, and the tracks, instead of going round the circumference, turn back at the level of the axle practically at right angles over the nose, and so along the top of the body.

But although everything was complete on paper, numberless experiments had to be made to produce a

THE SOLUTION

track strong enough to bear the heavy weight of the thickly armoured body. All manner of tracks were tested, but without success. It seemed as if at the last moment the inventors would have to throw up the sponge. In despair they tried a track of Balata belting, but even this was not satisfactory.

Then on September 22, 1915, Lieutenant Stern received the following triumphant telegram:

"Balata died on test bench yesterday morning. New arrival by Tritton out of Pressed Plate. Light in weight but very strong. All doing well, thank you.

"PROUD PARENTS."

Thus was announced the birth of the "Wilson" machine, which was later called H.M. Landship *Centipede*, and finally "Mother," as it was the first of all tanks. All tanks of this make were termed "Big Willies." A full-sized model was inspected by the military authorities and approved, except by some members of the War Office, who were highly annoyed to think that the Admiralty had a finger in the pie.

Running the track over the top solved the greatest problem, but created another. Where were the guns to be placed? Finally they were put in sponsons on each side of the tank—a "sponson" being the naval term for a structure projecting beyond the side of a ship, in which a gun is installed. This projection is essential to allow the gun to be fired clear of the side and directly ahead and astern. With the two 6-pounder guns and shields these two tank sponsons weighed about three tons.

So at last, in December 1915, "Mother," the first of all tanks, was completed by Messrs. Foster of Lincoln, and on her trial trip she behaved splendidly. But would she ever be used?

The enthusiastic Mr. Churchill was fully determined

that she should be. On 3rd December he wrote a paper to G.H.Q., called " Variants of the Offensive," suggesting that caterpillar tractors should be used to break through the enemy's lines, followed by infantry under cover of bullet-proof shields. He also proposed that the attack should take place at night with the aid of powerful searchlights.

On Christmas Day, 1915, Sir Douglas Haig, the new Commander-in-Chief, read the paper and pinned to it a slip on which he wrote in pencil : " Is anything known about the caterpillar referred to in para. 4, page 3 ? "

This slip turned out to be a real Christmas box, for it brought on the scene an actor who was to play one of the principal parts in the thrilling drama, " Tanks on the Western Front "—a young Lieut.-Colonel of the Royal Engineers named Elles. He was sent to England to obtain an answer to the pencilled query, and the mission changed his career, for he became a wholehearted champion of the new ideas of warfare, and later the general in command of the Tank Corps.

The construction of the first tank naturally had to be kept a great secret. Everybody connected with it was sworn to secrecy, and anybody suspected of talking was threatened with internment under D.O.R.A. (Defence of the Realm Act). Ladies who had heard about the mystery machines were told that if the secret reached the enemy thousands of lives would be lost. Those who knew about the existence of the Landship Committee were informed that all the experiments had failed, and that the people concerned had lost their jobs, a report which was readily believed.

At the office of the Landship Committee the plans were kept in a safe guarded at night by a civil servant, and the committee decided to change its name, lest the word " landship " should betray the secret.

THE ORIGIN OF "TANK"

In the earlier stages of its manufacture the machine resembled a cistern or reservoir, and it was decided to call it a "water-carrier"; but a difficulty arose. In Government offices committees are always known by their initials, and the secretary of the "Water-Carrier" Committee thought that the new title would be highly unsuitable, if not ludicrous! The name was therefore changed to "tank," and the committee was called the "Tank Supply," or "T.S." Committee. So originated the name by which these machines came to be known in every part of the world.

"Big Willie," or "Mother," was given an official trial on 2nd February at Hatfield Park, before an audience which included Mr. Lloyd George and Lord Kitchener. Everybody was very astonished and enthusiastic except Lord Kitchener, who called it "a pretty mechanical toy," and said most emphatically that the war would never be won by such machines. Forty tanks were ordered immediately by G.H.Q., France, and this number was increased by the War Office to one hundred.

Thus the tank came into being. It had not only been produced, but actually paid for, entirely from naval funds, and the design and experiments had been made almost entirely by naval men. It was in every sense of the word a real "landship," which the mere landlubbers at the War Office had failed to appreciate, and at times had tried hard to sink without trace.

The order for the first hundred tanks, which later on was increased to a hundred and fifty, was given to Messrs. Foster and Co., Lincoln, and the Metropolitan Carriage, Wagon, and Finance Co., Birmingham. It was one of the most remarkable feats of the war on the "home front" that these machines, of completely new design, were constructed in six months in absolute secrecy. The country at the time was short of steel,

TANK WARFARE

and the whole energies of the factories were devoted to making shells; but the British engineers proved that they could tackle the hardest tasks and complete them in a shorter time than any other country in the world.

When the first drawings of the proposed tanks were sent to the manager's office at the factory, the staff thought that the Tank Supply Committee must have been composed of madmen to submit such absurd designs. The secret was explained to them, and they were asked what sentries and methods of isolation they would require to preserve complete secrecy.

They decided, after due deliberation, not to have any secrecy at all. They simply told their employees and friends that these strange armour-plated monsters were water-tanks ordered by the Russian Government, and in order to make the lie more effective they had painted on every tank an inscription in Russian which read, "With care to Petrograd"! Apparently every one was ready to believe that the Russians were queer people, who would naturally order weird-looking designs of water-tanks, so no curiosity was aroused, and thus the construction of tanks went on quite openly.

In March 1916 the Heavy Section Motor Machine-Gun Corps was formed under the command of Colonel Swinton. Officers and men were volunteers from other regiments, and everybody had had previous engineering experience. All they were told was that they would be required for an experimental armoured-car unit. The camp was at Bisley, and two new arrivals were amazed when they were informed that the Motor Machine-Gun Corps had left two days before for Siberia. However, Siberia turned out to be the name of a camp not far away.

The mystified volunteers were trained in the use of Vickers and Hotchkiss machine guns, and sent to the naval gunnery school at Whale Island for a course in the

THE FIRST BATTALION

6-pounder gun. Wild rumours went round the camp regarding the wonderful new machines they would soon be driving, but nobody had any definite information.

In June the whole battalion was moved to a specially prepared training ground at Elveden, near Thetford, in Norfolk. Here the bewildered companies became more mystified than ever. They found themselves in an area about five miles square, which was completely cut off from the public gaze. All inhabited farms and cottages within the area had been evacuated, and a road running across it had been closed.

The ground itself contained an exact copy of a part of the line in France, and was hidden by three rows of plantations and guarded by six lines of sentries as well as cavalry patrols. No one was allowed to go in without a pass, and the troops were kept practically prisoners, as they could only leave the area on production of a special pass, which was very difficult to obtain. Aeroplanes were strictly forbidden to fly over this secret enclosure, and any who broke this rule were immediately fired at.

Prominent notices were posted up warning the public that it was a dangerous explosive area. Local rumour asserted that a tremendous shaft was being dug from which a tunnel was to be made to Germany!

Naturally the men of the Machine-Gun Corps Battalion were keyed up to the highest pitch of excitement. Eagerly they waited for the arrival of the mystery machines. It was rumoured that they could climb trees, swim across rivers, and hop about like kangaroos! False alarms were continually being given. Somebody would rush into a hut breathlessly announcing that he had distinctly heard the throb of a strange engine, and immediately the whole camp rushed out helter-skelter to see if the long-expected cars had come.

TANK WARFARE

Owing to labour difficulties the production of tanks was not going forward as fast as was at first anticipated, and amongst other things there was a shortage of 6-pounder shells, which were eventually obtained from the Japanese, who shipped 25,000 rounds back to England.

At last some " Big Willies " and a few " Little Willies " arrived at dead of night, and the training began in earnest. Every officer and man was bursting with keenness, and willing to devote all his time to learning how to drive and work the tank. They looked upon breakdowns as a delightful experience, which gave them the opportunity of putting their knowledge of the mechanism to a test, and though there were only a few machines available for training, so that many of the crews had no tanks of their own until they went to France in August, they soon mastered all that could be learned on the " home front."

The great surprise was now nearly ready.

CHAPTER 2

A chapter about machinery, which can be skipped by those who prefer to go straight on with the story in Chapter 3—What a tank is—How it goes—What it is capable of doing.

WHAT was it like, this strange new monster? And how did it work?

Seen from the side, the tank had the shape of a parallelogram with rounded corners. In the bottom corner, at the rear, were the sprocket wheels, whose deeply notched circumferences engaged with the links on the underside of the track plates, and drove the hull along the track. In the top corner, in front, was the "idle" wheel which guided the track over the nose of the hull, and could be adjusted to tighten up or loosen the track when required. Both tracks went right round the hull, and the weight of the machine was carried upon the track by means of rollers which ran right along the underside. These and other main features were common to all tanks, and this description of the earliest types will be clearer if the reader turns to the sectional drawing of a later type, Mark V., which appears on page 200, besides glancing at the pictures of the Mark I. tank in action, on pages 24 and 32.

The space in the steel hull between the caterpillar tracks contained the machinery and crew, and, being only just over 7 feet high, was none too roomy.

In the forward part of the machine, in a kind of conning tower or cab, were seated the tank commander

TANK WARFARE

and driver. The upper section of the tower was raised one foot above the level of the track, and in the forward wall, in front of each seat, was a rectangular window which could be closed from inside by a steel flap. Below the windows, the front wall sloped downwards as far as foot level, where it met the floor which here sloped upwards, thus making the front of the tank pointed like a fish. This shape was necessary to accommodate the feet of the tank commander and driver.

The driver, on the right, drove the machine and looked after the gear changing, whilst the officer, in the left-hand seat, manipulated the hand-brakes for steering slightly in either direction.

In the middle of the conning tower, between the windows, was a machine gun mounted on a ball-socket, which enabled it to be turned in any direction without displaying any gaps. The officer's seat was made slightly higher than the driver's in order to give more effective control of the gun. The positions of the crew and guns (in a Mark IV. type) are shown in the diagram on page 89.

The middle of the interior of the tank was occupied by the engine, on both sides of which was a narrow gangway. Two or more pipes led from the top of the engine to the silencer, from which a long exhaust pipe went down to the back of the tank, almost as far as the earth, thus preventing the flames from the exhaust pipe from being seen in the distance.

In the earliest model no silencer was provided, and consequently the noise, sparks, and flames emitted by the open exhaust pipes revealed the presence of tanks to the enemy. In their efforts to overcome this defect some of the crews fixed up silencers made out of oil drums, or damped out the sparks with wet sacks, or covered the exhaust pipe with clay and mud.

The rear portion of the interior was occupied by the

THE TANK INTERIOR

differential gear and cross shafts, with secondary gears from which the drive was carried by coventry chains to the driving sprockets. Between the differential and the engine was the gear-box, and above it the huge curved starting handle. Against the rear wall, behind the differential, was the radiator, with a ventilator, and from the radiator pipes ran along the roof to the engine.

From each side projected a sponson containing guns.

The type known as the male tank carried in each sponson a 6-pounder gun, protected by a close-fitting revolving shield, and a machine gun, its complete armament consisting of two 6-pounders and four machine guns. The other type, the female tank, had much narrower sponsons, each containing two machine guns behind revolving shields, and was armed with six machine guns but no 6-pounders. In both types the racks containing the shells and ammunition were situated in the space between the top of the engine and the roof.

The male tanks had small doors in each sponson, which were the cause of many sore heads to those careless ones who forgot to stoop when clambering in. The females had only a narrow door, some two feet high, underneath each sponson. One crawled in head first, and then pulled one's feet up; coming out, the feet were thrust through first on to the ground, and then the body was gradually lowered until the head could clear the sponson. If a tank was hit and set on fire these doors were practically useless as a means of escape for a crew of eight men.

There was also a manhole in the roof provided with loopholes, through which revolvers could be fired, and in the rear wall of the tank, near the radiator, was a horrible little opening through which a very skinny man might attempt to wriggle in a last desperate effort to escape.

TANK WARFARE

A fan sucked in fresh air through the radiator and helped to ventilate the stuffy interior, but in spite of this the inside of a tank, with an average temperature of 125° Fahrenheit, was hardly a health resort.

The original Mark I. tank trailed behind it two steering wheels, which, by means of a hydraulic lifting apparatus, could be raised from the ground or pressed down on to it, to help the tank over obstacles and to minimize bumping. These wheels were found to be in the way, and were later abolished. They can be seen in the pictures on pages 24 and 32.

The engine of the first tanks was a 105-h.p. Daimler, six-cylinder, sleeve-valve engine. Power was transmitted through a primary two-speed gear-box which was under the direct control of the driver, who could thus obtain first and second speeds, or reverse without other assistance.

The drive was then conducted through a differential, which carried a secondary two-speed gear-box on each outer end of the shaft. These secondary gears were operated by hand levers, manipulated by a gearsman, one to each track. The drive was then carried by chain to the driving sprockets at the rear of each track.

The two caterpillar tracks ran completely round the body, and consisted each of ninety hard plates of pressed steel. The tracks, however, did not actually move over the ground, but the sprocket wheels engaging with the links on the underside of the track plates drove the body along the tracks. In other words, the tank laid its own track, drove along it, then picked it up behind, and passed it over its head before laying it down in front again.

It was the all-round track which gave the tank its climbing power, because no matter at what angle the machine was to the horizontal it always presented a gripping surface. The fact also that the track was raised

TRACK AND ENGINE

in front gave an initial elevation, when an obstacle was encountered, which very greatly assisted in climbing banks and parapets. On the level, the machine rested on no more than four or five feet of its length, thus showing its derivation from the big wheel, and this gave it a slight rocking motion when it was on the move.

The point of balance was practically in the centre of the tank. A good driver could make the heavy machine sway in see-saw fashion on the edge of a jump, and also lower it quite gently over very steep drops. I believe that there is only one case known of a heavy tank turning turtle, and that was one that got out of control on a steep slope, and rushed headlong down a series of precipitous terraces.

When a tank was going into action, the driver first turned on the petrol and three or four of the crew swung round the big cranking handle until, with a great roar, the engine started up.

In the first tanks the petrol was carried inside the machine, at the sides of the front cab, and was transferred to the carburettor by gravity. When, therefore, a tank became ditched in a shell hole, nose downwards, the petrol supply was cut off, and in order to keep the engine running, the dangerous practice of hand feeding, or filling the carburettor straight from the petrol tin, had to be adopted. Later a pressure-fed system was installed, but as it was always going wrong and was decidedly dangerous, it was abandoned in favour of the " Autovac " system, which in the Mark IV. machine drew the petrol from the outside supply tank by suction, and then delivered it to the carburettor by gravity.

When the engine was running steadily the doors of the sponsons were closed and bolted from the inside, and the tank crawled out to battle. The driver was fully occupied in driving, peeping at the ground ahead, and making the necessary gear changes for turning. The officer, his map and aeroplane photographs on his knees, peered anxiously through the holes in the flap or through a periscope, picking up landmarks, directing the driver, putting the gunners on to targets, and occasionally firing bursts from his own Lewis gun as figures loomed up in front of the tank.

In the sponsons behind him, the 6-pounder gunner, kneeling on the floor, his eye glued to the telescopic sight, his finger on the trigger, swept his gun round in search of machine guns and enemy artillery batteries. As the gun flashed vividly, a terrific booming sound filled the tank interior, and the breech recoiled past the gunner's face, which was protected by a shield. His mate, crouched on the narrow floor, quickly unloaded and thrust another shell into the hungry breech. The empty shell cases fell on the floor and were thrown outside, through a small opening on the underside of the sponson door. The machine gun in the rear of the sponson was operated sometimes by the No. 2 of the 6-pounder gun, and sometimes by the gearsman, who sat on a seat near the differential.

In the other sponson the 6-pounder gun and machine gun blazed away in a similar manner. Sometimes all four guns were working at the same time and the din was tremendous, even drowning the steady throbbing of the 105-h.p. engine. The tank soon became full of petrol and cordite fumes, but the crew dared not open a flap or loophole to get fresh air for fear of the enemy machine-gun bullets, which beat against the armoured sides like hail.

The tank had a range of four speeds, from three-quarters of a mile an hour on bottom gear to four miles an hour on top gear, its average speed across broken country being two miles an hour.

GUNS AND GEARS

The driver was himself able to change from first to second speed, but if he wished to go faster he could only obtain third and fourth speeds by banging on the engine cover with his right hand. When he had attracted the attention of the gearsmen sitting at the back of the tank, he lifted up one or two fingers in the air to indicate to them which speed he required. They then altered their gear levers accordingly, whilst he helped them by careful manipulation of the clutch.

With the differential unlocked it was possible to make small changes of direction by the use of hand-brakes, which were controlled by the tank commander. When making a full turn, or "swinging," as it was called, the differential was locked and the gearsman on, say, the right-hand side was signalled to put his gears into "neutral." (The sign for this was a closed fist.) The right-hand track was thus disconnected, and the whole of the drive went on the other track. The officer then pulled the right-hand brake, and the right track, being at a complete standstill, the whole tank swung round in that direction, practically upon its own axis.

A skilful driver could make these turns without stopping the machine, but generally the tank stopped and then turned. As four men (the officer at the hand-brakes, the driver at the throttle and clutch, and the two gearsmen at the secondary gears) were necessary for this slow and clumsy operation, much time and labour was wasted, and tempers were often considerably frayed. When surrounded by the enemy, many valuable opportunities were missed, and the fighting capacity of the tank was reduced by half.

Both machines were 26 feet 5 inches long, and 8 feet 2 inches high. A male tank was 13 feet 6 inches wide, including sponsons, and weighed 28 tons. A female was 10 feet 6 inches wide, with sponsons, and weighed 27

TANK WARFARE

tons. The original or Mark I. tank, with its tail, was 32 feet 6 inches long, and the female of the species was 13 feet 9 inches wide.

A tank could move over flat ground at 100 to 120 yards a minute, over ground intersected by trenches at 30 to 40 yards a minute, and at night time at 15 yards a minute. Its radius of action was about 15 miles, and it could remain in action for about eight hours. This was about the limit of endurance of the crew. It could cross or go through ditches, ploughed ground, banks, walls, hedges, or fences. It could also go through barbed wire entanglements like a rhinoceros through a field of corn, and as it ploughed through it left behind it two paths of flattened wire, along which two single files of infantry could easily follow.

There were naturally several obstacles at which even a tank jibbed, such as tree stumps, very thick woods, large and deep ditches, very soft and greasy ground, and hills that had to be taken diagonally.

Where there was only a narrow track of earth just wide enough to take the track of a machine, as for example between two shell holes, the tank would probably become ditched. If a trench was wider than 12 feet, and deeper than 6 feet, the nose of the machine would probably drop in and bury itself in the perpendicular wall, without a chance of being able to rise vertically over the top.

The climbing powers of a tank were considerable. The limits of the gradients it could ascend were as follows : on dry ground, 1 in 1.2 ; on wet ground, 1 in 2.5 ; on very wet ground, 1 in 4. It could tackle a perpendicular bank of 6 feet, or if the slope was 1 in 1 it could mount 12 feet. On the other hand it could negotiate a sheer drop of 12 to 15 feet, but this largely depended on the softness of the ground and the skill of the driver. Trenches

WHAT A TANK COULD DO

8 to 10 feet wide could be crossed with ease, and usually a 12-foot width was no great obstacle.

Its strength may be judged from the fact that it was capable of pushing over single trees with diameters of 15 inches to 2 feet, but this had to be done carefully, otherwise the roots came up underneath the tank and it was "bellied"—*i.e.* its track could not grip the ground. Slender trees like poplar were knocked over with ease.

A tank could naturally not cross swamps, or streams with marshy banks, and could only go through ponds where the water was no more than 12 inches deep and the bottom of gravel, but on the other hand it could cross a stream 18 inches deep if the bed were firm. It avoided routes with too many sharp turns, and was loth to tackle a long and continuous gradient of over 1 in 2. Wherever possible it kept clear of metalled roads and the French *pavé* roads, as this kind of hard surface tended to break the track plates. When travelling through ruined villages it was advisable to beware of the fallen roofs of houses which often concealed a large basement, or shell hole, or some other kind of trap. Narrow and deep sunken roads, with cuttings on one or both sides, were also to be avoided, because the tank's range of vision became very limited, and hidden guns were difficult to spot.

Trench mazes were also given a wide berth, as a tank was liable to go over the tops of dug-outs, which might collapse and bury the machine.

A male tank, owing to its greater width and projecting guns, had to avoid rides or drives in woods which were less than 18 feet wide.

Although the tank may seem a very noisy machine it could be throttled down so that it could approach to within 250 yards of the enemy lines without being heard. When tanks moved up behind the line in this manner an

TANK WARFARE

artillery or machine-gun barrage was generally arranged to drown any noise that might arise.

The best kind of ground for a tank was hard, level ground, capable of sustaining a weight of 20 lb. per square inch. Ground containing a large proportion of chalk or gravel and stones was most suitable for tank operations. Where the ground had been very heavily shelled it was wise to look out for the remains of an old road, as this often afforded firm support to a machine in an otherwise very difficult bit of country.

Reconnaissance officers, whose duty it was to spy out the land and indicate likely routes, and tank commanders tested the ground by pushing an ordinary ash walking-stick into it. Ground capable of bearing 20 lb. per square inch renders firm resistance to the stick, and two hands are required to push it in a depth of 12 to 18 inches. Ground that can bear 12 lb. per square inch will allow the stick to be pushed in 12 to 18 inches with one hand. Where the earth is soft, or there is marshy ground beneath the surface, the stick can be thrust right in up to the handle. This shows that it will only bear a pressure of 5 lb. per square inch, and is useless for tank purposes.

CHAPTER 3

The curtain goes up on the Somme—Amazement and terror of the Boche—What the Tommies thought.

AT the end of July 1916 a momentous decision was made. The War Office ordered tanks to be sent out to France at once for use in the autumn.

The danger was clear at once to the Tank Supply Committee: very few tanks were available, and very few crews had been properly trained. Members of the committee immediately approached Sir William Robertson, Chief of the Imperial General Staff, and urged him to wait until the spring of 1917, when large numbers of tanks would be ready. They pointed out that tanks could only be effective in masses, and to use them before they were completely equipped, and the crews properly trained, would be to throw away the chance of springing an overwhelming surprise on the enemy.

The French too, who at that time had begun to build tanks of their own design, pleaded for delay until these machines were ready. They suggested that both English and French tanks should be used on the same day, so that both armies would benefit from the element of surprise, and deliver a decisive blow at the Germans.

But the Higher Command in France refused to alter its decision. The Battle of the Somme, begun on July 1, 1916, was still in progress, and though we had advanced about four miles our losses had been very heavy. On the first day of the attack alone the British Army had suffered 60,000 casualties. The flower of Kitchener's

TANK WARFARE

Army, the finest army of volunteers that the world has ever seen, was gradually being frittered away in vain efforts to batter through the powerful German defences. Flesh and blood had been sorely tried, winter was not far away; something had to be done to revive the spirit of the troops and to encourage them to fresh efforts. So the new weapon was brought into play.

The tanks at Thetford, however, were in such a state of repair that, with the inexperienced labour available, it would have taken at least three months to get them ready. Nevertheless Lieutenant Stern, a man with plenty of drive and energy, guaranteed to have all the machines ready in ten days. He asked for volunteers from the workmen of the Metropolitan Carriage, Wagon, and Finance Co., Birmingham, and immediately obtained a party of forty men. They were billeted at Thetford, but the Army could not supply food! Lieutenant Stern therefore appealed to the Great Eastern Railway, who actually put a restaurant car on a siding at the camp, and fed the workers until the job was finished.

On 15th August thirteen tanks left England. They were entrained at night at Thetford and sent by rail to Avonmouth, thence by boat to Havre, and so to the newly created training centre at Yvrench, where others joined them at intervals until, by the end of August, fifty tanks were assembled.

In those early days the difficulties of entraining were great, and each sponson (the part containing the guns) had to be unbolted and hoisted by means of a girder and tackle on to a separate trolley, as otherwise the machines would be too wide to travel by rail. Every sponson, with its gun, weighed 35 cwt., and in the journey from Thetford to Yvrench they were loaded and unloaded no less than five times, a very weary and back-breaking task.

OFF TO THE FRONT

After a certain amount of overhauling and tuning up, and some practice against wire entanglements and specially constructed machine-gun positions, the tanks were ordered up the line, and arrived in the forward area on 10th September.

Here the crews were kept feverishly busy, fitting in new guns, testing spare parts for the engines, fixing on anti-bombing nets, sorting out new equipment, and poring over a multitude of instructions, maps, and aerial photographs. As most of the tank commanders had never been taught what points to look out for in the mass of general orders issued to them, and many had never even seen an aerial photograph before, they were more puzzled than enlightened.

Each tank carried a spare drum of engine oil and one of gear oil, two small drums of grease, three water-cans, spare barrels for the Vickers guns, one spare gun, carrier pigeons in baskets, signalling flags, and a lamp-signalling set. In addition to this, room had to be found for two days' rations and the equipment of the crew, which included padded leather "anti-bruise" helmets.

The male tank carried 324 rounds of 6-pounder ammunition and 6,300 rounds of small arms ammunition; whilst the females absorbed as much as 31,000 rounds of S.A.A., all of which had to be carefully stacked in racks lining the interior.

At first the army commanders were uncertain as to how to use this new type of armoured car. It was feared that if the tanks started before the infantry, the noise made by the tracks, as they approached the front line, would startle the Germans and bring down their barrage on the infantry assembled in our trenches. Eventually each tank was given a fixed route, and it was arranged that they should reach their objective five minutes ahead of the infantry.

TANK WARFARE

To avoid destruction by our own artillery, lanes were to be left in our barrage down which the tanks could advance. They were to be used in sections of twos and threes, the males for attacking machine-gun nests and strong positions, the females as man-killers.

On 13th September the tanks were moved up to their points of assembly and filled with petrol and ammunition.

The majority of the crews had never been in France before. They were bewildered by the strangeness of the Somme battlefields, deafened by the ever-increasing thunder of the bombardment.

Moving at night, they found roads choked with motor lorries and ambulances. Strings of restless mules were dragging forward limbers, guns, and ammunition, and masses of infantry were ploughing steadily through the mud. Everything was crawling along at a snail's pace in an apparently hopeless state of confusion. By the side of the road were huge dumps of ammunition, stacks of food and bombs. The ground was scarred and torn, littered with rotting fragments of equipment, broken-down limbers, tin cans, dead mules, rusty wire, and dud shells.

All night long Very lights kept shooting up and down, revealing the clear outlines of jagged tree stumps, and here and there tumble-down brick walls which once had been a village.

Everywhere there was an atmosphere of great excitement. In the valleys behind the line were massed troop after troop of cavalry, including thousands of dark-skinned warriors in turbans, and jaunty, slouch-hatted Canadians. Rumours sped swiftly from unit to unit. It was going to be the great break-through this time. The cavalry were to get a chance at last. As for the infantry, they were talking of nothing else but the great new surprise we were springing on the Germans.

"Caterpillars they calls them, a funny-shaped kind of armoured car that can crawl through the thickest wire and climb over any trenches. They are stuck all over with wicked little guns, and can fight standing on their heads, so they say. A fellow from B Company saw one crawling up the road the other night, with two funny little wheels trailing behind. All the men inside them wear leather hats, so as they won't get bumped about. Full of shells they are. Stacks of ammo. My, I don't fancy Fritz's * chances when they go over. He won't half get it in the neck." So the talk ran on.

In the meantime the crews of the tanks were trying hard to find out what they were supposed to do. The orders, maps, and time-tables issued to the commanders were insufficient, only one set being available for three tanks; consequently they had to be almost learnt by heart and then passed on to the next tank.

But even this turned out to be useless, for at 5 p.m. on the day before the battle all orders were suddenly cancelled and fresh ones given verbally.

That night the tanks crept slowly to their starting-points, the spots immediately behind our lines from which they would move off to the attack half an hour before dawn.

* The nicknames given to the Germans by British soldiers changed as the war went on. In 1914 and 1915, when feeling against them was very strong, they were called *the Hun*, or simply *Huns*. During the Somme offensives of 1916 *Fritz* came into use, probably from a growing respect for the enemy's fighting qualities. As the war progressed, and the Germans made their great spectacular advances against us, the British Tommy regarded them more favourably, and the friendly name of *Jerry* was adopted and used all through 1918 to the end of the war.

Boche, adopted from the French, was used throughout the war, chiefly by officers.

TANK WARFARE

The night was pitch black; the ground, battered and dented by fierce bombardments, was riddled with shell holes; mud was everywhere.

Blindly the new monsters floundered in and out of the numberless craters. In one narrow sunken road a tank was obliged to squelch heavily over clumps of dead bodies. Many failed to reach their destination, some breaking down with mechanical trouble, others becoming hopelessly ditched. Out of the forty-nine that had set out on the approach march, seventeen did not arrive at their starting-points. The remainder were obliged to lie up near artillery batteries, which roared incessantly all night long. The crews were unable to get any sleep, though they had been on the move continuously for twenty-four hours, and the dawn found them utterly weary. But they were none the less determined to prove their worth.

. . . . .

At 5.30 a.m., trembling with excitement, they started up their engines and crawled forward on their great adventure.

It was seven months since the first order for building tanks had been given, seven months of secrecy and thrills, and now, on September 15, 1916, a landmark in the history of the Great War, the new landships, launched at last, were steadily ploughing their way over the perilous sea of no-man's-land.

Did they realize that in that hour they were changing the face of warfare for ever? Those brave pioneers knew only too well that much was expected of them. They felt instinctively that the future of a great weapon was in their hands, and they drove forward full of hope and confidence.

The driver, gazing anxiously at the reflector in front of him, or peeping through a periscope, was wondering no doubt if the engine would stay the course. Would the

THE FIRST ATTACK

old "Willie" break down suddenly when in the midst of the enemy? Would they cross the German trenches without getting ditched? He gazed ahead in horror. Phew! that was a narrow shave—almost ran over a wounded man!

The officer anxiously noted the shell-bursts which crept nearer and nearer. What happened to a tank if a shell came crashing through the front? Perhaps they would know only too well before the day was out. He did not want to think about that sort of thing. Ah! that heap of ruins over there, that was his objective. He touched the driver's arm and pointed. The latter banged on the engine cover and signalled to the gearsman at the rear, who pulled a handle, and then slowly the "Willie" turned in the required direction.

Crouching over their guns, the gunners peered anxiously through the narrow gun slits, looking for targets. Many a time they had fired away enthusiastically on the ranges, but now, somehow, it was quite different. They could see little grey figures falling stupidly to the ground a hundred yards away. It was queer; what was that ominous pattering like hail on the steel sides? Sparks and splinters seemed to fill the interior and stung one's face and hands. They had never been told about that when training in England. But nothing mattered so long as they could go on.

. . . . . .

The long line pressed forward, slithering in the mud, crunching over barriers, flattening lanes through the wire, dipping into holes, and nosing out again, swaying and plunging, while their crews gasped for breath in the poisoned air and the inferno of gun fire roared ever more deafeningly about them. The German trenches at last! More grey-clad figures running, crying out in horror, stumbling and lying still. The tanks crawled on.

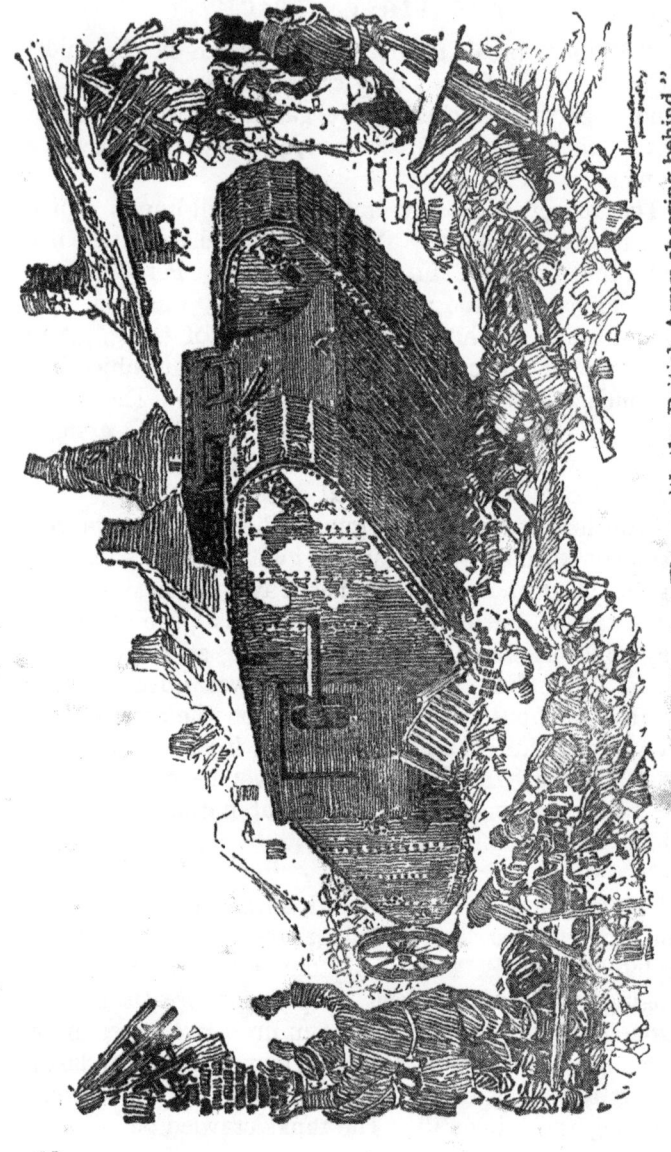

"A tank is walking up the High Street at Flers, with the British Army cheering behind."

THE GREAT SURPRISE

Some crashed through dug-outs and disappeared, or plunged into shell holes—helplessly ditched. Some broke down and crouched silently in the mist, while their crews laboured and cursed in vain at the engines. But the remainder did good work.

One tank led the way into Flers, the Germans flying before it in terror. Most of them bolted into the cellars, and the New Zealanders, who were following, simply had the job of rounding them up, and captured the village without a casualty. A low-flying aeroplane, acting as observer that day, sent back a message which was printed with great jubilation in every newspaper in the kingdom:

"A tank is walking up the High Street at Flers, with the British Army cheering behind."

Others assisted the infantry greatly by flattening out the enemy wire and crushing machine-gun positions.

Another bold tank straddled a German trench, raked it with machine-gun fire fore and aft, and then, crawling along behind it, took three hundred prisoners.

An adventurous male heaved its way through the wire to Gueudecourt, where it courageously attacked a battery of artillery. It succeeded in destroying one gun, but before the 6-pounder could get to work again a shell crashed through the cab and set the tank on fire. Only two of the crew managed to escape from the blazing wreck.

The Germans apparently had heard that we were going to use some kind of new weapon. It was afterwards rumoured that this information had been given to them by the beautiful Mata Hari, a Javanese dancer in Paris and one of Germany's most skilful agents, who was later shot by the French as a spy. They had warned their troops against panic, but the warning had little effect. As soon as they saw these fearful iron monsters lumbering out of the mist towards them, the majority turned and fled in terror. A few stout-hearted machine gunners

TANK WARFARE

stuck to their guns and blazed away defiantly at the creatures' sides, but when they found that bullets were powerless they, too, dived like rabbits for cover, just in time to escape the ponderous tracks that crushed their puny machine guns into the mud.

Documents captured later revealed only too well the terrifying effect of this handful of tanks on troops already unnerved by the pitiless bombardment.

The following description from a German newspaper correspondent shows the panic produced in the German ranks:

"One stared and stared as if one had lost the power of one's limbs. The big monsters approached us slowly, hobbling, rolling, and rocking, but always advancing. Nothing impeded them. Some one in the front-line trenches said, 'The devil is coming!' and the word passed along the line like wildfire."

The German High Command was staggered. Secret and urgent orders were issued to the German troops to hold their ground at all costs, and fight to the last man against these new and monstrous engines of war, which they complained were both cruel and effective. In their usual thorough manner they set to work at once to devise counter-measures of every description.

The spirits of our own troops, on the other hand, rose tremendously. At first, when they saw these slug-like machines slowly crawling over no-man's-land, they were filled with surprise. They had expected to see something startling, but these unwieldy monsters, their sides painted all the colours of the rainbow, their clumsy snouts snuffling in and out of shell holes, their closed portholes looking like two heavy-lidded eyes, their caterpillar tracks gliding up and down with a snake-like motion, their ridiculous tails bumping stupidly along behind, had the appearance of having escaped from some comic Zoo.

TOMMY'S NEW FRIEND

But when, a few minutes later, the tanks' 6-pounders began to bark, and the machine guns to chatter, when they plunged unconcernedly through the thickest wire and smashed up the strongest machine-gun nests; when for the first time the infantry were able to advance unmolested and unwounded, then their sense of ridicule gave way to one of admiration and pride. They had "put it over" on Fritz this time. "What about gas and flame-throwers now? Why, they were not in the same street with the good old tanks! They'll make old Fritz sit up and take notice this time, and no mistake!"

The Tommy henceforth adopted a tone of patronage. He had at last found a real friend, one who was perhaps slightly grotesque, a little slow in moving about, and not too steady in his gait, but nevertheless one who made short work of the troops' most dreaded opponents—barbed wire and vicious machine guns.

The following letter, written home by a Territorial, is typical of the humorous manner in which the troops regarded the tanks:

"'Old Mother Hubbard,' they called her, and lots of other funny names as well. She looked like a pantomime animal, or a walking ship with iron sides, moving along, very slow, apparently all on her own, and with none of her crew visible. There she was, groanin' and gruntin' along, pokin' her nose here and there, stopping now and then as if she was not sure of the road, and then going on—very slow, but over everything.

"It was her slowness that scared us as much as anything, and the way she shook her wicked old head and stopped to cough. It was a circus—my word! I only saw her for about ten minutes. She came humping out of the fog at one end of the line, and humped into it again at the other. The last I saw of her was when she was

TANK WARFARE

nosing down a shell crater like a great big hippopotamus, with a crowd of Tommies cheering behind." *

Weird and fantastic tales were told in the press by war correspondents with vivid imaginations who wrote their dispatches far from the battlefield. There was nothing the tanks could not do, from knocking down houses and smashing up woods, to flattening out trenches.

But the Tommy had sufficient sense of humour to poke fun at these journalistic extravagances. He went one better, as this letter from a soldier to his sweetheart shows:

"They can do up prisoners in bundles like strawbinders, and, in addition, have an adaptation of a printing machine, which enables them to catch the Huns, fold, count, and deliver them in quires, every thirteenth man being thrown out a little farther than the others. The tanks can truss refractory prisoners like fowls prepared for cooking, while their equipment renders it possible for them to charge into a crowd of Huns and, by shooting out spokes like porcupine quills, carry off an opponent on each. Though 'stuck-up,' the prisoners are, needless to say, by no means proud of their position.

"They can chew up barbed wire and turn it into munitions. As they run, they slash their tails and clear away trees, houses, howitzers, and anything else in the vicinity. They turn over on their backs and catch live shells in their caterpillar feet, and they can easily be adapted as submarines; in fact, most of them crossed the Channel in this guise. They loop the loop, travel forwards, sideways, and backwards, not only with equal speed, but at the same time. They spin round like a top, only far more quickly, dig themselves in, bury themselves, scoop out a tunnel, and come out again ten miles away in half an hour." †

* From *The Tank Corps*, by C. and A. Williams-Ellis.
† From *Tanks, 1914–1918*, by Sir Albert G. Stern, K.B.E., C.M.G.

SUCCESS AND FAILURE

The only people who were not too pleased with themselves were the tank crews.

These bold pioneers, boxed up in their narrow iron ship, perspiring with the heat, stifled by petrol and cordite fumes, deafened by the clamour of the engine and the roar of the 6-pounder guns, jolted this way and that with every lurch of their clumsy vessel, did not appreciate the funny side of the battle. Knowing what high hopes had been set on them, they were disappointed with the results achieved.

Of the thirty-two that reached their starting-points nine pushed ahead of the infantry and inflicted considerable losses on the enemy; nine did not catch up the infantry, but were very successful in clearing up strong points; five were ditched, and nine broke down with engine trouble.

Their machines had been made for use over dry and fairly firm ground, and on the Somme they had been obliged to cross an area pitted with craters and full of loose and crumbling soil. The breakdowns were due to faulty design and the unexpected wear and tear of rollers and sprockets. The crews had not had enough training, and insufficient preparations had been made regarding supplies and reconnaissance of the ground to be attacked.

It seemed to them a wasted effort. The tremendous secret had been revealed for the sake of a small advance and a few thousand prisoners.

The great break through had not taken place. Sadly the cavalry trooped back to their horse lines again.

If only the Higher Command had waited a little longer! The Germans themselves admitted that if we had attacked when one thousand tanks were massed ready, their line must have crumpled up like cardboard.

Yet the attack was not entirely useless; the tanks had certainly raised new hopes in the British ranks.

TANK WARFARE

They felt, from that day on, that they had something up their sleeves which Fritz did not possess. They had seen how the tanks had saved scores of lives, and they had watched the Germans bolting like rabbits. Instinctively the infantry soldier realized that here was the very weapon he had been waiting for, a combined shield and battering ram, which would do all his dirty work and at the same time attract all the unwelcome limelight of the battlefield.

On the other hand, the Germans began to lose confidence in their own invincibility. The finest infantry in the world are powerless against tanks, and the German troops, knowing this only too well, were haunted by the fear of further attacks.

Although the tank men themselves were conscious of a sense of failure, the Higher Command was highly pleased. Sir Douglas Haig was so much impressed that he ordered one thousand more tanks to be constructed immediately.

CHAPTER 4

The all-conquering "female"—Mud—Through snow and ice at Beaumont-Hamel.

IT is a remarkable feature of the first tank action that although many of the crews, working under entirely strange and unknown conditions, and hampered by slow and imperfect machines, performed feats which to the average infantryman were absolutely amazing, yet, with one exception, no record of any decorations awarded to them appears in the Tank Corps Book of Honour. Thus the astonishing exploits of this courageous band of pioneers, which would have provided such rich materials for future historians, remain so far unrecorded.

Perhaps it is because these men belonged to the original C and D Companies of the Heavy Section Machine-Gun Corps before they were expanded into battalions that the full details of individual deeds on this occasion are missing. Many awards were undoubtedly made, and a search in the archives of the Committee of Imperial Defence would perhaps enable the Tank Corps Book of Honour to complete its records and at the same time commemorate those bold spirits who first drove tanks into action.

An honour which was recorded, however, followed shortly, for on 26th September Second-Lieutenant C. E. Storey, in Tank D.14, performed a brilliant feat of arms and opened the infantryman's eyes to the possibilities of tank warfare.

The 21st Division had been held up in front of

Gueudecourt by a strongly fortified trench system called Gird Trench. The 64th Brigade, after fierce fighting, had just managed to obtain a footing in this trench at two spots some 1,500 yards apart, and in order to take Gueudecourt it was essential to clear the whole trench. The portion held by the Germans was strongly manned and well wired, the wire being uncut.

The G.O.C. 110th (Leicester) Brigade, which was attacking, knew the difficulties of the task, so he asked for the help of a tank, and Lieutenant Storey, in charge of a female, moved up at night, after a strenuous journey over very heavily shelled ground.

At 6.30 a.m. the tank started forward, followed by bombers. Storey plunged through the wire and, turning, waddled alongside the trench, blazing away with his machine guns. At first he met with a stout resistance, the Germans bombing furiously and turning all their machine guns on him, but up and down he went, remorselessly driving them, yard by yard, to the southern end, where our infantry was waiting, bombs in hand. At the same time a low-flying aeroplane skimmed the trench, machine-gunning as it went. The Germans, huddled together at the southern end, were caught in a trap.

Storey, through the porthole, saw white handkerchiefs fluttering in sign of surrender, and gave the signal to the bombers who were following the tank. They took eight officers and three hundred and sixty-two men prisoners. The total number of our casualties was five. Storey then went on with the infantry and helped in the attack on Gueudecourt, fighting until his petrol gave out. He came out of action with all his crew wounded except two.

For this wonderful show of courage and determination he was awarded the D.S.O.

GREAT HAULS

He had conclusively shown that it was possible for eight men in a tank to capture 1,500 yards of trench, inflict heavy losses on the enemy, and take three hundred and seventy prisoners in the space of an hour, an operation which would have taken an infantry brigade many hours of hard fighting, and cost hundred of casualties.

On the other hand, the success of this lone tank encouraged infantry generals to demand them for use in twos and threes, and as tanks were constructed to be used in masses this idea did them more harm than good.

Meanwhile they continued to have astonishing adventures, though they were often defeated that winter by their worst enemy, mud.

On 14th November, for instance, two tanks managed to cross the enemy's front-line trench at Beaumont-Hamel, and then became hopelessly stuck. Undaunted, the crews blazed away with their guns at everything within sight, until the officer of the leading tank suddenly noticed that the trench nearest to him was covered with some flickering white substance. Bewildered, he opened the flap, and saw to his astonishment that the German troops in the trench were all vigorously waving handkerchiefs, papers, pieces of cloth, or anything white they could find, in sign of surrender.

The tanks were in a dilemma. They were unable to move, and had only sixteen men to take some four hundred Germans prisoners! They signalled frantically to the infantry, who luckily came up and took over the prisoners before the latter discovered that their conquerors were completely ditched.

The ground ahead of these tanks was so bad that "fatigue parties" were employed to dig them out and make firm tracks for a further advance in a few days' time, but when they succeeded in freeing themselves from the mud, after hours of labour, they had not gone far before they stuck again, and only one, by violent exertions, managed to get going once more and reach firmer ground.

This tank was ordered to attack, on the 18th, a strong position called the Triangle, near Beaumont-Hamel.

To make sure that it would not lose its way, Captain Hotblack, the reconnaissance officer, marked out a route during the night with a long white tape. Cold weather had now set in, and frost had hardened the ground. The tank crew were congratulating themselves that the going would not be so difficult; but fate intervened once more, for just before dawn snow came down and blotted out all trace of the tape.

It seemed as if the tank would have to disappoint the infantry after all, but Captain Hotblack, who had previously reconnoitred the ground, volunteered to lead it on foot. In the cold misty dawn he set out over our front line, followed by the clumsy "Willie"; sheltering in shell holes thick with ice and slush, and miraculously dodging the machine guns that were turned on him, he managed to guide it right up to the Triangle without being hit. The tank then opened out with its guns, and Captain Hotblack retired to report progress.

In the meantime our infantry had been held up elsewhere, and sent up an S.O.S. for the tank. As there were no effective means of signalling to the machine, Captain Hotblack ventured forth once more over the bullet-swept area and, hailing it cautiously, succeeded in attracting its attention. The tank turned round and followed him back; but, meanwhile, the wind had changed and a thaw had set in. The frosty ground returned once more to its quagmire condition, making the ground impassable, and the new attack had to be abandoned.

This action had nevertheless shown the value of

CAPTAIN HOTBLACK BLAZES THE TRAIL

reconnaissance, or "spying out the land," which was to be a most important feature of every future tank engagement.

It was realized that owing to the very limited vision of a tank commander, who often had to rely only on a periscope, it was vital to get to know the ground beforehand. This was done by studying maps and aeroplane photographs, and by actual glimpses from observation posts.

The system of taping out routes, originally suggested by Colonel Swinton, was adopted by every tank unit, and it was largely due to Captain Hotblack's courageous "blazing of the trail" that a high and fearless standard of efficiency was kept up throughout the corps.

CHAPTER 5

Mark II.—The tank loses its tail—Bellying and ditching—The struggle for existence.

IT will be remembered that after the Battle of the Somme orders for one thousand tanks had been immediately placed in England. It was arranged that deliveries should take place monthly, the complete thousand to be in France by the end of 1917, and that the tanks should be of a new type—labelled Mark II. by the authorities—with a number of improvements which experience on the battlefield had very quickly suggested.

The first of these was the abolition of the " tail." A tank which had its tail wheels shot away in action found that the loss made no difference to its steering, and this discovery relieved the tanks of their clumsiest feature.

The engineers were seriously considering other problems also.

When a tank ran over some obstacle, such as a tree stump, raised from the ground, but narrow enough to go between the tracks, the probabilities were that its belly would lie heavily on it, thus lifting the tracks from the ground and preventing them from getting any grip at all. No matter how fiercely the engine was raced, the tracks would simply revolve helplessly in the air. This was commonly called being " bellied," and it was sometimes disastrous, but no complete remedy could be found.

If, again, one side of a tank slipped into a deep trench, the belly would fall on the parapet and the full weight of twenty-eight tons, pressing hard on the crumb-

THE CORPS BEGINS TO GROW

ling earth, would make the tank heel over at an awkward angle, so that both caterpillar tracks would be only feebly gripping the loose surface, and it was ditched.

On soft, muddy ground, as can be well imagined, ditching was all too frequent, for it is obvious that if the caterpillar tracks are only cutting into oozing mud no grip is obtained, and the machine sinks deeper with every effort. This trouble, fortunately, could be cured. Iron shoes, or spuds, were placed on the track plates to enable them to get a firmer grip on soft ground, and a cigar-shaped splinter-boom, about 6 feet long, was fixed on the top of the tank. When machines became ditched the boom was attached to the caterpillar tracks on each side by chains, so that it was pulled underneath by the revolution of the tracks, until it was jammed in the earth. The tracks then having something solid to grip, the tank climbed out of the mud.

The exhaust pipe was also carried to the back of the machine and a silencer introduced. In the first tanks the exhaust belched forth flames on top, often revealing its presence at night and causing fires to break out among the tarpaulins.

The highly coloured camouflage painting was abandoned, and all tanks were henceforth of a neutral brown colour, and provided with camouflage nets. It was found that the shadow cast by a tank proclaimed its identity to enemy airmen, and that the best way to prevent this was to spread the new net right across to disguise the shape.

New cast-iron track rollers and sprockets were also fitted, which gave a longer lease of life to the tank, for the old steel ones wore out very quickly.

While all these mechanical improvements were being made, an equally important problem was tackled: the training of crews for the great new fleet.

TANK WARFARE

Companies A, B, C, and D of the Heavy Section Machine-Gun Corps were expanded, in France, into four battalions, under Colonel Elles, who had been appointed to the command on September 26, 1916. Every week great batches of men arrived at the training area near Bermicourt—such a strange medley of volunteers from infantry, cavalry, flying corps, non-combatant units, and even the navy, that they were nicknamed "Fred Karno's Army," after a well-known music hall comedian.

Some one in authority gave them an even less complimentary name : he called them "a regular rabble." And a rabble they were in those early days, but a rabble lured by adventure; a rabble keen and enthusiastic; a rabble not afraid of living dangerously; a rabble which, with all its lack of strict discipline, built up a tradition of devotion to duty and patient heroism unsurpassed in British military history. Most of them had come from that glorious mob of civilian volunteers who created Kitchener's Army. They were volunteering for the second time, and it was a fortunate thing for the tanks that such rich new blood was forthcoming.

The old tank hands became instructors, and soon courses in machine guns, 6-pounders, driving, mechanism, and so forth were in full swing. Boxing, games, and drill also played their valuable part in the training. Owing to the shortage of tanks in France many companies rehearsed with wooden dummies, which were carried on the shoulders of six men. As these strange twelve-footed creatures staggered across country, often a man in the middle, who could not see anything at all, tripped up and fell, bringing the whole clumsy contrivance to the ground amidst loud laughter from the onlookers.

In addition to the formation of the four battalions, each of which was to have seventy-two tanks (afterwards reduced to thirty-six), an area of 24 acres was taken over

WAR OFFICE *VERSUS* TANKS

near Erin for the building of workshops, stores, and tankodromes, where five hundred Chinese labourers were employed. The depot at Thetford, in England, was moved to Bovington in Dorset. A lonely stretch of open heathland near Wool was reserved for tank driving and manœuvres, and the old companies E and F were expanded into five battalions and a reinforcement depot.

The order for one thousand tanks had been increased to twelve hundred and fifty. Grants had been made by the Treasury, old factories were enlarged for the production of engines, armour plate, steel castings and guns, and entirely new factories were springing up for the construction of the new machines. After strenuous efforts the highly complex machinery of tank production had been set in motion at last, when suddenly it was threatened with a complete stoppage.

On October 10, 1916, the Army Council cancelled the order for one thousand tanks!

It was the first move in the senseless campaign waged by the War Office against tanks—a campaign which at times threatened the very existence of the Tank Corps, and continued ceaselessly until August 1918.

Naturally the cancellation of the order came as a bolt from the blue to the Tank Supply Committee. Lieutenant Stern immediately complained to Mr. Lloyd George, then Secretary of State for War, saying that he could not possibly cancel the orders that had been placed, and that he was prepared to resign rather than do so. Mr. Lloyd George was surprised—he had not been informed of the cancellation; he said he would make investigations. Next day the order for the one thousand tanks was reinstated. The War Office had lost the first round of the fight. But it countered swiftly, for with one cunning blow it knocked out the founder of the tanks, the brilliant originator of tank tactics and ideas—Colonel

TANK WARFARE

Swinton. He was removed by the simple process of "promoting" him to a position in the Committee of Imperial Defence.

Requests were also received by the British Government from the Russians, French, and Belgians for supplies of tanks. The Russian Government asked that plans of the tanks should be sent, but knowing that Russia could not possibly have any need for the plans, as she had not the means to carry out the construction, the Tank Supply Committee strongly suspected that they were intended for Germany, and consequently informed the War Office that they were much too busy to get them ready. The Intelligence Department of the War Office, however, continued to make requests, and in order to satisfy the supposed Russian inquirers, childish drawings full of incorrect details were carefully prepared and sent to Russia.

The Tank Supply Committee were inundated with letters from every part of the world, some correspondents suggesting all kinds of wonderful improvements, and others claiming to be the real inventors of tanks! One such letter, addressed to the "King's Secretary, Christal Palace, London," is quoted by Sir Albert G. Stern, and read as follows:

"Thursday,
"May 31, 1917.

"SIR,
"I Wright Having discoved the first Tank Pattern now hused at the War and Dementions for huse I sent it to the Admarality wich brought it out i have not received enything for same Pattern and Dementions for huse I feel i should have recived Something for same unles mistake as been made Patterns Advertsed for in Paper. God Save the King."

Such gleams of humour were very welcome in a situation which was otherwise all too gloomy.

CHAPTER 6

Smashing through at Arras—The cruise of the *Lusitania*—In the snow at Bullecourt—The lone fight at Monchy—Armour-piercing bullets—Undaunted crews.

DURING December 1916 there were only sixteen tanks in France in full working order and available for practice, and even by the end of March 1917 only sixty could be assembled for the Battle of Arras, and these were mostly old ones which had been renovated, or training tanks plated with mild steel, which was not strong enough to resist armour-piercing bullets. Nevertheless it was decided that two tank battalions were to take part, although the officers and men were far from being fully trained, and in January preparations for the battle were begun, for it is one of the most important features of a tank attack to ensure that each machine has a full supply of oil, petrol, and ammunition. Four supply dumps were chosen, and all the supplies, including 20,000 gallons of petrol, had to be taken by hand from the railhead to the dumps, a heavy task, which occupied a thousand infantrymen for several weeks.

In Arras itself tanks were hidden in the Citadel, in a ditch forming part of the old fortifications. Here, well covered with their green and brown camouflage nets, they lay secure from the prying eyes of German aeroplanes.

As Arras was undermined by a vast system of chalk quarries, the infantry was able to hide comfortably in the numerous tunnels, untouched by the fiercest shelling. The military authorities had also obtained the plans of the old sewers from the French, and these were enlarged and linked up with the chalk quarries, the whole being lit up by electricity, and provided with signposts like the London tube. It was estimated that three divisions of infantry could hide safely in this underground shelter.

The bombardment began on 4th April, and continued with great violence for four days, during which period our air squadrons were constantly attacking the German airmen, to prevent their coming over to take photographs or spy out the movements of our troops. They were successful in keeping the Germans on their side of the line, though not without fierce aerial fighting. Forty-six enemy machines were crippled and brought down, but we lost forty-eight of our own.

On 8th April the weather was fine, and there was a lull in the bombardment. A sinister quietness reigned along the front. That same night the fickle weather changed, and rain came down in torrents, followed by snow.

Our batteries were still quiet, only growling occasionally.

In the darkness a group of tanks met with an unfortunate mishap. They had decided to make a short cut in their journey up to the line, and the ground they were to cross not being considered too safe, a path had been constructed of brushwood and sleepers. When they were half-way over this causeway the apparently solid surface of turf broke beneath their weight, revealing a slimy bog into which six tanks slowly slithered.

Knowing that the infantry would be waiting for them at dawn, the crews toiled desperately to release their heavy machines. The night was black as ink, the wind howled round them, rain and sleet drenched them as they

BREAKING THROUGH

floundered about in the swamp, while not far away an ammunition dump, exploded by a German shell, roared and flamed like a dying volcano.

All their efforts were useless, for it was not till daylight came that they were able to get the tanks on to firm ground again, too late to take part in the attack, though they were used later on.

At 4 a.m. our bombardment was renewed with great violence, and at 5.30 a.m. tanks and infantry began their Easter Monday celebrations by going over the top in the pouring rain.

By 9 a.m. the Canadians, attacking with great dash and vigour, had captured practically the whole of the famous Vimy Ridge. The eight tanks detailed to assist them were unable to get into action, as the ground was sodden with rain and so churned up by shelling that it crumbled at the least pressure.

The forty tanks fighting with the Third Army, however, were scattered along a wide front, and were able to give tremendous assistance to the infantry. By battering down the thick wire entanglements and crushing machine-gun positions they helped the assaulting troops to capture the powerful stronghold known as the Harp, though this was over half a mile long, and, as Mr. John Buchan remarks in his *History of the Great War*, " Such a place as in the early days of the Somme would have baffled us for a month or more." Another strong point, called "Telegraph Hill," was also overrun, and our troops swarmed over the German Second Line and broke into the Third Line.

Except for the weather, everything now favoured a complete break through, for the Germans were only holding our tired infantry by a few thinly-manned machine-gun positions. Had we then been able to send forward a company of light, swift tanks, the last barrier

TANK WARFARE

would undoubtedly have collapsed, and Germany would have been defeated—in April 1917.

But, alas, the light tanks were still in the experimental stage in English factories, and the war was to drag on its terrible course for another nineteen months of bloodshed and destruction.

The Mark II.'s put up some wonderful fights, the most interesting being the Bank Holiday cruise of the *Lusitania*, commanded by Lieutenant Weber.

When zero hour came, this officer was in a state of great anxiety, for his tank developed trouble in the secondary gears. The crew grimly set about trying to repair it, and after a three hours' struggle the good ship *Lusitania* was ready to put out to battle. No sooner had they started than an urgent message came from an infantry colonel : " A machine gun is holding us up. Please investigate." The tank crawled slowly towards the stubborn machine-gun position, opened out with 6-pounders, and soon silenced its spiteful chatter.

Then the infantry went forward with their new friend, following so closely that when the tank ploughed through the wire, and poked its wicked nose over the German parapet, it could not treat the trench to a dose of 6-pounder medicine for fear of hitting our own troops. But the remedy was not necessary, for the Germans, thoroughly scared at the sight of a 6-pounder gun waggling about in threatening fashion over their heads, threw up their hands and surrendered forthwith.

The *Lusitania* then steered along the railway, treating a stronghold known as the Feuchy Redoubt to broadsides of 6-pounders and Lewis guns. Here the enemy decided not to wait for the tank's call, and quitting the redoubt, went to earth in a dug-out near a railway arch.

This only made the *Lusitania* more determined. It made for the arch, but was so keen on the chase that the commander overshot the mark and ran into our own barrage. Shells were falling thickly, and in a few minutes a British shell would probably have put an end to a British tank, so hastily it turned round and ambled back again until it came in touch with the advancing infantry. Then returning once more, it stood patiently by whilst the bombers ferreted the Germans out of their burrow.

A high bank came next, but the *Lusitania* had become so hot with its exertions that it refused to take the steep slope.

Lieutenant Weber decided to stop his vessel and give the engine a chance to cool down. Hardly had he heaved-to than the crew flopped down to sleep, completely drowsed by petrol and cordite fumes, tired out with lack of rest, and enervated by the great heat.

When the engine became cooler, and the sleepers were aroused, the *Lusitania* clambered up the slope and, putting on speed, plunged into battle once more. Passing the infantry, it battered its way through more barbed wire and, blazing away with its guns, chased the enemy from another redoubt and rounded up two troublesome snipers.

A little later on in the day came another S.O.S. from the infantry. Once more the *Lusitania* cruised up to an enemy trench and swiftly settled accounts with two machine guns. But by this time the battle-scarred ship was growing weary, petrol was running low, the magneto failed to function, and the tank came to its journey's end.

This did not dishearten the crew, for they still fired away incessantly, causing heavy losses in the German ranks.

Darkness came and they were still stranded; the engine could not be coaxed back to life. Against the steel sides the German bullets pattered like hail. Switching on their small cabin lights the crew strained again and again at the heavy starting handle, but without result. The Germans redoubled their fire, aiming at the loopholes and chinks, through which the light gleamed treacherously.

Soon the splash from their bullets became so uncomfortable that all lights were switched off. It was 9.30 p.m.; for twelve long hours the *Lusitania* had been cruising in troubled waters. Its petrol tanks being almost dry, Lieutenant Weber decided to abandon ship and return to our lines. But first of all it was necessary to find out where our lines were. The gallant skipper did not know if he was entirely surrounded or if the Germans were only immediately in front of him.

Sergeant Latham volunteered to spy out the land. Earlier in the day this sergeant had shown himself to be a man of great courage. Barbed wire, becoming entangled in the tracks, had dragged the camouflage net over the outlet of the exhaust, and in a few seconds the whole net was blazing fiercely. Without waiting for orders, Sergeant Latham got out of the tank, climbed on top under heavy machine-gun fire, and managed to throw the burning mass overboard.

Now, creeping out of the sponson door, he crawled warily into the darkness. Over his head British and German bullets sped their different ways. He came at length to a trench and, listening anxiously, heard the welcome sound of English voices.

Softly he called, waited for a reply, and then clambered quickly over the parapet. The troops in the trench were astonished; they had only just taken over, and had not been informed about the tank out in front. Sergeant Latham told them to fire high, as the tank crew would be coming in shortly. If the sergeant had not managed to give a warning most probably they would have been mistaken for German raiders and shot dead.

AHEAD OF THE BARRAGE

Next day, still keen on getting his landship safely back, Lieutenant Weber obtained a new magneto and set out with some of his crew.

On their way they met a battery commander, who eagerly questioned them about the derelict. Not knowing about the *Lusitania*, he had been heavily shelling that part of the front, and having made a direct hit on it, realized too late that it was a tank. He was much relieved to hear that the crew was not inside.

Thus perished the *Lusitania* after an exciting and memorable maiden voyage. The commander and crew had done their best to avenge the foul torpedoing of their illustrious namesake,* and for their strenuous and gallant efforts Lieutenant Weber was awarded the Military Cross, and Sergeant Latham the Military Medal.

April 9, 1917, is memorable, moreover, for something even more important than the *Lusitania's* adventures. Eleven tanks, operating with the Fifth Army, were due to attack Bullecourt on 11th April, but on 9th April it was suddenly suggested that the tanks should go over without a preliminary bombardment. Only when they reached the German front line would the barrage come down to protect the advancing troops. This idea of a surprise attack without a warning bombardment, with tanks concentrated on a narrow front instead of being scattered in pairs over a wide front, was the first attempt to introduce those tactics which afterwards surprised and overwhelmed the German armies. It is a landmark in the story of tank warfare.

The attack was fixed for the morning of the 10th April, but on their way to their starting-points the tanks ran

* The giant Cunard liner, *Lusitania*, was sunk by a German submarine off the Irish coast on May 7, 1915, with a loss of 1,198 lives, including 124 Americans. This atrocity aroused the horror of the civilized world.

into a violent blizzard. The snow came down so thickly that at times the driver of the leading tank could not even see the officer who was leading the way on foot, a yard or two in front. The pace of the whole column was reduced to a crawl. Snowdrifts had blotted out all landmarks, the wind rose to a gale. Slowly and laboriously the eleven blinded monsters crept on and on. Dawn came and they were far from the starting-points, the crews were almost exhausted—it was too late. The Australians were withdrawn from their assembly position, and the attack was postponed.

Next day, under cover of the usual bombardment, tanks went forward at dawn, followed by the Australians. The attack was a failure. The tanks were blackly silhouetted against the snow and heavily shelled, nine being knocked out by direct hits; and the infantry, unable to resist the temptation of following the tank tracks in the snow, became easy targets and suffered heavily.

In one tank a shell came through the front, blew the driver's head off, and exploded in the engine, filling the interior with fumes, flames, and brains. The officer was blinded and stunned, the corporal wounded. As the crew crawled painfully out of the narrow sponson doors, another shell hit the roof with a fearsome crash.

In another a shell hit the petrol tank, which in these tanks (Mark II.) were situated forward, near the driver and the officer. The tank immediately burst into flames. The officer and driver, caught like rats in a trap, were burnt alive. Only a sergeant and two men succeeded in escaping from that raging furnace.

A third tank was hit twice. All the crew were wounded, the officer being badly hit in the leg. He kept grimly on, however, and fought until his ammunition gave out. When returning, he climbed out of his tank

AT BULLECOURT

to see what damage had been done. A vicious shell exploded near the tank and wounded him once more in the leg. The crippled crew, salving what they could, then evacuated the tank, hobbling away with their wounded commander on a stretcher. They had no sooner quitted than the tank was hit repeatedly and set on fire. Even when they had almost reached the dressing station their ill luck did not desert them, for a vindictive shell exploded close to the stretcher and wounded the officer for the third time that day.

One adventurous tank managed to get straight in to Bullecourt, where it began to clear up the village in great style. It was met by a terrific fusillade of rifle and machine-gun bullets, and bombs were hurled at it from the ruins of the houses. To his astonishment, the tank commander discovered that he was entirely unsupported; no British troops were in sight. Suddenly, in the middle of the street, he came to the edge of an enormous shell hole. The tank stopped; the driver tried to reverse, but could not get the clumsy secondary gears to work; the " bus " came to an absolute standstill.

The wily Germans rushed up a field gun, and hiding it in a ruined house, shelled the tank at close range. The crew could not persuade the machine to move, their ammunition was running out, and they realized only too well that in a few minutes the tank would be blown to pieces. The commander decided to get out. Slipping quietly through the doors, with a couple of Lewis guns and some ammunition, the crew fought their way back, yard by yard, until they came in touch with the foremost Australians.

Two more of the tanks broke clean through the Hindenburg Line and, followed by batches of Australians, rattled victoriously through the village of Hendecourt. They were seen later, by an aeroplane, ploughing over the open country towards Riencourt, still followed by the elated Australians. This village was five miles beyond the trenches. They never came back. A vigorous German counter-attack cut them off entirely. They may have run out of petrol, or been knocked out by field guns, but neither tanks nor infantry were ever heard of again.

This disaster had unfortunate results. The Australians attributed their heavy losses and the failure of the attack to the tanks, and refused to have anything more to do with them. It was not till over a year later that the Australian Corps could be induced to operate again with tanks, but their intense dislike was then converted into intense admiration.

Far worse was the fact that for the first time two tanks had fallen into German hands. They experimented thoroughly, and discovered that the steel sides of these Mark II. tanks (which in reality were only practice tanks armoured with mild steel) could be pierced by armour-piercing bullets. They acted swiftly. From that time every German infantryman was supplied with five rounds of "K" (armour-piercing) ammunition, and every machine gun with several hundred rounds.

On 11th April three tanks met a strange fate at Monchy-le-Preux, a village standing on a hill.

Zero hour had been fixed for 5 a.m., and six tanks were to assist the infantry; a brigade of cavalry was also standing by, ready for a break through.

On their way up in the dark two of the tanks broke down with mechanical defects, the other four took up their position and moved forward at the time arranged. One became ditched, but the remaining three kept steadily on over no-man's-land in the falling snow. The tank commanders thought it strange that no barrage had yet come down, because they had been instructed to follow

THREE LONE TANKS

behind our barrage. Stranger still, not a single infantryman seemed to be following them. They cruised about no-man's-land for some time, but there was still no movement from our trenches. Dawn was lighting up the sky, showing up the tanks clearly against the snow. It was dangerous to loiter, so the commanders decided to go on alone. Methodically and patiently the three tanks drove the Germans from Monchy. Yard by yard they blazed their way down the main street and came out on the other side. If they had been supported by the infantry, a company of the latter could easily have taken possession of the entire village.

Meanwhile the Germans, seeing that no infantry was following, regained courage, and creeping up out of cellars and dug-outs, worked their way back to the village in the rear of the tanks.

The latter, after fighting beyond Monchy, suddenly noticed that the Boche had reoccupied the village behind them, and turned back to clear the way once more and to look for our own troops. This time they met with a more determined resistance. Bombs were hurled at them from windows, and machine guns spat at them from doorways. One tank was surrounded by Germans who fiercely attacked it with incendiary bombs in an attempt to set it on fire and smoke out the crew. All the gunners were wounded or killed, but the gallant commander grimly kept his forward gun going, and fought a passage through.

The three tanks had now been fighting in and around Monchy for an hour and a half without any support. They once more dispersed the Germans who had reappeared in front of Monchy, when down came our own barrage, and one by one the unlucky machines were knocked out by British shells.

Zero hour had been postponed for two hours, and

nobody had taken the trouble to inform the tank commanders !

Some one had blundered. So deadly was the fire of our artillery that one tank was actually blown to pieces, five of the crew being wounded and one killed.

The infantry now advanced, and after very heavy fighting succeeded in capturing the village, which the three tanks had taken unaided an hour and a half previously.

The cavalry also staged a charge in the good old style, but barbed wire and a few machine guns held them up completely, and they retired in confusion after what can only be called a useless massacre. It was proved conclusively that day that one machine gun behind barbed wire, manned by a stout-hearted gunner, could easily hold up a brigade of cavalry.

On 3rd May another attack was made on the tremendously strong position of Bullecourt. Eight tanks worked in front of the infantry and succeeded in reaching their objectives, but only after fierce opposition on the part of the enemy.

The infantry, however, could not follow, so most of the tanks were obliged to retire again.

The Germans had learnt their lesson, and had made great anti-tank preparations. Realizing that the sight of tanks had a demoralizing effect on their infantry, the German Higher Command had been at great pains to advertise to their troops that they could easily be riddled by armour-piercing bullets, and if vigorously attacked by bombs, machine guns, and even trench mortars, could be put out of action in a very short time.

Unfortunately the tanks fighting on this occasion were all armoured with mild steel only, and consequently the crews suffered heavily from wounds caused by bullets which pierced the sides. They also were armed with

ARMOUR-PIERCING BULLETS

Lewis machine guns instead of the handy Hotchkiss carried by the early tanks. This change had been made by an officer who had once been in charge of the Lewis Gun School at St. Omer, and who consequently thought that it was the finest gun in existence. The tank experts, knowing the vulnerability of the outer cover of the Lewis gun, and the size of its barrel, which made it very unsuitable for use in loopholes, protested vigorously against this decision, but they were over-ruled. All the Mark IV. tanks were armed with Lewis guns, and it was only after their unsuitability had been proved over and over again in battle that tanks were again fitted with the light and effective Hotchkiss gun.

In this action at Bullecourt one tank ran into a perfect storm of armour-piercing bullets, which penetrated the steel sides and wounded the officer and four of the crew. No less than five of the six Lewis guns were rendered useless, the large barrels being shattered. As a fighting machine the tank was hopelessly crippled, so the crew painfully crept out to the nearest shell hole. Immediately the German machine gunners opened out on them; but the officer, with the last Lewis gun, gallantly replied to their fire, and covered the retirement of his crew from shell hole to shell hole until they reached the safety of a British trench.

A remarkable proof of devotion to duty was given by the officer and crew of another tank. It met with such violent opposition in Bullecourt that the officer himself and four of the crew were wounded, leaving only three unwounded men to fight and drive the landship. Undaunted, the commander turned round and made his way back again to the starting-point. Here he unshipped his wounded and took fresh men on board. But the driver refused point-blank to be relieved. He had driven the tank from the start, he said, and he was determined to drive it to the end. It was *his* tank ; he knew all its funny little tricks, and besides, if his officer, a wounded man, was going into action again he was going with him. So Lance-Corporal Wateridge was allowed to keep his seat.

Then a gunner, Private Anderson, spoke up ; he was blinded in one eye by bullet splash, but still keen. He had not such a good case as the driver, for the loss of one eye is a serious handicap to a gunner. He did not assert his right to remain, but pleaded to be taken into action again. It was pointed out to him that, as the tank's steel was not thick enough to stop armour-piercing bullets, he was liable to be hit in the other eye and completely blinded. He replied that he knew that, but did not want to let the old tank down ; could he see her through this trip at any rate ? His wish was gratified.

So back the tank crawled to Bullecourt, and soon the gunner with the blind eye was hard at work emptying drum after drum at troublesome machine guns ; the officer, feeling rather faint, directed operations doggedly and skilfully, and the driver drove as he had never driven before. For seven long exhausting hours the tank battered through wire, crushed machine guns into the ground, and blazed away at the powerful defences of the enemy ; then the commander wearily turned for home. Every man in the crew was wounded ; nearly every round of ammunition had been expended. The driver slowly and carefully brought the landship to a safe anchorage at the starting-point once more.

Only men filled with courage and determination could have accomplished two such voyages in one day. The commander, Lieutenant Knight, was awarded the Military Cross ; the driver, Lance-Corporal Wateridge, the Military Medal ; and Private Anderson the Distinguished Conduct Medal.

Thus ended the Battle of Arras as far as tanks were

A GALLANT CREW

concerned. Every available tank had been used, and out of the original sixty, one battalion had no tanks left at all, and the other only a mere handful. They had not performed miracles, they had only been used in small batches to mop up strong machine-gun positions and force a way through the enemy's wire.

As yet the Higher Command had not fully realized their capabilities, but Sir Douglas Haig was greatly impressed. On April 24, 1917, he told Colonel Stern, who organized the manufacture of tanks, that a division of tanks was worth ten divisions of infantry, and that after aeroplanes tanks were the most important arm of the Army, as they were such tremendous life-savers.

The surprise capture of Monchy-le-Preux by the three tanks (which was due to a mistake) showed that tanks should be used without any preliminary bombardment and, to be effective, must be sent forward in masses. The need for greater co-operation with the infantry was also obvious, as although tanks could capture trench systems and villages, they could not hold them.

The casualties of the tank men had been high, but they felt, nevertheless, that they had accomplished more than the original tanks on the Somme. The crews were better trained, and therefore there were fewer mechanical breakdowns. They also had a clearer idea of what was expected from them, and how to set about attaining their objectives.

The newspapers in England had exaggerated their feats on the Somme at such length, and with such a wealth of impossible detail, that they had become the standing joke of the British Expeditionary Force. At Arras they had determined to prove what they could really do, and the dogged spirit shown by all ranks, even in the face of disaster, was a triumphant vindication of those who had once been termed a " regular rabble."

TANK WARFARE

Just before the Battle of Arras a form was introduced for all tank commanders, called the "Tank Battle History Sheet." On this form the officer recorded the experiences of his tank in action. The following is a typical example of the kind of fighting that took place at Arras:

BATTLE HISTORY OF CREW No. D.10.   TANK No. 784.

Date, 23/4/17.

Commanded by Second Lieutenant G——.

Unit to which attached	98th Infantry Brigade.
Hour the tank started for action	4.45 a.m.
Hour of zero	4.45 a.m.
Extent and nature of hostile shell fire	First three hours artillery fire not very heavy, but from then very heavy fire until rallying-point was reached. No direct fire by anti-tank guns.
Ammunition expended	290 rounds 6-pounder; remainder on tank could not be used owing to the shells sticking in shell cases on tank. Eight pans for Lewis gun ammunition.

BATTLE HISTORY

Casualties . . . . . . Nil.
Position of tank after action . . Factory Croisilles, 12 noon.
Condition of tank after action . . Good—only required refilling and greasing.

Orders received.—To advance from starting-point on British front line at T.4.b.4.5 to Hindenburg Line at point T.6.a.0.5, from which point infantry were to bomb along Hindenburg Line (front and support) to river Sensée at U.7.a.4.4. Tank to assist infantry and, after objective at river taken, to proceed to Croisilles.

Report of Action.—I started from starting-point at T.4.b.4.5 at zero, and made for Hindenburg wire at T.6.a.0.5, crossing same and getting into touch with our infantry, from whom I received report that they were held up by machine guns along the trench. I proceeded to this point and cleared the obstacle. I then travelled parallel to the trench, knocking out machine-gun emplacements and snipers' posts all the way down to point U.1.c.5.0. The infantry kept in touch all the way down, moving slightly in rear of tank, and after emplacements were knocked out they took the occupants prisoners. In two cases white flags were hoisted as soon as the emplacement was hit. The shooting was very good. Up to point U.1.c.5.0 the shelling had been casual, but when we reached the N. bank of the sunken road at this point, and were firing into emplacements towards the river, we were in full observation from the village, and the artillery fire became very heavy. The supply of 6-pounder ammunition now became exhausted, and the ground on the S. side of sunken road being very bad, I decided to move back along the trench, and then crossed the wire, and crossing sunken road at about T.12.b.5.3, made for rallying-point at Factory at Croisilles, where I arrived at 12 noon. I was of opinion that the Hindenburg front line was too bad (wide) to cross, and so could not deal with support line, and was unable to observe this line from front line. I sent two pigeon messages at 9.30 a.m. and 12 noon. I had only one message clip, so had to fasten second message with cotton.

(Signed) G——, Second Lieut.,
O.C. Tank D.10.

In one or two instances where the tank commanders had been either killed or seriously wounded, the N.C.O.'s immediately took charge and continued to direct the tanks towards their objectives.

One of the drawbacks of tanks in battle is the total lack of any means of communication with other tanks. When once inside, with doors bolted, flaps shut and loopholes closed, one can only make signs to a tank very near at hand by taking the great risk of opening the manhole in the roof and waving a handkerchief or a shovel.

At Bullecourt, when right on top of the German front line, a tank commander had a most important message to send back to his section commander (the captain who is in charge of the four tanks in a section). As this officer was back with the infantry, the journey was a perilous undertaking. The tank commander asked for a volunteer from the crew, and to his great astonishment and pride the entire crew volunteered. Private Savage was eventually chosen, and slipping out ran across a bullet-swept area to the indicated spot. He could not find the section commander, but was informed that he had gone into action in another tank, so without hesitation he went forward again to this tank, which was at that moment ploughing its way through the German wire. Every German machine gun in the neighbourhood was firing

DEVOTION TO DUTY

at the machine, but undaunted, and thinking only of his errand, Savage ran on and actually delivered his message to the section commander untouched.

In addition to armour-piercing bullets the Germans had also constructed tank traps. These were holes filled with water and covered over with a light layer of turf. They might have seriously impeded the tanks if it had not been for the intelligent courage of a tank sergeant. The first tank to enter the danger area stumbled on one of these traps, fell through the sham surface of turf, and became bellied in the crumbling earth. Other tanks were following. The sergeant of the bellied tank got out, and though heavily shot at, ran back to warn the other tanks. He succeeded in diverting them to safer ground.

One driver, when his tank was being machine-gunned at very close range, found the machine heeling over to one side. Knowing the danger, he deliberately opened the flap to get a better view, as he could not see clearly through the glass prisms. He observed what was wrong, and began to right the tank. As he was doing so, a bullet struck him in the eye, causing intense pain, but he grimly stuck to his job, and with tremendous pluck managed to swing the tank out of its dangerous position; then, without a word, he collapsed against the engine, unconscious.

All these incidents show that the guiding motive of that period was undoubtedly a great devotion to duty. Brave deeds were accomplished, not in the heat of the moment, but after cool reflection. The team spirit was emerging. Individuals sacrificed themselves without hesitation for the good of the whole, and the Tank Corps was winning its spurs, not in feats of showy brilliance, but in the hard and dangerous task of saving the lives of the unprotected infantry.

CHAPTER 7

Training at home—Strenuous times at the Cadet School—The depot at Wool—Thrills of the first tank ride.

IN England a large training centre had been opened at Wareham, where men were trained in discipline and drill, and then sent on to the Wool Depot, at which courses were given in tank driving, maintenance, etc. Those who had applied in France for commissions in the Tank Corps were sent to the Machine-Gun Corps Cadet School at Pirbright, where much knowledge was forced into them in a remarkably short space of time.

All the cadets were as keen as mustard, and the Army authorities took full advantage of their keenness. From 6.30 in the morning until nine at night they were kept hard at it, drilling, attending lectures, and studying. Everything was done at the double.

Though it was a Tank Cadet School, cadets wore the Machine-Gun Corps badge on their white bands, and the existence of tanks was hardly ever mentioned. The only special tank subject taught was the 6-pounder Hotchkiss Q.F.; otherwise the training was on infantry lines.

The drilling staff was composed of warrant officers and N.C.O.'s of the Rifle Brigade, war-stained veterans who knew how to use their lungs on a parade ground. The regimental sergeant-major, a much feared and respected autocrat, was nicknamed "Magog," owing to his resemblance to the famous red-cheeked and red-nosed statue of that name in the Guildhall at London.

CADET SCHOOL CHARACTERS

He was a terror on parade, but could be as charming as a prince in his less military moments. Beneath his benevolent sway numerous sergeants rushed hither and thither on the parade ground, harrying squads of bewildered cadets.

One particular sergeant had a profuse flow of Cockney banter which he hurled at his squad on every possible occasion. He loved to remind them that their future depended entirely on him. The company poet makes him speak thus :

> " You finks you'll all be wearing stars
> Wivin a week or two ;
> I bet you'll wish for prison bars
> Afore I've done wiv you.
>
> Look 'ere ! If you'll be pals wiv me,
> Then I'll be pals wiv you ;
> We'll work togevver, doncher see—
> I guarantee I'll get you through.
>
> But if you don't—well, s'elp me Gawd !
> Me name it isn't Bates,
> If I don't make an awkward squad
> For you and all your mates.
>
> I'll learn you 'ow to stand at ease
> And 'old your 'eads up in the hair !
> I'll show you 'ow to lift your knees
> And double rahnd the square !
>
> And then I'll learn you at the last
> Wiv whistles and your 'ands
> To dror attraction wiv a blast
> And issue all commands."

He certainly taught his squad how to acquire fog-horn voices, though many became speechless in the process.

The presiding genius of the school was for a short time a colonel who earned the name of " The Peacock." He was small and stout, and very fond of making elaborate entrances on to the parade ground, whilst the whole school of cadets stood rigidly to attention, hardly daring to breathe. His short, strutting stride and his pompous carriage made his resemblance to a peacock so marked that he only required a train of feathers to complete the illusion.

Nothing pleased him more than to set up a metronome in the centre of the square and make the companies march round as fast as they could go, in time to its quickened beat. As the step became faster and faster, and long legs and short legs strove hard to keep pace, the N.C.O.'s pursued them relentlessly, yelling, " LEF' RIGHT—LEF' RIGHT—LEF' RIGHT ! " as though they were possessed. The company poet, in a satirical poem called " The Peacock," describes the scene in these words :

> " Then on the square, the tom-tom beat,
> The howling sergeants roared aloud,
> And hurried on the hastening feet,
> And cursed and chased the helpless crowd."

Perhaps the worst shock to the cadets' feelings, however, came a week after they arrived at the school. A cross-country run of some five or six miles was announced for the following Saturday. Every cadet had to take part, and every man was timed in at various points on the route. N.C.O.'s were stationed to see that the cadets were keeping on the run, and that nobody was attempting a short cut. Besides causing considerable loss of breath, this test weeded out the aged, the weary, and the infirm.

After thoroughly learning squad, section, and platoon drill, there came the fateful day when a nervous cadet had to take a company in company drill. By his side stood the all-powerful colonel and the adjutant, notebook in hand. The company was marched far, far

SOMETHING TO LEARN!

away, right to the other end of the square, and then the colonel gently purred, " Now, march the company through those two markers without touching them."

The two markers had been placed in the centre of the square at a very awkward angle. Shouting to the full extent of his lungs, and yet feeling that his voice could hardly be heard, the unhappy cadet somehow struggled through the ordeal.

Other subjects in which he had to pass were: Military Law, Administration, Topography, First Aid, Sanitation, Bombing, Gas, the Lee-Enfield Rifle, the Lewis Gun, the 6-pounder Hotchkiss Q.F., Signalling, Bayonet fighting, and " Physical Jerks."

The P.T. (Physical Training) instructors were familiar figures at the Cadet School. They were arrayed in sand-shoes, long blue trousers, and striped jerseys of vivid hues. They were always bouncing up and down like Jack-in-the-Box, and buzzing from one end of a squad to the other, all the time rapping out commands in fierce voices. They were nicknamed " The Wasps," and they were experts in the art of delivering stinging rebukes. They were seen at their best in their blood-curdling demonstration of bayonet fighting. The savage fury with which they attacked the inoffensive sacks stuffed with straw, the intense pleasure they showed as they thrust and stabbed with one lightning jab after the other, their hair-raising cries and yells as they exhorted their clumsy pupils to further bloodshed, was at the same time impressive and repellent. It was rumoured that in spite of their lurid and bloodthirsty language they had never seen any actual fighting, and most probably this was correct, for it is one of the peculiarities of war that the farther away a man is from the firing line, and the safer his job, so much the more does he breathe the spirit of slaughter and revenge.

TANK WARFARE

A subject in which all cadets had to pass, under penalty of R.T.U. (Return to Unit), was topography, or the art of reading and making maps, and studying the natural features of the countryside. Nobody who has not attempted it can imagine the feeling of utter helplessness which descends on a beginner when he is told to go forth and explore a certain tract of countryside and make a map of it. He wonders what to start on, what to put in, and what to leave out, and his first effort somewhat resembles a blend of a futuristic painting and a crossword puzzle.

A favourite sport of the topography officer was to give every pair of cadets a series of difficult compass bearings with the distances to be marched on each bearing. When they had plotted out their directions and marched the required distances, they had to mark on the map the spot reached, which was checked back by the officer on their return.

Lost and wandering pairs of cadets could be seen all over the countryside, some forcing their way through brambles and undergrowth, some striving to jump across wide streams, some brought to an early finish by high walls, others ending up in the middle of a field of bulls or in the heart of a swamp.

When this exercise took place by the light of the moon, many cadets were so baffled that they gave up the quest as hopeless, and retired to the nearest place of refreshment.

On a really dark night a party of eager cadets would be taken on foot by this same enterprising officer across country. He twisted this way and that, climbed hills, plunged into valleys and through sombre woods, until he called a halt at some remote and unrecognizable spot.

Then, turning to his puzzled pupils, he pulled out his watch, looked at it by the light of an electric torch, and

LOST IN THE DARK

said: " It is now exactly 10.15 p.m. I want you to make your way back to my hut in pairs. You must promise me on your honour that you will keep at a walking pace. The first pair to arrive will be timed-in and given points accordingly. The rest will also have to mark the time of their arrival. I shall be there waiting for you. Goodnight." And he suddenly slipped away into the darkness.

The night was black as ink. Nothing could be seen but the dim outline of bushes; nothing could be heard but the murmuring of the wind among the trees.

In a few moments the cadets had split up and blundered off in different directions, blindly groping their way towards the camp. Some clever ones, with an uncanny sense of direction, soon found their way home over hill and dale, but the majority wandered aimlessly over the open heathland, stumbling over roots, continually tripped up by brambles, and at times falling abruptly into sand pits.

These exercises, though the cause of much grumbling and grousing at the time, proved very useful in France, when tank commanders often had to lead their tanks over unknown country in the depths of the night.

In order to increase their powers of observation the topography officers would also often take them for route marches, and then request them to write a full account of everything they had seen on the way. He was very fond of quoting extracts from his pupils' papers, much to the confusion of the one so honoured and the delight of the rest of the class.

After one march in the neighbourhood of Brookwood cemetery he quoted with glee one pupil's report: "The road ran *dead* straight through the cemetery." The funny side of this remark was increased by the fact that the victim was totally unable to see any humour in it.

Life, however, was not altogether a joke at the Cadet

School. Hard work and long hours were the order of the day. There were so many different subjects to study in so short a time that it was a wonder nobody suffered from congestion of the brain. Every cadet drilled hard and studied hard, for over his head there always dangled the sword of R.T.U., which meant that if he failed he would be returned to his unit in disgrace, and owing to the changing policy of the War Office, who would one day decide to increase the establishment of tanks and the next week to reduce it by half, no cadets were ever sure of gaining their commissions.

Ugly rumours went round that out of the previous company only a mere half-dozen were granted commissions, so an anxious atmosphere pervaded the school. When the end of those strenuous three months drew near and examinations were the order of the day, there was considerable uneasiness in the camp. It was like going to school again; cadets of all ages, now armed with pens, scribbled furiously sheet after sheet of military wisdom.

In the practical subjects things were not so difficult—especially in signalling, because the signalling sergeant had a knack of placing an experienced signaller near his most backward pupils. Messages were received by two cadets, one who called out the letters as he watched the flags wagging, and the other who wrote them down. The expert, generally a cadet who had come from an R.E. signalling company, shouted the letters in a loud voice, so that everybody at hand could hear. The sergeant, who naturally wanted all his pupils to pass, walked to and fro, apparently to prevent any cheating, but when he reached the expert he did not tell him to subdue his voice: he prodded him gently in the back, whispering, " Louder ! Louder ! "

There were no failures in signalling.

GETTING THE PIPS

When the fateful examinations were over and the commissions awarded, the jubilant cadets celebrated their last night at the Cadet School by driving a borrowed steam-roller around the square. Thus did they satisfy their yearning for tanks!

They had had three months of intensive cramming; they knew how to handle a company on a parade ground, how to mount and inspect guards, and how to tackle the finer points of military law. They had learnt the mechanism of the 6-pounder gun, they had passed tests in rifle and Lewis gun shooting, and knew how to adjust every stoppage and to give a detailed description of all the parts.

They had mastered the art of signalling by means of flags, buzzers, and shutters. They could put a squad of recruits through any exercise in physical training, explain to them fully the mysteries and use of gas masks and bombs, or teach them the elements of squad and rifle drill. They were experts at map reading and the use of the compass; they were physically fit, alert, and disciplined, and were eager to begin their real training—the driving and handling of the mysterious tank.

The fully-fledged second lieutenants were posted to the Tank Depot at Wareham, in Dorset, where they were first put through their paces on the square, in order perhaps to reduce any tendency to swollen heads which might arise from the wearing of a brand new " pip."

But Wareham was not the Promised Land, for the keen subalterns were still unable to quench their thirst for tank knowledge. They had to content themselves with minor courses, such as revolver shooting. One of the strangest courses was that concerned with pigeons. A squad of officers was marched into the pigeon hut, where a sergeant explained to them, with great detail, how and when to feed a pigeon, how to release it from its basket, how to roll up and attach a message to the clip on its leg, and how to start it off on its journey.

One weary pigeon acted as a demonstrator. Each officer advanced in turn, grabbed the poor bird in one hand, attached the message with the other, and replaced the pigeon in the basket. These lessons were going on all day long, and the wretched bird had become so used to being clumsily handled by scores of officers that it scarcely made a movement, realizing perhaps that passive resistance was the wisest plan.

It is interesting to recall that when a pigeon is released with a message from a tank in action, it is thrown downward so that its wings will open out, and it can then rise swiftly and fly away.

After a few weeks spent in this miscellaneous training the new officers were sent to Bovington Camp, near Wool, highly pleased to think that at last they were going to drive a real tank.

Wool is a picturesque and sleepy old Dorset village, and the tank camp at Bovington, a mile or so away, had been erected on the edge of a vast stretch of open heathland, which extended to the borders of Wiltshire. It was an ideal place for tank manœuvres and training, as it was far from main roads and prying eyes.

When the first tanks were driven from Wool station along the lonely road to Bovington Camp, tremendous precautions were taken to prevent any unauthorized person from discovering the "great secret." Military policemen were dotted all along the route. All traffic was stopped, and the inhabitants of all the farms and cottages bordering the road were requested to draw their blinds and keep in their back rooms.

This "hush-hush" business went on for some time, until one day a farmer informed the military authorities that he was only too pleased to help them in any way to keep this great secret, but he thought they ought to know that a few days before a tank had broken down and had been towed into his yard with the help of his horses! He also casually remarked that the tank stayed in his yard for forty-eight hours, without any attempt being made to hide it at all.

On their arrival at Bovington the tank aspirants were issued with a pair of dark brown dungarees, and next day the mechanism and structure of a tank was explained to them by instructors in the workshop hangars.

To one who was not well versed in engineering it was rather a bewildering process. Each separate part of the mechanism had a separate instructor, who rattled off his monotonous explanation to a bunch of officers, and as these instructors were sometimes quite close to each other their high-pitched voices often clashed. The eager officer on the outer edge of a group, hearing a lecture on the magneto, would suddenly find that he was listening to a talk on the carburettor, or that strange phrases about sprockets and pinions were also floating into his ear.

But what he failed to pick up from the instructors he soon learnt from his brother officers, who were so keen that they talked of nothing but tanks and tank mechanism from morning to night.

The first lesson in driving was given in a stationary tank, on the use of the clutch, the throttle, and the foot-brake, gear-changing, and the manipulation of the hand-brakes.

To a novice the array of levers and brakes was very mystifying, and when the engine started up the sudden roar was deafening and confusing. The instructor would suddenly lean forward and bellow in one's ear, " GET HER INTO NEUTRAL! " A trembling hand grasped the nearest lever and pulled hard, there would be a terrible grinding sound as if the tank was going to break in half, and the enraged instructor yelled, "NO, NOT THAT ONE! THE OTHER!" Afraid that the tank might fall to pieces at any moment, the officer quickly pulled everything within reach, to the accompaniment of ear-splitting sounds, until the engine suddenly stopped and the instructor, doubled up with laughter, spluttered out, "This is a tank, not a blessed signal-box."

After a time, however, the prospective landship commander found his sea legs and began to know his way about his strange craft, and that same evening, at twilight, he had his first view of tanks returning after a day's drive.

It was a most impressive and fearsome sight. Over the brow of the hill, dimly outlined against the dusk, loomed a herd of strange, toad-like monsters. The noise of whirring engines and the weird flap-flap-flap-flap of the tracks, like the padding of gigantic webbed feet, filled the air. The vast snouts went up and up, and then suddenly dipped down abruptly as the creatures breasted the slope.

Then, lurching, slithering, and stumbling, they raced for home. They made one shiver: they were so repulsive, so inhuman, so full of menace. Even though there was no danger, one felt fear creeping through one's veins. The impulse was to turn and run for dear life, but instead one stood there rooted with horror and admiration.

Was it a nightmare? Had these uncanny brutes emerged from some dim prehistoric age and come prowling forth into the world again?

Nearer and nearer they came, roaring fiercely and snorting flames in their frenzy to crush and devour. What soldiers in the world could be expected to stand against these thick-skinned monsters? The very sight of them, crawling relentlessly forward, was enough to

THE FIRST RIDE

inspire terror in the bravest man. With guns blazing, and machine guns chattering, they must have been the very symbol of ruthless destruction to the terrified troops of the enemy.

Suddenly the whole herd slowed down and stopped, and out of their steel sides dropped figures in overalls.

The spell was broken: the human element had appeared; terror gave way to curiosity. To-morrow the greenhorn himself would be driving one of these strange machines.

The first ride in a tank is a thrilling experience. I shall never forget mine. Climbing in cautiously through the narrow sponson door I was surprised to find I could not stand erect. I wormed my way past the engine to the driver's seat. The first impression of the interior was of its narrowness. How could eight men go into action boxed up in such a small space? There was just room to move down the narrow gangways on either side of the engine, and for a seat over the gear-box on which sat the controllers of the secondary gears.

The large cranking handle, situated just over this box, was turned by the united efforts of three or four men who handled it very cautiously, for when the engine back-fired the handle swung back with great force. It once happened that a man, straining on the handle, slipped and fell face downwards on the box; the engine back-fired at that moment, and the heavy handle struck him on the back of the neck and killed him.

When the 105-h.p. engine started up the din was terrific. The instructor shouted, " Get her into third ! " and the machine jolted forward at a tremendous pace.

There was a note of urgency from the engine, the tracks seemed to be devouring the ground, the hull was throbbing with the speed. Looking through the flap in the cab I was suddenly astounded to see somebody calmly *walking* past. We were only going two and a quarter miles per hour !

We clambered up slopes, we climbed down banks, and then right in front of us appeared a deep shell hole. " Go forward and take it quietly. Don't rush her too much," shouted the instructor. We came to the edge, the nose of the tank went out and out, and then dipped slightly down and down until we appeared to be driving straight into the ground. Then gradually the nose tilted upwards once more, and I was looking at the sky. Up and up we went as though we were about to jump off the ground. Then slowly and gradually we heeled forward, and soon I was looking out over level ground once more. We had crossed the crater.

We crawled over trenches at all angles. The driver is not bumped about as much as one would imagine, but automatically seems to change position with the machine. At one moment he is lying almost on his side, at another on his back, and at times he is staring straight into the ground, but if he nurses the throttle carefully, sooner or later the tank comes back to the horizontal. It is a very similar sensation to that of a ship riding the waves.

The crew in the rear of the tank are the only people liable to be thrown and bumped about, and they often have to hang on like grim death, to avoid contact with red-hot pipes and engine covers.

During the first day's driving I experienced an almost irresistible desire to fall asleep in my seat, everything was so warm, the atmosphere was so drowsy, but frequent halts and breathers in the fresh air kept me awake. This stupor, caused by the petrol fumes which pervade the inside, is common to all crews riding in a tank for the first time. After a few days' driving, however, I became accustomed to the fumes, the close air, and the heat.

Another driving exercise was to go slowly down a

DRIVING TESTS

very long and steep slope. Half-way down, the instructor gave the signal for the foot-brake to be applied, and to my great amazement the huge tank, weighing no less than twenty-eight tons, was pulled up in a few yards.

As we climbed slowly out again up the almost perpendicular side, the instructor motioned for the brake to be applied once more and the engine to be stopped. The motionless tank seemed to be hanging on to the slope like a fly on a wall. "Now put her in reverse and let go the brake," said the instructor. I did so, and the heavy machine began to slide down backwards in an alarming manner, but at the same time the engine spluttered and came to life again.

"Change gear quickly and climb up once more!" came the order, and by careful manipulation we soon clambered to the top.

This method of starting up a tank, when it is lying at such an angle that it is impossible to use the crank handle, often proved very useful to tank commanders when in action.

The tests for driving included the driving over a taped course, which had frequent turns and bends, and driving through a sunken road. The latter was very difficult, as the road was narrow, and had a series of right-handed turns. It was essential to be in the centre of the road and to be able to judge the right minute for turning, otherwise the tail of the tank swung round too sharply and hit the bank. The driver of any machine which touched the bank at all was disqualified. As turning necessitated signalling to the gearsman in the rear of the tank to put the secondary gear on one side in neutral, the operation required exact timing and a fair amount of skill.

In order to test the mechanical knowledge of tank drivers the track instructors often entered the tank, unseen and unheard, and interfered with the engine so that it stopped. The bewildered driver was then cross-examined and asked to give the cause of the stoppage.

I was one day driving up a small slope, when suddenly the engine spluttered and, in spite of my efforts at throttling, " conked " out immediately. I naturally thought that it was due to my bad driving, for I had never acquired the professional touch, when a loud voice rang in my ears, " What was the reason for that stoppage ? "

Somewhat startled, I turned round in my seat and, to my horror, saw the most severe of track instructors.

" Why—er—I perhaps did not—er," I began to stutter, when suddenly I caught sight of one of the gearsmen, who was standing right behind the dreaded examiner and making dumb show with his lips. I understood his message immediately, and stopping short in the middle of my speech, I adopted an air of profound wisdom (or the nearest I could get to it), and after a minute or so of intense thinking I raised the engine cover and, giving a rapid glance in the manner of an expert, I said, " You can't expect the engine to go when the pencil is missing." He laughed, produced it from his pocket, and jumped out again. Needless to say I thanked the gearsman heartily for his prompt assistance.

The climax of the course was to take what was humorously known as the " Swallow Dive." This exercise, which every driver had to tackle, was discussed by all novices with bated breath. Rumours of nasty jolts and jars, and tales of severe bruisings abounded. It was an alarming plunge into a deep shell hole, and no tank man was fully " blooded " until he had piloted a tank through this ordeal.

The tank was driven slowly up a small incline. When it reached the top, the driver was told to go cautiously on and on until it was rocking gently on its centre of

THE SWALLOW DIVE

balance, on the very summit of the incline. The machine then stopped. "Now, look down," said the instructor.

The startled novice peered down through the flap. He seemed to be perched in mid-air. The nose of the tank was well off the ground, and right below loomed the depths of a vast crater. The drop appeared to be tremendous. To his anxious eyes it seemed at least fifty feet! Surely it was impossible for a tank to leap down there!

But the instructor was merciless. After he had let the driver feast his eyes on the "jump," he told him to drive backwards a little way. "Now, change gear, go forward and over the top. Keep your hand on the throttle, and don't forget directly you feel yourself falling, throttle down. Don't open out until the tracks hit the ground"!

With that he clambered out on to safer ground. He was going to be the audience for this act.

Slowly the tank went forward, inch by inch it crept over the top of the incline. His heart in his mouth, the driver fingered the throttle nervously. He dared not peep through the flap into that bottomless pit. Suddenly the nose of the tank tilted forward, and the huge machine went down, and down, and down. He had the sensation of dropping gently through space. The throttle was almost closed, the engine was just ticking over; without warning the tank plunged violently downwards and, with a terrific bump, the heavy snout struck the ground. The tank, for a second, practically stood on end. One of the gearsmen in the rear, taken unawares, was hurled clean out of the sponson door. The others clung wildly to anything within reach, their feet sliding and scraping over the steel floor. Grease drums, oil cans, and stray tools shot forward in a clattering mass, landing on the driver's back and spraying him with oil.

TANK WARFARE

The driver himself was at such an angle that he looked straight into the earth a couple of feet in front of his face. But the throttle was now opened out full, and as the engine raced, the caterpillar tracks gripped firmly, and foot by foot the tank crawled up to the top of the crater. Then, slightly shaken but triumphant, the driver got out to watch the next tank go over.

The "Swallow Dive" was a striking demonstration of the capabilities of a tank. To plunge into a pit twenty feet deep and then crawl out unscathed is a feat which many a motorist would class as a "tall story." Often, however, a trembling driver forgot to throttle down when taking the leap, with the result that the nose of the tank, hitting the ground with increased violence, stuck in the earth, and the engine petered out, leaving the unlucky crew badly shaken and almost standing on their heads.

At the end of a day's driving a most disagreeable job had to be done. The tank is a monster with a voracious appetite, and besides devouring huge quantities of petrol, has to be fed daily on grease. This was injected by means of grease guns, and as many of the apertures for greasing the tracks and rollers were placed at the base of the tank, it was necessary to lie flat on the ground to perform this sticky rite. When the ground was muddy, the language of the grease-gun brigade must have made the ears of the tank inventors tingle furiously.

The officers and men at Bovington Camp moved in an atmosphere of keenness and petrol. They were all desperately eager to learn all they could about tanks, and a few bumps and minor accidents (I had a finger nail ripped off whilst manipulating a troublesome secondary gear), or a constant aroma of petrol, oil, and grease, did not deter them in the least.

To emphasize the naval aspect of the landship, all

SIX-POUNDER PRACTICE

officers took a course in the ship's compass. This was conducted by an ancient mariner, who explained its uses and mysteries.

Even art was not neglected, for a well-known R.A. could be seen daily, mounted on a ladder, busily painting wonderful designs for camouflage nets.

As a change from petrol engines and machinery, some of the officers used to hire traps in the village of Wool and drive over to the beautiful cove at Lulworth on Sunday afternoons. The delightful country lanes, the freshness of the air, and the steady trot-trot of the horse were a pleasant contrast to the grim interior of a tank, the smell of petrol, and the roar of engines.

When the tank-driving and maintenance course was finished, squads of officers were marched back along the dusty highway to Wareham, and then, on the following day, they tramped the long weary road to Lulworth Camp.

Here, in the most beautiful surroundings, they were taught how to fire a 6-pounder gun from a tank. The targets were situated on the land side of a great cliff, and were bombarded from across a valley.

The flash and boom of a 6-pounder with a shortened barrel was very startling on first acquaintance, especially when bottled up inside a tank, but one soon became used to this handy little gun and came to respect its accuracy.

As it was a naval gun installed in a landship the firing practice was similar to that done by battleships, except that the targets did not move. The tanks crawled over the undulating downs, whilst the gunner glued his eye to the telescopic sight. There were no targets visible to the naked eye, but flashes were made to denote battery positions, and the gunner had to hit the spot from which the flash came.

TANK WARFARE

It seemed tremendously difficult at first, the more so as the tank kept going up and down with every rise and fall of the ground. The secret was to keep the eye fixed to the sight and the finger on the trigger. Whenever a flash appeared one switched the centre of the telescopic sight, at the point where the lines crossed, on to the desired spot and waited till a second flash came, then immediately pulled the trigger. Invariably one hit the mark.

To fire a 6-pounder in the cramped interior the gunner knelt on the floor, with his No. 2 crouched beside him waiting to reload. The recoil of the gun sent the breech back almost as far as the engine cover, but the gunner was protected from injury by a shield of steel. At times the trigger was pulled and no explosion resulted. Anxiously one waited a long minute of suspense, fearing that at any second the shell might explode in the breech. Then, gingerly opening the breech, the tank commander seized the offending shell and, taking it boldly in his arms, flung it quickly through the opening at the bottom of the sponson door. Luckily this was a rare occurrence.

Other interesting courses at Wareham were those on that most important subject, reconnaissance. Parties of officers, notebook in hand, were sent to make a detailed report on Poole station from the tank point of view. They had to discover whether it were a junction or a terminus, the type of country on each side of the line, the gauge, the number of lines and how they were laid, the type of rail with weight in pounds per yard, the gradients, the measurements of the platform and the materials of which it was made, the type of signalling, the rolling stock, the number of engines, details of tunnels, cuttings, and embankments; the position and measurements of the ramps and their suitability for unloading of tanks, the condition of roads leading to

INVADING A RAILWAY STATION

the station, the water supply, the facilities for night entraining, and the position of level crossings, etc.

Swarms of officers clambered over the rails and sidings, noting and measuring. Others seriously paced the platforms or stormed the signal-boxes in search of information. Astonished railwaymen gaped at them open mouthed. Had the British Army gone mad? They might have been confirmed in their diagnosis had they seen the results of this mighty investigation on some of the weird scraps of paper which were handed in under the heading of " Plan of Poole Station."

All future tank commanders were taught also how to read aeroplane photographs by ascertaining the direction of light at the time the photograph was taken and intently studying the shadows.

So the good work went on. Then one day they would suddenly find themselves on a draft for France, and within a week they would be proud commanders of a tank in a fighting battalion, with an opportunity of putting their knowledge to the supreme test.

CHAPTER 8

Improvements—The Mark IV. tank—Blowing up the Boche—The unditching beam—The "hush-hush" scheme

IN the meantime the new Mark IV. tanks were arriving in France. They were not so wide or so heavy as the original "Willie"; they did not carry so much ammunition, and they contained several improvements.

The petrol tanks, which in the Mark I. were situated in the interior of the forward part of the machine, near the seats of the officer and driver, were now combined into one heavily-armoured tank large enough to hold sixty gallons, placed outside at the back. This improvement made the cab of a tank less of a death trap, as in the first tanks a direct hit in front generally resulted in the officer and driver being burnt alive.

The tracks had wider shoes and the armour was much thicker all over, so that now the German "K" bullets could not penetrate. The 6-pounder gun was shortened, and the track rollers and links made of cast iron, thus enabling them to stand much greater wear than previously.

The sponsons were also considerably modified. In the male they were reduced in size and weight, and after being unbolted could be pushed in together with the gun. The female was supplied with a double door under each sponson, which could also be swung in. Besides abolishing the tedious system of unbolting and lowering by means of girders on to separate trolleys, the new sponsons gave a much better chance of escape to the crew. The old

THE MARK IV. TANK

female tank only possessed a small door, two feet high, in each sponson, and when a tank was hit and set on fire only one or two of the crew managed to crawl out of these narrow doors before the interior had become a blazing furnace.

The double glass prisms, let into the flaps of the cab for the purposes of observation, were also replaced by steel plates pricked with minute holes.

They were all armed with Lewis guns, although a military committee had decided in May 1917 that this type of gun was useless in a tank, and recommended that

Diagram showing position of crew and guns in Mark IV. tank.
Left to right: Gearsman—Lewis gunner, who was also No. 2 of 6-pounder—Six-pounder gunner—Driver—Tank commander, with Lewis gun. The shading shows the position of the engine.—*From a sketch by Capt. R. L. Phillips*, R.A.S.C. (T.A.).

it should be replaced by the Hotchkiss. As it was the War Office which had forced the Lewis gun on the tanks against the advice of the tank experts in November 1916, this change of face showed that even the military mind was capable of learning by experience, though often that experience was gained at the expense of others. However, the decision came too late for the tanks used in 1917, and it was not till the Mark V. appeared on the scene in 1918 that the Hotchkiss once more came into its own.

The next action in which tanks appeared was the

TANK WARFARE

Battle of Messines, in June 1917. It had for its object the capture of the Messines ridge, and was a very carefully planned and swiftly successful operation.

For a year beforehand our tunnelling companies had been burrowing their way, yard by yard, under the enemy's lines. They had dug no less than five miles of galleries. We intended not so much to go over the top and drive the Germans out, as to blow them up from below.

Twenty great mines were carefully and secretly laid. These contained altogether over a million pounds of ammonal. As the day approached for exploding these mines our listeners, crouching in remote galleries far beneath the earth, heard the unmistakable tap-tap, tap-tap of German tunnellers. They were driving a gallery right in the direction of our great mine underneath Hill 60! Would we be countermined and all our efforts made useless? Anxiously the listeners waited and listened. They calculated that if our attack took place on the date arranged, the German countermine would just fail to reach us. So we let him carry on, all unsuspecting.

Seventy-two tanks were to help the infantry, and for the first time we used twelve old tanks to bring up supplies. Each supply tank held sufficient "fills" for five fighting tanks. A "fill" is the amount required to fill up a tank, and consisted of 20 gallons of water, 60 gallons of petrol, 10 gallons of oil, 10 lb. of grease, 10,000 rounds of small arms ammunition for a female, and 200 rounds of 6-pounder ammunition and 6,000 rounds of small arms ammunition for a male.

A thunderstorm of great violence raged on 6th June, rivalling the fierce and incessant bombardment of our artillery. At three o'clock the guns died down, and for a few minutes there was an uncanny silence. At ten minutes past three the mines were detonated.

BLOWING UP THE BOCHE

First came a low, insistent rumble, then a mighty growl that swiftly burst into one tremendous roar, making the air vibrate with terror. Great spouts of earth and volcanoes of flame shot up from the German line. The crimson sky was barred by flying fragments of gold, great masses of earth vomited forth against the rising sun, and then, while the ground still shuddered in anguish, down came our barrage with a resounding crash, and infantry and tanks went forward to the attack.

The German front line had been completely wiped out. Here and there in the reserve lines, pale, nerve-shattered creatures crouched trembling and shaking in the pitiful remains of a dug-out. Everywhere the attack was successful. The tanks were hardly needed, so well had the mines and the artillery done their task, and so quickly and surely did the infantry advance.

One tank reached its objective in one hour forty minutes, and as its route lay across two miles of scarred and churned-up ground, this was very good going.

Three tanks of "A" Battalion, after mopping up machine-gun positions near Joye Farm, patrolled up and down whilst the infantry was consolidating its position. In the dusk they became ditched, and as darkness followed quickly they waited until dawn to start unditching operations. When it became light, however, they discovered that the enemy was massing for a counter-attack, so they decided to turn themselves into forts.

The Lewis gunners took their guns outside the tanks and formed strong points in shell holes. As the Germans came on down the valley the 6-pounders opened out on them, the Lewis guns chattered away, and they were stopped. They fired streams of armour-piercing bullets at the ditched tanks, and were astonished that these had no effect. They had not reckoned on meeting tanks with thicker armour.

TANK WARFARE

Repeatedly they came on to the attack, but each time the 6-pounders cut up their ranks and brought them to a standstill.

At last, after this handful of tank men had held the enemy at bay for over five hours, our artillery put down a violent barrage, which effectually damped the ardour of the attackers.

Their morning's " good deed " having been accomplished, the crews set calmly to work to unditch their tanks, but in this they were not so successful, and after an hour or two of laborious efforts the tanks had to be abandoned and the Lewis guns handed over to the nearest infantry.

When tanks had to be evacuated in no-man's-land it was always the rule for the officer in charge to dismantle the telescopic sights and breech blocks of the 6-pounder guns and bury them near at hand, either in the parapet of a trench or at a spot which can easily be recognized. The place of burial was carefully noted by the tank commander, and the map reference given to the adjutant of the company, who arranged for a salvage company to collect them at a later date, if that was possible.

The Lewis guns were handed over to the infantry, but the tank officer must retain a receipt for them or else woe betide him ! He might lose half his crew and hand over the other half to the Field Dressing Station as wounded, but they were merely human flesh and bone, and no receipts were required for them. But one Lewis gun not accounted for would involve him in endless correspondence and bring down upon him the wrath of those mighty ones who pursue their exalted careers far from the mud and blood of the common firing line.

It can easily be seen, however, that it was most important not to leave Lewis guns in the tank, or any 6-pounder capable of being fired, or the enemy might have

"TANK CORPS" AT LAST

gained possession of the tank and turned our own guns on us.

After the Battle of Messines, on June 28, 1917, the name of the Heavy Section Machine-Gun Corps was changed to the Tank Corps, the War Office realizing at last that the existence of tanks was no longer hidden from anybody!

Another change, too, was made in the equipment of a tank, the narrow torpedo-shaped boom being replaced by the "unditching beam." This was a huge baulk of teak, 12 feet long and weighing 9 cwt., strengthened at each end by iron. It had been evolved at the central workshops in France, and was intended to assist a tank to escape from the very frequent fate of being hopelessly stuck in the mud or bellied in loose earth. Under battle conditions it was placed crosswise on top of the tank, resting on guide rails, which lifted it clear of the conning tower or any other obstacle on top. The ends projected slightly beyond the tracks, the beam itself being attached to the girder rails by clips, to prevent it falling off when the tank was climbing in and out of steep shell holes. It can be seen across the back of the Mark IV. tank in the frontispiece.

When a tank became ditched one of the crew climbed out of the manhole in the roof and, releasing the clips, attached the beam to the tracks on each side by means of a pair of heavy chains. The differential gear then being locked and the clutch released, the revolving tracks carried the beam over the snout of the tank, where it swung to the full extent of its chains until it was carried under the belly. When it was firmly jammed between the ground and the tracks the latter could grip its solid surface, and the tank climbed out again. Sometimes, however, when the ground was particularly swampy, the beam was dragged right underneath and came up behind,

TANK WARFARE

dripping with mud and slime, whilst the tank still floundered helplessly in the morass.

Generally these beams were very useful and helped tanks to get over very difficult ground. The great drawback was that they had to be adjusted from the outside, usually under heavy fire from the enemy, a task requiring great courage and coolness of mind.

During the next few months the Tank Corps was fighting one of the most hopeless series of fights in its existence. The dreaded Salient of Ypres, which had become the graveyard of the British Army, was chosen as the scene of a vast offensive, and three brigades of tanks (216 machines) were detailed to assist.

The object was to drive the enemy from the ridges overlooking Ypres, and then advance along the Flanders coast against the German bases, especially the submarine bases. At that time the unrestricted submarine campaign was gradually throttling the English Mercantile Marine, and threatened to cut off England's food supplies.

One part of this offensive was known as the "hush-hush" scheme. It was a bold and original plan to attack the enemy in a spot where he least expected it. Whilst the main armies were pushing forward in front of Ypres and along the coast, a small force was to swoop down on the Belgian coast at Middelkerke, a seaside place between Neuport and Ostend, and tackle the enemy in the rear.

The bold raiders were to be carried on three vast pontoons, each 700 feet long, which were built in the Thames and conveyed to Dunkirk harbour. The pontoons were to carry, in addition to the infantry of the 1st Division, several batteries of 18-pounders and 4.5 howitzers, a couple of companies of the Royal Engineers, some motor lorries, and nine tanks.

The places selected for the landing had been chosen

THE HUSH-HUSH SCHEME

after very careful examination of numerous aerial photographs at all states of the tide.

Under cover of a dense smoke barrage and a heavy bombardment by the warships of the Dover Patrol, monitors lashed together in pairs would push the vast barges with their human freight on to the shelving beach just before dawn. The sea front on this coast is protected by a steep sea wall of concrete about thirty feet high, which had a projecting coping. On top of the wall is an esplanade, and across the roadway a row of villas. There was barbed wire on the beach, and field guns concealed along the wall and in the sand dunes. The esplanade, too, was thickly wired, and the ground floors of the villas had been made into concrete machine-gun positions.

Altogether the place bristled with defences, and we could only hope to smash through them by surprise. For this purpose the nine tanks were to be used. Once on the beach, the sea wall had to be surmounted. The infantry might perhaps storm the esplanade, but in order to hold the position they would require guns, ammunition, and supplies. These would have to be hauled up and over the steep sea wall by the tanks.

The wall had not been long built, and luckily the Belgian architect who had designed it was a refugee in France. When he was traced the military authorities found to their delight that he had his drawings with him, so a model was built in an isolated camp near Dunkirk, where the infantry patiently practised and re-practised the assault.

A similar concrete model was erected in the lonely sand dunes at Merlimont, near Paris-Plage, and a detachment of tanks, manned by volunteers, set about the difficult task of climbing the wall.

The surface was very smooth and steep, and for a tank to scale it was an awkward proposition. This, however, could have been overcome by fixing special shoes on the tracks. The difficulty of the overhanging coping still remained. Many experiments were made by the tank engineers, and at last a solution was found. Each tank was fitted with a large steel ramp a little wider than the tank itself, and supported on girders to which were attached a pair of wheels. When the tank reached the foot of the wall, the ramp was lowered by means of tackle until the wheels rested on the slope. The tank then trundled it up the incline, like a wheelbarrow, until the wheels came to a stop against the coping. The wheels were then detached, and the tank, after disengaging itself, was able to climb up over the ramp on to the esplanade.

After dealing with the barbed wire and machine-gun positions, the tanks had then to haul the guns and motor-lorries up the wall. Naturally these vehicles would be subjected to severe strain if dragged straight up the steel ramp and then bumped on to the flat surface of the esplanade. So a strong gangway was fixed on the top of the ramp. The guns and other vehicles were to be hauled up this gangway, and on reaching the point of balance, their weight, tipping it over see-saw fashion, would enable them to run gently on to the esplanade.

When these difficulties had been finally mastered, the tanks rehearsed daily the scaling of the wall and the hauling up of guns and motor-lorries, until everything went without a hitch. No stranger sight could be imagined than these gigantic slugs slowly crawling up the model sea wall. It seemed as if at any moment they would fail to grip the steep incline, and that their huge weight would cause them to crash helplessly to the ground. But the wonderful climbing powers of the tank, which under the delicate touch of a skilled driver could climb an almost perpendicular slope, never failed, and not a single accident is recorded.

PASSCHENDAELE

In order to allay the curiosity of chance onlookers, the rumour was spread about that the tanks were rehearsing an assault on the forts of Lille.

Unfortunately, or rather fortunately for those who were appointed as actors in this drama, the "hush-hush" scheme was never tried out. It still remains a plan on paper only. The strip of land near the coast, beyond the mouth of the Yser, which had only just been taken over by the British and which was a vital jumping-off point for any offensive along the Belgian coast, was suddenly snatched from us by a swift German attack. The Boche had forestalled us and won the first move in the game! We still held Nieuport, but the bridgeheads, which were necessary for any concentration of troops, were in German hands.

In addition, the forward sweep of the victorious armies in front of Ypres had been reduced to a mud-crawl. It was expected that the village of Passchendaele would have been taken in three days. Instead, our sorely-tried troops were still floundering through the swamps three months later, and Passchendaele, which in the first few days was a symbol of hope, had become a portent of doom.

In such circumstances there was no chance of support for any attack from the sea. So in October the "hush-hush" brigade crept quietly back to their units, and the little *plage* of Middelkerke slept on undisturbed.

Would the attack have been successful? If a few field guns had survived the naval bombardment they could have blown the pontoons sky-high directly it grew light enough, and the little force would then have been stranded. Again, one field gun situated on the esplanade and manned by courageous gunners, could have caught each tank at point-blank range as their great noses were slowly thrust over the top of the wall.

TANK WARFARE

It was a desperate scheme, and one likely either to succeed completely or to fail disastrously. Considering the strong defences, the steep wall, the acres of barbed wire, and the nests of machine guns, that audacious force, drifting in slowly on their frail rafts, seemed doomed to extinction.

But there are two things to remember: the human factor and the element of surprise. Imagine those German gunners, with rumours creeping back to them that the British Army had taken the Passchendaele Ridge and was wheeling forward to Ostend, and that another army was attacking up the coast not far away.

They would be full of anxious excitement, wondering how long it would be before they were called hastily up to the line to stem the British tide or perhaps, even worse, to prepare for a retreat. Then suddenly, out of the dawn, a hurricane of shells came bursting round their quiet villas, and before they had recovered from the shock nine vast forms loomed up in the mist over the sea wall and, battering through the barbed wire, came straight for them, spitting bullets and vomiting shells.

How could they be expected to stand and fight these iron monsters that had crawled from out the very bed of the sea? Rather would they not desert their guns and fly as their brothers did on the Somme, screaming, " The devil is coming ! "

CHAPTER 9

The dreaded salient—Treachery—Ugly rumours—How to empty a " pill-box "—Fighting for sixty-two hours—Fray Bentos holds up the Boche.

THE Third Battle of Ypres, which ended in the capture of the Passchendaele Ridge, makes one of the most tragic stories of the war.

The country in this part of Flanders is flat and swampy. The Germans were firmly seated in a semi-circle on a ridge of low hills which overlooked Ypres and the British lines from three different directions. Behind the German lines was a swampy valley, and in the rear of that another low ridge of hills. Our object was to attack across the marshy ground, capture the first line of hills, descend into the swamp on the other side, and then advance uphill once more to storm the second ridge.

A hundred years before, Ypres had been a seaport, and acre by acre the neighbouring countryside had been reclaimed from the sea by an intricate system of dykes which drained the land. But for three years the British and German armies had faced each other there, and continual shelling had destroyed the dykes, blocked the streams, and rendered the whole salient one vast marsh.

Yet it was across this type of ground that our infantry was to attack, and for some unknown reason heavy tanks were chosen to assist them. The tank chiefs protested vehemently; they pointed out that no tank could cross such water-logged ground, that tanks were not submarines, and that, if they were used, it would simply be throwing away highly-trained men and wasting valuable machines. But the decree had gone forth; the Higher Command was intent on its battle, and it had been ordained that tanks should be used. Arguments were of no avail.

Week by week the concentration of troops and guns increased. The enemy observed it all with great interest, and shelled every road, every railway, every wood, and every possible place where troops could shelter. At night his aeroplanes came booming over, dropping bombs on huts and dug-outs. Some sections were so harassed by shelling that it became impossible for anybody to go up to the forward areas by daylight. All rations and shells had to be taken up by night. All working-parties went forward as soon as the darkness descended, dug gun-pits and trenches, constructed roads and duckboard tracks, and crept back before dawn came. Every night and all night the roads were shelled, and the wastage of lives was considerable, but our men stuck to it grimly.

The methodical habits of the Germans even extended to their shelling. At certain spots our troops knew that shells would drop every five or ten minutes. They came at length to know these fixed intervals. They waited for the shelling to cease, and then everybody dashed hastily across the danger zone before the next batch of shells was due to arrive.

The 1st Tank Brigade had formed a tankodrome at Oosthoek Wood, the tanks arriving by night and being very carefully camouflaged. Not long after their arrival the wood was shelled by day and bombed by night. Nobody could understand how the Boche had discovered their hiding-place. Next week a raiding-party captured a German document which revealed the cause of the trouble. It contained the information given by a British prisoner, one Sergeant Phillips, who, when cross-examined

THE THIRD BATTLE OF YPRES

by his German captors, had told them everything that he knew. Along with other statements, he gave exact information about the hiding-place of the tanks, their approximate strength, and their movements.

The result of his treachery was that, owing to the constant shelling, the wood had to be evacuated by all the officers and men, only a handful being left to guard the tanks. The name of the traitor, together with the official account of his baseness, was read out on parade to all tank units to warn them of the great need for secrecy. This account mentioned that when Sergeant Phillips returned to England after the war he would be tried and punished in the only way suitable for traitors.

For tanks to move up to the line across this country of dykes and swamps, it was necessary to build miles of causeways. Bridges had also to be constructed over the canals. This work was done by the 184th Tunnelling Company of Royal Engineers, and as the Germans had a complete view of everything that was happening, they naturally did all they could to prevent any progress. Shrapnel, high explosive and gas shells were rained down on the unfortunate workers, who were often toiling away in mud up to their knees, and were compelled to wear gas masks for long periods. After strenuous efforts they would succeed in laying down a useful stretch of causeway, when over would come a batch of shells and destroy their handiwork in a few minutes.

As most of the prominent landmarks had completely disappeared under the continual shelling, the reconnaissance officers of the tank battalions set to work to map out a series of compass bearings, taken from well-known spots, to points in the enemy's lines. By use of these a tank commander could keep direction across the flat marshy land in which it was so easy to lose one's way.

In preparation for the battle the tanks had been given

several new articles of equipment, the strangest of which was a carriage clock mounted in brass. It was really a handsome affair, more fit for a spacious dug-out or a comfortable Nissen hut than the cramped interior of a greasy tank, and demands for these clocks to replace those alleged to have been destroyed by shell fire became so excessive that the issue was stopped after the Third Battle of Ypres.

The next most prized item was a pair of binoculars, and it was really astonishing how many of these, too, were stated to have been destroyed by shell fire. Electric hand-lamps, six periscopes and signalling shutters were also in the list, in addition to a very complete medical haversack containing splints, iodine, small tins of ammonia tablets to sniff when gassed, shell dressings, and remedies against burns. These thoughtfully provided and ominous medical " comforts " were not, however, so popular with the crew as the other more ornamental fittings.

From the stationery point of view the tank was also well provided, as the tank commander possessed a log-book in which to record the daily running of his landship, a battle history sheet on which to inscribe in full detail the record and movements of his tank in action, a list of spare parts and tools, and last but not least, pigeon message forms. The poor pigeons were taken into action in a basket which, for lack of room, was often placed on top of the engine. In the heat and excitement of a battle they were sometimes overlooked, and when the basket was opened at last there emerged a decidedly overheated and semi-asphyxiated bird.

The moving of the petrol tank to the rear left two vacant spaces in the interior of the cab, which were converted into cupboards. One was just near the officer's seat, and was the only hint of luxury in the machine.

TANK CORPS.
DAILY TANK LOG.

Form TK22

Battalion..................................
Date.................................... Manfrs. Tank No......................

DUTY.

Batt. Tank No.	Fighting
Company	Training
Hr. Eng. Run	Trekking
Gals. Petrol	Testing
,, Track Oil	Not Running
,, Engine Oil	Under Repair
Lbs. Grease	Weather—Wet or Dry

TANK PARTS REPLACED BY NEW MATERIAL.

Material Mark or No.	Part No.	DESCRIPTION.	Reason Renewed.

INVOLUNTARY STOPS—CAUSE.	Minutes Lost.

DETAILS AS TO GROUND PASSED OVER.

Signature of Tank Commander..

TANK WARFARE

Here one could stow away bottles of liqueurs, vermouth and whisky, and water-bottles of rum, so that it was possible for all to have a quiet drink when in the very midst of fierce fighting.

For any big engagement two days' ordinary rations were carried, in addition to the emergency ration, and sometimes extras were issued in the shape of chocolates, biscuits, oranges, and lemons. When these arrived the crew immediately knew that they would soon be setting out on a pleasant trip into the enemy's territory.

The attack was due on 31st July 1917. For sixteen days our massed artillery, the largest concentration of guns ever made by the British Army during the whole of the war, fiercely bombarded the enemy's lines, until it seemed as if no human being could possibly survive that tempest of destruction. It tore great holes in the ground, completely smashed up the dykes, diverted streams from their courses, and made the whole area absolutely waterlogged. No sooner were shell holes created than they became immediately full of water.

On 31st July we attacked at dawn on a front of seven miles, and practically everywhere our troops gained their objectives. In the afternoon it began to rain. The enemy counter-attacked, but we still held the captured ridge. All night long he kept on attacking, and all night long it rained steadily. Next day we were going to deliver another great blow, but the rain kept on, washing away all hopes of victory. For four endless days it came down ceaselessly. The shell holes brimmed over and became ponds, the ponds turned into lakes, the lakes merged into one vast sea of muddied water.

Lying in shell holes full of slime, our brave troops, drenched to the skin, endured endless misery. The only tracks by which they could cross the sodden wilderness behind them were continually shelled. To leave the track

UGLY RUMOURS

was to take the risk of drowning, and at night mules and men often plunged into a watery grave.

The tanks had naturally not accomplished miracles in that first attack. Although they gave valuable assistance to the infantry, they could not swim. Most of the day's history for tank commanders could be summed up in the fateful words, " Bellied in boggy ground." Many, by use of their unditching beams, managed to struggle out of the oozy slime, but the majority sunk lower and lower, until the water came in through the sponson doors and stopped the engines.

As they wallowed in the mud they were attacked by aeroplanes, and subjected to direct fire from the enemy artillery. Many of the crews were killed and wounded without getting to grips with the Germans at all.

The depressing effect of rain, rain, rain, day and night, and the postponement of their hopes of driving back the enemy, made the army commanders sullen and embittered. They looked round for a scapegoat, and found it in the numerous tanks stranded on all sides in that desolate swamp. Tanks are no good, they said ; they can't cross bad country, and as a battlefield is always very badly churned up they will always be useless in battle. A report was framed ; ugly rumours circulated ; the Higher Command in France, it was whispered, was in favour of the total abolition of tanks. The stout heart of General Elles, the young commander of the Tank Corps, was stricken with horrible doubts and fears. The corps which he had fathered and championed, the great invention in which he had such complete confidence, was on the point of being suddenly extinguished. He had seen his precious tanks being wilfully misused, he had seen his highly trained men wantonly sacrificed in the mud ; and now, to crown all, they were going to wipe out the Tank Corps in a moment of pique and despondency.

TANK WARFARE

"If only they would give me a chance," he said to himself. "I'll prove to them yet that, used in the right way over the right ground, my tanks will lead the infantry to victory." So, though the outlook was black, he still hoped and planned.

Then on 16th August, nearly a fortnight after the first attack, the weather improved and the second big attack was launched. It encountered the new German method of defence. He held his first line, a series of fortified shell holes, with a few men only. When attacked they fell back through what was known as the "pill-box" zone. These "pill-boxes" were small forts of concrete, with walls at least three feet thick, holding garrisons of thirty to forty men, and plentifully supplied with loop-holes through which peeped the wicked noses of machine-guns. Some of them only stood a yard or two above the ground, whilst others were built into the ruins of farms and houses.

The German artillery was drawn well back, ready to shell the attackers held up in the pill-box zone. His reserves were in the second line, waiting for an immediate counter-attack directly the advancing troops had expended their initial energy. Our infantry, toiling slowly through the mud, came to a standstill against these walls of concrete. Light field guns failed to destroy them, bombs had no effect on them, and so our men fell like leaves in autumn.

After the action, a little cluster of pill-box fortresses near St. Julien still remained uncaptured. There were four of them, one called the Mont du Hibou held by eighty men, and the largest, called the Cockroft, manned by a garrison of one hundred, its walls in places being eight feet thick. It was vital that they should be taken, as they were holding up the whole advance. The corps commander was informed by his generals that to capture

EMPTYING "PILL-BOXES"

them would cost about a thousand casualties. General Sir Ivor Maxse, however, was one of the few commanders who had any faith in tanks. He arranged that a batch of tanks should advance at dawn along the road, as the open ground was in such a terrible condition. There was to be no warning bombardment, but the artillery would put down a dense smoke barrage just beyond the pill-boxes, thus blinding the enemy and cutting him off from observation of the tanks' movements. Two tanks were to attack each stronghold by getting behind it and blazing away at its one weak spot, the entrance door.

Everything went with a swing.

At dawn down came the great wall of smoke, shutting off the doomed pill-boxes, and the tanks crawled forward. The first fortress, Hillock Farm, must have been held by men seized with panic, for no sooner had the first tank drawn up alongside and treated it to a vigorous broadside than the whole garrison fled helter-skelter across the mud.

At the Mont du Hibou, which was a two-storeyed pill-box, a determined male tank left the road and plunged into the mud to tackle the fortress from the rear. It kept going until it became bogged. By a lucky chance one of its 6-pounder guns was pointing straight at the back door. The 6-pounder boomed away, and in a few minutes had blown a nasty hole in the door. Stolidly the 6-pounder kept on with its good work, and fired forty rounds into the ever-widening gap.

The garrison was bewildered. Well protected by their thick walls, they had confidently awaited an attack from the front, and now here was a savage gun actually dropping shells in their very midst from the rear! They could stand it no longer, and bolted like rabbits. Some escaped, but the remainder were shot down or surrendered to the infantry, who followed closely behind.

TANK WARFARE

The third pill-box, Triangle Farm, was manned by gunners of a stouter breed, for they fiercely replied to the fire of the tanks, but the two machines eventually got the upper hand, and the infantry, forcing their way in, shot or bayoneted the whole garrison.

Owing to the ditching of a male tank, one female had the difficult task of attacking single-handed the biggest strong point, the Cockroft. Undaunted she set out over the mud, her machine guns spitting away valiantly. When within fifty yards of the thick walls she became firmly stuck, but her appearance on the scene was quite enough for the large garrison. They decided not to await the same fate as their comrades, and swiftly departed. The tank commander immediately signalled to the infantry following behind by waving a shovel through the manhole in the roof. This was the prearranged signal that the pill-box had been evacuated, but no notice was taken. He then sent his sergeant back with a message to the infantry to come forward and occupy the deserted strong point. Once more nothing happened. Apparently the infantry could not conceive that one female tank had forced a hundred men to quit a strongly fortified and practically impregnable pill-box. Their own experience was one of hopeless attacks against those concrete walls, in which the unfortunate attackers were mown down like ripe corn. Finally the tank commander himself went back, found the colonel of the regiment, and induced him to send men forward to take over the abandoned Cockroft.

The tanks, having completed their round-up, retired down the road again, and reached their rallying-point just in time to escape the German barrage, which, now that the smoke had cleared away, descended furiously on the road.

This brilliant little action was remarkable for the fact that although on a front of a mile we had advanced 600

THE TANKS REPRIEVED

yards and captured powerful strong points, yet instead of the anticipated casualties of one thousand men the only losses sustained by the infantry had been fifteen men wounded. The Germans must have lost almost fifty machine guns, in addition to many killed, wounded, and prisoners. The tank casualties, which were heavier than those of the infantry, included two killed and twelve wounded.

Coming in an hour of deep pessimism this tank exploit was sufficient to tip the scales in favour of a further lease of life for the tanks. While not at all convinced of their general usefulness, the Higher Command decided not to abolish them entirely, but to keep some on the off chance that they might occasionally assist the infantry to clear up troublesome machine guns or flatten out awkward patches of wire.

Although the general offensive had been a failure, attacks were still carried on. Weary infantry, caked with mud from head to foot, were flung again and again against the unyielding enemy. Tanks, too, were thrust forward through the mud. If one in ten ever succeeded in getting into action the crews thought they had done remarkably well.

The men were depressed in spirit. All their laborious preparations seemed to end by their tanks becoming bogged. The iron monsters, baffled by the clogging mud, floundered helplessly in the morass, or, after thrashing away in vain with their unditching beams, their engines became overheated and they slid back exhausted into the depths of the muddied waters. Some foundered heavily, sinking and sinking, until the water swirled round their conning towers.

Still, whenever a tank got ahead of the infantry, the crew fought with great determination. They had heard the rumours that were going round, they knew that tanks were considered useless by many infantrymen and, clenching their teeth, they patiently scraped the mud off their guns and machines, drove desperately in the dark along the battered roads, and when they arrived in action fought as though the honour of the whole Tank Corps depended on the result. If their tanks broke down or became ditched, they had orders to get out and form strong posts with their Lewis guns. As the stranded tank was often ahead of the infantry, this was a decidedly dangerous task, but no tank crew ever flinched from doing its duty.

Listen to this thrilling tale of perseverance and courage:

On 22nd August the gallant Tank F.1, commanded by Lieutenant Hill, set out at dawn from Spree Farm. Its name, *Fray Bentos* (taken from the familiar brand of bully beef), was boldly painted on its side. The section commander, Captain Richardson, had decided to be a passenger for this particular journey. The object of the voyage was to harass and drive the Germans from three strongholds with the high-sounding names of Somme Farm, Gallipoli, and Martha House. The first call was made at Somme Farm; several 6-pounder shells were dropped in as visiting cards, but the occupants hastily decided that they were not at home to blustering " males " of this sort, and left at once for a quieter spot.

Gallipoli was a tougher proposition. Its machine guns spouted streams of armour-piercing bullets against the front cab of *Fray Bentos*. Lieutenant Hill was wounded and began to bleed profusely, then suddenly he fainted from loss of blood. Captain Richardson came to his assistance, staunched his wounds, and, lifting him gently from his seat, took his place; but in the confusion the tank became ditched. Without hesitation Captain Richardson attempted to climb out on the roof to fix the unditching gear, but so heavily was he fired at that he also was wounded and was obliged to abandon his efforts.

The infantry had, in the meantime, entered Gallipoli, driven out the Germans, and advanced slightly beyond it.

The Germans, now thoroughly roused, counter-attacked, swiftly drove our infantry back, recaptured Gallipoli, and swarmed forward. They had not reckoned with *Fray Bentos*, which, although ditched, was very much alive, and their startled troops were suddenly brought to a standstill by a broadside of 6-pounder shells and machine-gun bullets. The leading waves of the enemy wavered. More shells burst in their ranks, bowling them over like skittles. They could stand it no longer, but broke, and the counter-attack faded away.

Fray Bentos was now completely isolated, being 500 yards ahead of our line. Captain Richardson thought hard. What could he do next? The tank would not move. The enemy was watching him closely; if he attempted to return on foot with the crew they would probably all be caught by machine-gun fire directly they got away from the safe shelter of the tank. Confound it! Why should he retire? Why not convert good old *Fray Bentos* into a real pill-box, one with walls of steel, not concrete? They had two handy little 6-pounders and four Lewis guns, with plenty of ammunition: they would stick there and fight it out. "Let them all come!" that was *Fray Bentos*' motto.

So they stayed and fought. The morning passed, and the afternoon was slipping away when, in addition to sniping from the front, the gallant crew found that they were being fired at from the rear. Our own troops were shooting at the stranded tank, thinking, no doubt, that it had been captured by the Boche.

This was adding insult to injury. If they did not succeed in stopping the fire of our infantry the next thing would be a nice big hole in the roof, and our artillery blowing the tank sky high.

Life was full of problems. Some one must go back to warn the infantry before any further damage was caused. Sergeant Missen volunteered for the job. He peeped out of a flap and saw snipers practically surrounding the tank. It was going to be a difficult journey! He waited for a lull in the firing, and then, slipping quietly out of the sponson door, he wormed his way back on his belly through the mud. Yard by yard he dragged himself along. Huge shells were falling near at hand, smothering him with slime, snipers' rifles cracked, vicious bullets whined past his head, but he kept on. The mud camouflaged him. Only when he moved did those keen eyes spot their elusive target. He had only fifty yards farther to go when there was a loud chattering, and a stream of bullets whistled above his steel helmet. He had got in the path of one of our own Lewis guns! Luckily the bullets went high, and so, inch by inch, he crept up to the astonished infantry. He warned them not to fire on the tank, as the crew were still in occupation and intended to hold out as long as possible.

"How many men are there in the tank?" they asked.

"Eight," replied the sergeant, "including two officers, who are both wounded."

The infantry looked at each other in amazement. "These tank fellows are crazy," they thought.

Night came, and the little band of warriors in the tank prepared for trouble. Whilst some slept others watched and waited, their fingers on the triggers.

Through the gun slits and the flaps they could faintly see dim figures closing in round them. Suddenly there were flashes, followed by loud explosions against the sides of *Fray Bentos*. Bombs were being thrown! The

STILL HOLDING OUT

6-pounders roared, and the Lewis guns barked out savagely. Then the shadows melted quickly, and there was quiet, save for the thud of stray bullets against the steel. Other attacks followed, but they, too, were beaten off, and at last the dawn came.

Captain Richardson watched the happy beams of sunshine dancing through the chinks and loopholes. He felt light of heart. Day had come. The strain of peering into the darkness and the anxious waiting for the next blow from an unseen foe had made them all nervy and irritable. But now the good revealing light had appeared. Soon, no doubt, our infantry would advance again, and the crew of *Fray Bentos* would be relieved. Lieutenant Hill was in a weak condition and had already fainted several times; the sooner he could be taken to a Field Dressing Station the better.

The morning slowly passed, the afternoon dragged on, but still no movement from the direction of our trenches. The enemy was getting bolder; bullets pattered continually at loopholes and flaps. The snipers were taking careful aim. It was dangerous to peep through the loopholes. Already some of the crew were wounded by splash. Yet the Germans kept their distance. They feared the flash and roar of the 6-pounders, and had no desire to be caught by shells at close range. Nor did they fancy the streams of bullets that came from the Lewis guns as they scoured right and left.

Night descended once more. Captain Richardson looked round at his crew of wounded and weary men. Should he try to get back to-night? They might do it under cover of the darkness. But, on the other hand, he still had plenty of ammunition and enough food, for they had carried two days' rations into action as well as the " iron " ration for emergency purposes.

The Boche had not been able to touch him yet, and

they could not advance whilst *Fray Bentos* stood on guard. The infantry was almost sure to relieve them to-morrow. The crew was still cheerful and willing to fight on, so the courageous skipper determined to stay in his steel fort for a second night.

Nothing happened for some time; there was no sign of movement anywhere. He felt that mischief was brewing. The gunners strained their eyes, peering into the black night, watching and waiting. Even the pattering bullets had ceased. Had the enemy decided to leave them alone for the night?

Then a gunner shouted in alarm, "What's that?" and pointed upwards. There was a noise on the roof! A party of Germans had managed to creep up unobserved, and had climbed on top of the tank.

"Get your revolvers ready," murmured the captain, and at a signal the loopholes in the conning tower and manhole were opened and revolvers flashed forth. On the roof there was a clattering of feet, shouting, and explosions, but the revolvers fired again and again, and the raiding party retired, throwing bombs as they went.

"That will keep them quiet for a bit," thought the brave skipper; but the Boche was only baffled, not dismayed. In the darkness a machine gun was brought up close to the tank, and before the startled crew realized it streams of deadly armour-piercing bullets were hammering against the sides of *Fray Bentos*. The interior swarmed with steel splinters, one man was killed and others wounded, but they fought back grimly, and the dangerous machine gun was forced to withdraw.

Although in the ordinary way the steel of a tank could not be penetrated by armour-piercing bullets, yet naturally at very close range the bullets struck the steel sides with such force that numerous chips of steel were

SIXTY-TWO HOURS

dislodged from the inner walls and shot all over the interior like sparks.

With similar alarms the night passed, and dawn at last came round again. Throughout the morning of this third day the captain looked hopefully back for the long-expected infantry. His food supply was running short, his men were tired, all day long German bullets kept up a steady tattoo on the sponsons and front cab, but no relief came.

Cooped up in that narrow space the brave crew gamely stuck to their posts. One dead body lay across the tool-box, and on the floor the badly wounded rested in pools of blood and oil. The mingled stench of cordite, blood, and petrol pervaded the close atmosphere. No engine raced. All was silent and still, save for the groans of the wounded. Now and again a machine gun hastily chattered or a 6-pounder emitted a deep booming roar.

Darkness descended for the third time. What new devilment would the Germans devise?

Captain Richardson decided to get back. There was not enough food to last out until the following day, the ammunition was falling low, and his wounded badly wanted medical attention. He considered also that he had assisted the infantry to the best of his ability. The crew had done their duty like good tank men. There was nothing left now but to return. His gunners blazed away at the German lines with the object of keeping the enemy in their trenches, and then at 9 p.m. on the 24th the weary but still cheerful crew dragged themselves slowly back to our lines.

They had held out during the day of the 22nd August, the night of the 22nd-23rd, all day on the 23rd, the night of the 23rd-24th, and the whole day of the 24th up to nine o'clock in the evening—a total of sixty-two hours. The two officers were both wounded, one man

TANK WARFARE

was killed, and four were wounded, one being wounded twice.

For this superb exhibition of endurance and determination Captain Richardson and Lieutenant Hill were awarded the Military Cross, Sergeant Missen and Gunner Morrey the Distinguished Conduct Medal, and Gunners Hayton, Arthurs, Budd, and Bentley the Military Medal.

CHAPTER 10

Swallowed up in the mud—Captain Robertson wins the V.C. and establishes a tradition—The Poelcapelle disaster—Whitehall loses faith—Salvage.

THROUGHOUT September and October we continued to attack, but Passchendaele was still beyond our grasp. The rain fell with depressing regularity. The conditions under which the infantry fought were appalling. There was mud, mud, mud everywhere and in everything. It caked the muzzles of rifles, slithered into the barrels of Lewis guns, clung to the food, sucked down the marching feet. It was truly "the abomination of desolation." Men tramped across the swampy wastes on duckboard tracks which were shelled with sickening regularity. Often they would see the flimsy track blown up in front and behind them, yet they dared not move from the path. Whole regiments were laid up with "trench feet." Troops hobbled to the attack, their rifles and guns wrapped round with flannel. Misery was piled on misery; it was not war, but a muddy massacre. Yet the Higher Command kept stubbornly to its purpose. Whatever happened Passchendaele must be captured, and so the senseless slaughter continued.

It was at this stage impossible for the tanks to use any route except the roads, now pitted with shell holes. The approach marches had become sheer agony. Crawling at night with no lights, they had to be on the watch all the time lest they fouled light railways, damaged timber tracks or bridges, or became entangled with telephone wires or air lines. One tank, when crossing a light railway (sleepers were laid down for this purpose), was butted off in the dark by an engine which suffered severely from the collision. The rate of progress was extremely slow, as the tanks often became mixed up with supply wagons and limbers, or surrounded by crowds of jibbing mules, whose drivers cursed the tanks heartily. The crews had been working hard all day, and would be working part of the next day and trekking again the second night, so they became thoroughly tired out before going into action.

The roads, too, were heavily shelled, but the tanks could not leave their fixed routes, so the crews shut themselves inside and trusted to luck. Generally the tank commander guided them on foot, often he would trip up over barbed wire or stumble into a shell hole, and unless the driver was all attention the tank would go over him in the dark. Across several of the roads, just taken from the enemy, the latter had felled trees which created very difficult barriers. If one tank got hung up whilst struggling to cross these obstacles, it completely blocked the narrow road and held up all the tanks behind.

How bad the ground was the following incident will show. After managing to get into action at St. Julien, a tank was hit by a shell which crashed through the top, killing the officer and sergeant, and wounding three men severely. The senior man left was a lance-corporal, who immediately tackled the problem of getting the wounded back. Fearlessly he got out and, splashing through the mud, hailed another tank. By this time the enemy machine gunners had spotted him, and when he attempted to carry a wounded comrade to the safety of the second tank he was fired at heavily, but he stuck to his task and saw his patient safely on board. He could easily

SWALLOWED IN MUD

have climbed in as well, but tank men are taught never to desert their comrades. So back through the slush he trudged, the bullets whistling round his ears. With great difficulty he managed to pull the other two wounded from the battered derelict, and, after attending to their wounds, placed them gently in the driest shell hole he could find.

Now the next part of a tank crew's duty is to assist the infantry by forming strong points with Lewis guns. The earnest lance-corporal was rather puzzled. His officer and sergeant were dead, and he could hardly form a strong point with two badly wounded men. Still he decided that he would do the next best thing, so he got into touch with the nearest infantry and handed over the Lewis guns to them. On returning, he could find no trace of his two wounded comrades. It was impossible for them to have even crawled away, and yet they had completely disappeared.

With shells falling all round he scrambled from one crater to another, searching in despair. Suddenly, in the spot where he thought he had placed them, he saw something white moving. He crawled nearer, and stared horrified. It was a human hand. The wounded men had actually been buried in the mud by shell fire!

Frantically he tore at the dirt and slime with his hands; but thank God it was not too late, they still breathed faintly. He worked hard to revive them, and then, by a tremendous effort, he succeeded in getting them to a dressing station.

Thus did a lance-corporal do his duty.

It was about this time, too, whilst tanks were wallowing in the gloomy " Slough of Despond," that a great feat of heroism shone out over the marshy wastes like a beacon. On 6th October Captain Robertson, of A Battalion, gained the V.C.

TANK WARFARE

To win this supreme honour it is essential that the evidence of three independent witnesses be available. Generally it is earned in one of two ways. Either a man, stirred by the excitement of battle to superhuman courage, accomplishes some extraordinary feat, such as capturing a trenchful of the enemy single-handed, or else he shows an intense devotion to duty, combined with complete self-forgetfulness and a grim determination to carry on, even to the extent of sacrificing his life. Captain Robertson belonged to the latter class.

His section of tanks was due to go into action against Reutel. As the condition of the ground was bad, he set out, accompanied by Private Allen, who had volunteered to assist, to tape out a route. Working all night, and with very little sleep during the day, this task occupied them from 30th September to 3rd October. On 1st October Private Allen had been blown up by a shell and severely shaken, but with great determination he stuck to his self-imposed duty.

It was not until half-past nine on 3rd October that Captain Robertson had plotted out a satisfactory route. He returned and, without a break, went forward once more, leading his tanks up on foot. They reached their starting-point safely by 3 a.m. on 4th October. Except for a few hours he had then been continuously on his feet since 30th September. He now rested for a couple of hours, and at 6 a.m. went forward again to guide his tanks into action. He knew that there was a great danger of the tanks missing their way, so with great determination he led them on foot.

To attack Reutel they had to cross a stream called the Reutelbeek by a bridge which was under direct enemy fire.

The ground had suffered an intense bombardment, trees, hedges, roads had disappeared, but by some strange

CAPTAIN ROBERTSON, V.C.

chance the bridge still remained. Captain Robertson was certain that if the tanks, blundering from one muddy crater to another, failed to see this bridge the action was lost. Deliberately he made up his mind. He would guide them over to the other side of the stream. So, slowly and patiently, he walked on, and his brave assistant accompanied him.

The German barrage came down furiously, rifles cracked, machine guns spluttered, but the two lone figures went ever forward.

They were well ahead of the infantry now, the only two living creatures to be seen. Bullets whistled by them, flattening with a dull sound against the thick hides of the following tanks. Shell-bursts flung showers of mud over them, but they walked on, unhurt and undeterred. At last they came to the bridge. Quietly and calmly Captain Robertson crossed it and guided the tanks over, one by one, by motions of the hand. The machine guns, near at hand, chattered savagely, but Captain Robertson might have been on point duty in a country town for all the notice he took. The last tank crawled over. They were not far from their objectives now; once they hit the road they could not miss their way.

The brave captain could then have taken shelter in a tank, but his task was not completed—there was still a little way to go; so, without hesitation, he walked forward once more. It seemed as if all the rifles and machine guns were concentrating their fire on him. The tank commander of the leading tank was amazed to see him still go untouched. It was a miracle. At last the road was reached, and simultaneously Captain Robertson, his mission accomplished, fell forward shot through the head.

The faithful Private Allen, even in this tragic moment, did not hesitate in his duty. The enemy was only a few yards away, but he knelt by the side of his dead captain and gently took all maps and papers from his pockets. They must not fall into German hands. Then sadly he arose and staggered to the friendly shelter of the nearest tank.

Thus did Captain Robertson sacrifice his life. His tanks went forward and successfully drove the enemy from their strong points. Private Allen was awarded the D.C.M. for his splendid devotion to duty, but it was not long before death claimed him also.

The path thus taped out by this heroic martyr to duty was one often followed by section commanders in the Tank Corps, especially by those of A Battalion, to which he belonged. Being an entirely new corps, lacking in history and precedents, the officers and men felt that it was essential for them to maintain a high standard of conduct when in action. Captain Robertson's example created a tradition which, noble in itself, was responsible for the sacrifice of some of the finest men in the Tank Corps.

When tanks go into action the captain of a section has a somewhat peculiar task. He is naturally responsible for the good or bad work of his tanks, but it is practically impossible for him to exercise any control over them. Once it has started out over no-man's-land the tank is a self-contained unit, working entirely on its own. The officer and crew, boxed up in their narrow iron machine, are entirely cut off from the outside world. The officer knows what his objective is, and directs his tank accordingly. If the tank breaks down, becomes ditched, or is knocked out, the tank commander himself has to decide what to do next. There is no appealing to a higher authority when surrounded by the enemy!

The section commander has three courses open to him: (1) He can remain with the headquarters of the

SECTION COMMANDERS

infantry battalion with whom his tanks are fighting; (2) he can go into action in one of his own tanks, generally a male tank; or (3) he can make the perilous choice of leading his tanks into action by walking in front of them, exposed to the deadly fire of rifles and machine guns.

The last course was almost sheer suicide, for it must be remembered that tanks go over the top ahead of the infantry, and consequently meet the full blast of the enemy's fire. Nevertheless section commanders often guided their tanks on foot and endeavoured to direct them by running from one to the other, out in the open, in full view of the Germans. Naturally many were killed, but this did not deter their successors, who faithfully followed the Robertson tradition of sacrificing themselves for duty's sake.

It is sad to reflect that this sacrifice, made by so many brave men, was not absolutely necessary, and, except in a few instances, made scarcely any difference at all to the result of the action.

Unlike their comrades in the infantry, a tank major or colonel never led his company or battalion into action, but watched developments from the rear. The major of a tank company practically corresponded to the general of a brigade of infantry, and during a battle he received the reports of his tank commanders at Brigade Headquarters, while the colonel of the battalion generally remained in contact with Divisional Headquarters. Thus deaths amongst the higher ranks of tank battalions were rare, as a glance at the casualty lists will prove.

. . . .

On the 9th October eight tanks made a despairing effort to get into action against some strong points on the Poelcapelle road. Conditions had gone from bad to worse. Day and night, night and day, the enemy shelled the road. The surface was pitted with shell holes. For thirty long hours the rain had teemed down. The highway was one long series of slushy puddles, strewn with smashed limbers, and made foul by the bloated bodies of dead horses and fragments of human limbs.

Despondently the tanks picked their way up this nightmare of a road to their starting-point, the cross-roads near Poelcapelle. The night was pitch dark, the pitiless rain beat down upon them in torrents. One tank, getting too near the edge, suddenly slipped over on one side, and slid helplessly into the gurgling water. The others reached the cross-roads. Shells were pouring down upon the dismal ruins of Poelcapelle in a frenzy of destruction.

The leading tank suddenly plunged into a new shell hole and became bellied. It strove so fiercely to climb out that the unditching gear broke. The second tank pulled up on the side of the road, waiting to pass, when a shell landed on top and set it on fire. These two maimed creatures blocked the way. It was impossible for the others to get by, so they slowly and cautiously turned round and crawled back again. Unfortunately the last tank had run into the ruins of a derelict and, swerving sideways across the road, became irretrievably ditched. The four remaining machines could now neither go backwards nor forwards : they were trapped ! There was no shelter anywhere, no hope of escape from the fierce storms of shells.

The four baffled monsters, puffing and snorting, turned helplessly this way and that. In a last despairing effort a couple plunged wildly off the road, only to become immediately bogged in the slimy water. The others were hit and mutilated. Before they recovered from the shock more shells descended and completely disabled them. Most of the crews were killed or wounded.

The rain still came down steadily. So did the shells.

THE ROAD TO POELCAPELLE

In a few minutes nothing stirred on that ill-omened road. Only eight huge carcasses remained, some battered beyond recognition, others lifting their snouts pathetically above the slimy waters.

It was a tragic end to a series of tragic battles for the tanks. After this disastrous episode no more tanks were used in the Ypres sector.

The road to Poelcapelle was now completely blocked by the derelicts, and supplies being thus cut off from the troops in front, it was essential for the obstructions to be shifted immediately. This dangerous task was undertaken by the chief engineer of the 1st Brigade of Tanks, with his stalwart salvage gang, who slaved every night to clear the road. In spite of intense shelling he managed to blow up most of the wrecks with heavy charges of guncotton, and within a week the road was free again.

The appalling scenes witnessed on the road are described in the following letter by an engineer officer who took part in the salvage work:

" I left St. Julien in the dark, having been informed that our guns were not going to fire. I waded up the road, which was swimming in a foot or two of slush; frequently I would stumble into a shell hole hidden by the mud. The road was a complete shambles and strewn with débris, broken vehicles, dead and dying horses and men; I must have passed hundreds of them as well as bits of men and animals littered everywhere. As I neared Poelcapelle our guns started to fire; at once the Germans replied, pouring shells on and around the road; flashes of the bursting shells were all round me. I cannot describe what it felt like; the nearest approach to a picture I can give is that it was like standing in the centre of the flame of a gigantic Primus stove. As I neared the derelict tanks the scene became truly appalling; wounded

TANK WARFARE

men lay drowned in the mud, others crawled and rested themselves up against the dead to raise themselves a little above the mud. On reaching the tanks I found them surrounded by the dead and dying; men had crawled to them for what shelter they would afford. The nearest tank was a female. Her left sponson doors were open. Out of these protruded four pairs of legs; exhausted and wounded men had sought refuge in this machine, and dead and dying lay in a jumbled heap inside." *

Meanwhile in England the fate of the tanks wavered in the balance. On 11th October Mr. Winston Churchill, Minister of Munitions, told Colonel Stern, who supervised the output of tanks, that the War Office considered that tanks were a failure. They complained that they were being lumbered up with useless tanks at the front, and that millions of public money was being wasted. In their opinion there had been a total failure of design, no progress had been made, and their belief in mechanical warfare was at such a low ebb that they proposed to give it up entirely.

A few days later the then existing construction programme of 4,000 tanks for 1918 was cut down to 1,350. Colonel Stern immediately saw the Chief of the Imperial General Staff, and pointed out that the reduced programme was totally inadequate. Next day Colonel Stern was dismissed from his job, and side-tracked into a new position connected with the development of tanks in France and America.

Colonel Stern had forgotten that he was dealing with the military mind. He, a mere temporary colonel, had dared to suggest to a powerful general that the infallible War Office was wrong. What was the world coming to? These jumped-up civilians must be taught a lesson. So

* From *Tanks in the Great War*, by Colonel J. F. C. Fuller, D.S.O.

THE WAR OFFICE AGAIN

Colonel Stern, one of the staunch pioneers who had laboured and fought ceaselessly for tanks from their birth, was dismissed, and in his place an admiral was appointed who had never even seen a tank!

Thus, from the rear, the Tank Corps was dealt a heavy blow by enemies more dangerous than any German—the strongly-entrenched Almighties of Whitehall.

The tank units were all withdrawn from the dreaded salient by the latter part of October to refit and gird up their loins for new efforts.

The infantry and artillery remained to stagger on through the swamps. The weary and dispirited troops gathered up their ebbing strength into one supreme effort, and in the first week of November the heights of Passchendaele were stormed. The Third Battle of Ypres had ended at last. The cost to the British Army was nearly 400,000 casualties.

No battle could better illustrate the immense and criminal futility of war. Four hundred thousand of some of the best troops in the British Army were squandered to obtain a muddy ridge which, only four months later, was hastily abandoned when the Germans advanced.

The Tank Corps withdrew from the salient in a state of gloom. They had achieved so little at so great a cost. Every infantryman trudging over the duckboards could see the scores of derelict tanks lying helplessly in the slime. Everybody was remarking, " Tanks are no good ; look at them stuck in the mud all over the place."

In one way, however, good came out of misfortune, for the Germans, too, were now firmly convinced that as an instrument of warfare tanks were useless. They considered that they had been highly over-rated, and took no steps to build tanks in large quantities.

The task of salving the derelicts fell to the tank salvage companies, who had no less than 190 broken-down machines to get out of the mud. They often laboured under heavy shell fire, and had many casualties, and they carried out their rescue work with the aid of very primitive tools, for although they had to repair and get out of the mud tanks of 28 tons' weight, their main implements consisted of a few spanners and crowbars, numerous empty petrol tins, lengths of rubber tubing, and baulks of timber. Often these appliances, even, were "scrounged" from the nearest dumps and wagon lines. Yet they succeeded in getting the most hopeless crocks on their tracks again, and when confronted with apparently immovable derelicts their ingenuity was amazing.

One battered old hulk, sunk deep in a shell hole full of water in the Ypres area, was rescued in the following manner:

First of all the water was baled out of the shell hole by means of empty petrol tins. It was then discovered that the cylinders of the tank had seized, and that the radiator was holed by numerous bullet and shell marks. New cylinders were obtained and fitted in the engine, but there still remained the problem of the water system. At length some one hit on a bright idea: the petrol tank at the rear was filled with water, a pump was quietly "lifted" from a water-cart, and with the aid of a hose pipe the water was then pumped into the interior.

The petrol tank being thus misused, the next problem was how to maintain a flow of petrol. This was accomplished by placing a petrol tin on the roof and attaching a length of rubber tubing which led to the carburettor.

All now being ready, the engine was started up, but the old "bus" could not climb out. Baulks of timber were fetched and placed under the tracks, but they only sank into the mire. More timber was brought, and finally the resurrected "Willie" crawled out of its muddy bed.

A TANK'S FULL STOP

Owing to the congestion on the roads, and the fact that a few days previously a salvaged tank had broken down and completely obstructed the traffic, the salvage company was strictly forbidden to use the roads or to cross railways. This particular gang drove the old " bus " across country, but finding the ground too boggy, they decided to risk crossing a light railway. They therefore carefully built up a small ramp on each side of the railway with timber, and everything promised well, but as the old tank crawled up the side of the track and bumped down to the level she stopped abruptly, right across the rails. A pool of water on the roof, dislodged by the sudden tilting, had fallen straight into the magneto!

The light railway could not have been blocked more effectively. Truck after truck, full of shells and ammunition, urgently required in the front line, was held up. The salvage men grew frantic. They tried again and again to start up the engine, but it was hopeless, and by this time ten trucks were waiting in a line, and a small crowd had gathered round the broken-down crock. Visions of courts-martial floated before the eyes of the salvage officer. In desperation he sent back a runner to Headquarters to procure a new magneto by hook or by crook.

Meanwhile the crowd grew. So did the line of trucks. Angry voices asked when " that confounded tank was going to come down off its perch." Eventually a new magneto arrived, and luckily the old " bus " decided to move. The angry spectators climbed back, and their trucks moved on once more.

The salvage men drove the tank cautiously, parallel to the road on the driest ground they could see, but their troubles were not yet ended. Gradually the rear walls, loosened by rust and the long immersion in water, began to slip and bulged out beyond the tracks on each side, giving a concertina-like effect to the tail. There were ominous rattlings, and it seemed as if "Willie" would soon fall to bits. They stopped once more, and sent back for two strong steel bars which they fixed between the tail, riveting the two rear walls firmly together.

All now seemed propitious for the final journey to the railhead, but the salvage men were taking no more chances; they drove her along the road.

The progress on that last lap would have appealed to Charlie Chaplin. Perched on the back like a footman, one man worked steadily away pumping water from the petrol tank into the interior. On the roof sat another man superintending the flow of petrol from petrol tins through a piece of rubber tubing. Inside, a third man supervised the intake of petrol into the carburettor and kept a watchful eye on the water system. Meanwhile, yet another man continually darted off the road, filling up empty petrol tins with water from shell holes in order to keep the petrol tank at the rear supplied.

In this strange manner, stage by stage over a period of several days, did the enterprising salvage gang bring home their rescued derelict.

CHAPTER 11

The Only Way at Cambrai—The general leads his land fleet—Triumph of the tanks—Captain Wain achieves the impossible—The lone gunner—A tank commander at bay.

IN June 1917 the name of the Heavy Branch Machine-Gun Corps had been altered to the "Tank Corps," and it was decided to increase the number of battalions from nine to eighteen; and in that month the staff of the brand new corps began to make plans for a new type of battle.

Till that time both sides had conducted their battles on similar lines. Artillery was massed, and blazed away at the enemy's wire and trenches for weeks on end. Then, over the heavily mutilated ground, the unfortunate infantry stumbled forth to the attack. Usually they ran up against large patches of uncut wire, and were mowed down by machine guns, and even if these obstacles were overcome they soon became exhausted by such terribly difficult going, and could not possibly advance more than 4,000 yards or so.

The shelled area hindered the forward movement of guns also, and the infantry reserves, tramping up over craters and trenches, became too tired out to continue the attack.

Moreover, the element of surprise was entirely missing. In order to collect the great mass of guns and shells required, railway lines had to be extended and roads constructed, the ordinary traffic behind the line was enormously increased, and enemy aeroplanes and spies soon found out what was going on.

TANK WARFARE

The Tank Corps staff now proposed to attack in an entirely different manner. There was to be no previous artillery bombardment to put the enemy on the alert and to churn up the ground. The main element was to be surprise. At dawn a fleet of tanks would set out over no-man's-land, crush its way through the barbed wire, and make straight for the enemy's guns. Meanwhile aeroplanes would be busy bombing the enemy's field guns. Second and third lines of tanks would then follow, spreading panic and demoralization amongst the enemy, whilst our heavy guns concentrated on knocking out the enemy artillery and shelling villages and the roads by which he would retire.

The whole operation, which was really to be a gigantic raid, was to be over in twenty-four hours. It can be summed up in three words: "Advance, Hit, Retire," and to attain these results it was to rely on surprise, audacity, and rapidity of movement. It aimed at destroying the enemy's guns and killing his troops, not capturing ground or holding trenches.

Having worked out their scheme, the Tank Corps searched for a part of the line where the ground was not swampy or scarred with shell holes. They found it in the country near Cambrai, a region of undulating chalk downs covered by a thin growth of grass and coarse weeds. It was one of the most peaceful parts of the line, a haven of rest for weary and shattered German divisions. In some places no-man's-land was over 1,000 yards across.

So the Tank Corps chiefs, full of eagerness, approached General Headquarters and explained their simple and entirely original plan. G.H.Q. listened, and talked to them condescendingly, like parents to foolish children. "Do you realize that this sector is defended by the famous Hindenburg Line, which is considered to be impregnable? Do you know that there are three lines

PREPARING FOR CAMBRAI

of trenches, and that in front of the main line there are acres and acres of barbed wire everywhere over fifty yards deep ? " they asked.

"We are fully aware of all that," replied the tank staff, "and that is why we chose this sector to show how easy it will be for our tanks to plough their way through the wire. Besides, we calculate that if the artillery have the job of cutting the wire the bombardment will last five weeks and will cost at least twenty million pounds. Ours is a much cheaper and better way."

"That remains to be seen," said G.H.Q. "Perhaps you don't know that in the Hindenburg Line the trenches are in most places from 12 to 18 feet wide, and your tanks can only cross a trench 10 feet wide. Your whole scheme is therefore unworkable."

But the tank chiefs were not to be discouraged. "We have foreseen that," they answered, "and we have devised a means of crossing by using huge fascines."

G.H.Q., however, were not to be persuaded, and went on with their plans for the Third Battle of Ypres. The tank staff, undaunted, set to work to reconnoitre the Cambrai area with great thoroughness. The more they looked at that dry, firm region the more their mouths watered. Their precious tanks were, at that time, being wilfully thrown away in the swamps of Ypres, whilst here a country made for tanks remained untouched and undisturbed.

So, in September, Brigadier-General Elles, the Tank Corps commander, visited Sir Julian Byng, the Third Army chief, and conferred with him about an attack at Cambrai. He managed to convert him to the tank point of view, and General Byng himself approached G.H.Q.; but the latter still would not sanction any action outside the Ypres area. It was Passchendaele or nothing with them.

A few weeks later it was obvious to everybody, even

to G.H.Q., that the Third Battle of Ypres was a failure, so reluctantly they approved of the tank battle scheme.

" Let them have a cut at the Boche if they want to. We don't really believe they can do what they promise, but if they like to commit suicide let them carry on. It is their funeral, not ours. If it does chance to be a success, so much the better for all of us." Such was the attitude of the Higher Command.

The original tank plan, however, was altered from a raid to a battle, and was to last forty-eight hours. An attempt was to be made to seize Cambrai and Bourlon Wood, and the cavalry was to push on towards Valenciennes. To carry out this ambitious project the only infantry provided were six divisions of the Third Army, of whom many were in a very tired condition, having just come from Ypres, where they had suffered heavy casualties. The additional forces supplied were two divisions of cavalry, who were expected to go right through the gaps and accomplish miracles. The artillery was also increased to one thousand guns, and a strong force of French cavalry and infantry was held at our disposal on the left flank.

The attack was authorized on 20th October, and was to take place on 20th November. Thus, after a delay of three months, the Tank Corps proposals were sanctioned.

Only four members of the Tank Corps staff knew about the scheme, and with great joy they set to work to prepare for action. The day had come for which they had so eagerly and patiently waited. At last the tanks were to be given a fair trial over good ground.

General Elles determined to use every tank in France; the whole of his nine battalions were to be flung into the fight at the hour of attack. It was a question of do or die. If the tanks failed, then the Tank Corps was doomed; but the bold general was confident that there

SLEDGES AND FASCINES

would be no failure, and in those few hurried weeks before the battle he made sure of success.

On 24th October orders were given to the Tank Corps Central Workshops for the construction of 110 tank sledges, to be used for hauling up supplies, and 400 fascines. These fascines consisted of 75 bundles of brushwood bound together by chains, making one huge cylindrical bundle $4\frac{1}{2}$ feet in diameter, 10 feet long, and weighing $1\frac{3}{4}$ tons. The fascine was carried on the nose of the tank; when a wide trench was reached a quick release was pulled inside, and the fascine fell into the trench, thus enabling the tank to cross easily.

To complete these orders the workshops toiled day and night. The sledges required some 3,000 cubic feet of wood, weighing 70 tons, which had all to be sawn out of logs. For the fascines 21,500 ordinary bundles of brushwood, weighing about 400 tons, were procured, as well as 2,000 fathoms of chain to bind them together, and eighteen tanks had been especially fitted up for this task. The steel chains were wound round and round the bundles, and then two tanks pulled the chains in opposite directions, thus binding the bundles tightly together. It is related that some months later an infantryman, looking for firewood, filed through the chain binding a fascine, and the bundle suddenly sprang open with such force that it killed him.

The work was done mainly by the 51st Chinese Labour Company, about a thousand strong, who were attached to the workshops. Each fascine was pushed through the mud to the railway trucks by twenty of these Chinese coolies, chanting a weirdly monotonous refrain. The steadiness of their work was fully shown on one occasion when no less than 144 fascines were loaded on to trucks in twenty-four hours.

In addition to sledges and fascines, an order was given

for the overhaul and repair of 127 machines, most of them salved from the swamps of Ypres. These tremendous tasks were completed in three weeks, during which time the workshops were working twenty-two and a half hours out of twenty-four.

The tank battalions at Ypres and Lens were withdrawn immediately from the line to training areas where they could practise co-operation with the infantry. It was vital that the latter should have complete confidence in the tanks. They were therefore asked to construct the biggest and strongest wire entanglements possible. The tanks then quietly waded through the lot, much to the joy and surprise of the infantry. After the demonstration the tanks were fitted with their fascines, and carried out a special form of drill devised by Colonel Fuller, the brilliant chief of tank staff.

As three lines of trenches had to be crossed, and each tank only carried one fascine, which could not be picked up again after once being dropped, the following plan was adopted.

The tanks were to work in sections of threes. The leading tank was to go straight ahead through the enemy's wire, and then turning left, without crossing the trench, was to blaze away to keep the enemy down and protect the two following tanks. These made for the same spot, the second approached the trench, cast its fascine, crossed over on it, then turned left and worked its way down the back of the fire trench. The third tank crossed the fire trench on the fascine already there, made for the support trench, dropped its own fascine, crossed over, turned left, and worked down the back of this trench. Meanwhile the first tank had swung round and, crossing over the fire and support trenches on the fascines already in position, moved forward with its own fascine for the third line.

THE TANKS ASSEMBLE

The infantry followed in single file, and were also divided into three groups. The first were " Trench Clearers," who followed immediately behind the tanks and helped to clear up trenches and dug-outs. The leading wave planted red flags at the gaps made in the wire by the tanks. The second were " Trench Stops," who were to block the trenches at various points. The third were " Trench Garrisons," who occupied the captured trenches.

Naturally these exercises with the infantry roused the enthusiasm of the tank crews. After the weariness and futility of Ypres, the men were in a state of deep depression. They knew that the Tank Corps was considered to be useless, and they had crept away from that ill-omened swamp with their tails between their legs. Now they felt that, at last, they were going to be given a fair chance. As yet they were in the dark as to where and when the battle would take place, but their spirits mounted at the thrilling rumours that swept round the camps. They were keen and eager to show their mettle, and were fully determined to stage a " come-back " that would startle both the Germans and the Higher Command.

The next great task was the moving up of the tanks and the arranging of supplies.

As there were not sufficient railway trucks available, a number of old French heavy trucks were used. Movements were made only at night. New ramps and sidings had to be built at the railheads to take this heavy traffic, yet with the exception of a couple of minor accidents everything went like clockwork.

Thirty-six train loads of tanks were actually carried to the assembly positions by 18th November, two days before the battle.

The light railways of the Third Army accomplished

astonishing feats in forming dumps of stores. In just over a fortnight they carried no less than 165,000 gallons of petrol, 55,000 lb. of grease, 5,000,000 rounds of small arms ammunition, and 54,000 rounds of 6-pounder ammunition.

Great precautions were taken to keep everything absolutely secret. All movements were made after dark, and any reference to the battle in telephone conversations was completely forbidden.

It was all quiet on the Cambrai front. The usual number of aeroplanes droned over the sleepy line, the artillery fired the usual number of daily rounds, and the usual infantry held the peaceful front line. The attacking forces were to pass through them, and so those in the line were kept, as far as possible, ignorant of the attack. In fact an order was circulated asking for the names of all officers and men who knew Italian, the idea being to spread a rumour that the divisions concerned would soon be going to Italy.

The presence of tanks in the neighbourhood was explained as being due to the establishment of a training area, and the Tank Corps Headquarters at Albert was called " The Tank Corps Training Office."

At the 1st Tank Brigade Headquarters at Arras a more subtle method was used. A locked room, containing elaborately faked maps of other sectors and numerous " secret " plans, had the sign " No Admittance " painted in bold letters on the door. It was hoped that enemy agents or over-curious persons would thoroughly search the room and obtain much highly confidential and thoroughly misleading information.

Farther north, a different ruse was employed. Every night six tanks detrained at a siding and trekked across country to a wood. They then entrained again at another siding on the far side of the wood, and returned to their

CAMOUFLAGE

tankòdrome. This was repeated nightly for a few weeks. Naturally the district swarmed with rumours of a great tank concentration. The agents of the enemy were not long in informing him of this important bit of news, and in due course the wood was heavily shelled, showing that the Boche had been thoroughly hoodwinked.

At Cambrai the tanks themselves were mainly hidden in Havrincourt Wood, and where no woods were available they were camouflaged with canvas, painted to represent bricks and tiles.

The plans of the attack were not told to the section and tank commanders until three days before the battle, and reconnaissance had to be carried out in a very stealthy manner.

On the night of the 18th–19th the Germans raided our trenches and took back some prisoners. It was not known how much these men knew about the forthcoming attack, or if they would give away any information when cross-examined. All that could be done was to wait and see what fate had in store.

On the night before the attack the tanks cast aside their camouflage nets and crept slowly forward along routes marked out by a special black-and-white tape which had been laid down at dusk. Their engines were just ticking over, so that they made as little noise as possible.

The Grand Tank Fleet, consisting of 378 fighting machines gathered together from every part of the line, was eagerly waiting for the fateful dawn. Every driver, every gunner, and every tank commander in France was going over the top.

Besides the fighters, 32 machines had been fitted up with towing gear and grapnels to clear a path through the wire for the cavalry, 54 tanks carried supplies, 2 carried bridging materials, 1 was to carry forward tele-

TANK WARFARE

phone cable, and 9 were fitted with wireless apparatus. The grand total of tanks employed was 476. There were no reserves whatever.

Every man was aware that the fate of the Tank Corps would be decided that day, and every man was determined that if a knock-out blow was to be administered it was not the Tank Corps who would get it, but the unsuspecting Boche.

When the company officers first looked out over that firm chalk land at the acres of barbed wire and cunningly sited trenches, they all had but one opinion.

" If the Boche doesn't tumble to it before the show, it's an absolute gift ! "

On the evening of the 19th November, Brigadier-General H. J. Elles, the commander of this battle fleet of landships, issued his famous order :

"SPECIAL ORDER, No. 6.

" 1. To-morrow the Tank Corps will have the chance for which it has been waiting for many months, to operate on good going in the van of the battle.

" 2. All that hard work and ingenuity can achieve has been done in the way of preparation.

" 3. It remains for unit commanders and for tank crews to complete the work by judgment and pluck in the battle itself.

" 4. In the light of past experience I leave the good name of the corps with great confidence in your hands.

" 5. I propose leading the attack of the Centre Division.

" (Signed) HUGH ELLES,
" B.-G. Commanding Tank Corps.

" November 19, 1917."

THE GENERAL LEADS HIS FLEET

The last paragraph filled everybody with astonishment and pride. The fleet was going into battle led by the commander in person in his flagship, the *Hilda*. Every crew felt that the eye of the chief would be watching them, and they swore not to betray his trust.

Throughout the whole of the war, on no matter what front, no general in command of any large body of troops ever led his troops into action. A general's place during a modern battle is well in the rear.

General Elles was the one outstanding exception, but then he was a young man under forty, in charge of a young corps engaged in an entirely new form of warfare. His task was not to follow precedents but to create them. He fully realized, too, that his fleet of landships, designed and brought into being by naval men, should go into action in naval fashion. An admiral always leads his battle squadrons into action, and shares the same dangers as every sailor. General Elles went one better : he ran up the Tank Corps flag on his landship, and proposed to lead the very centre and spearhead of the attack. This flag, which was designed at Cassel in August 1917, was of three colours—brown, red, and green. Brown represented the earth or mud ; red, fire, or the fighting spirit ; green, the fields, or " good going." These colours symbolized the ambition of the Tank Corps, which was to fight its way through mud and blood to the green fields and open country beyond.

By flying the flag the general would inevitably attract attention to his tank and be in the very forefront of danger, but when great issues are at stake to take great risks is the prerogative of a great leader, and the brave flapping of that lonely flag was, that day, easily worth another hundred tanks to the enheartened Tank Corps.

At 4.30 a.m. on 20th November the enemy suddenly came to life, and there was an ominous burst of shelling and trench-mortar fire. Had the Germans discovered our plans ? Was everything doomed to failure at the eleventh hour ? The tanks, thickly wrapped in mist and darkness, held their breath and waited anxiously. In half an hour the shelling died down and a strained silence took its place.

By 6 a.m. all the tanks were ready in front of our trenches in one long line stretching for six miles. The leading tanks were 150 yards ahead of the rest, and behind, at the gaps in our own wire, the infantry stood silently waiting. There was a thick mist, and it was cold. Rum was served to the tank crews.

Sunrise was at 7.30 a.m. At ten minutes past six the tanks began to move forward in the semi-darkness, the infantry following quietly in single file. Ten minutes later a thousand guns opened out and a fierce barrage of high-explosive and smoke shells descended like a hurricane on the German outpost line, 200 yards in front of the advancing tanks. Overhead squadrons of bombers boomed past, dropping their deadly eggs on German Headquarters and gun positions. Above the roaring of their engines and the thunder of the bombardment the tank crews could hear the rending and snapping of the barbed wire as their machines trampled a way through.

The amazed Germans were completely overwhelmed. As scores of these monsters loomed up out of the mist, with their weird humps on their backs, the defenders of the line fled in panic, throwing away their arms and equipment as they ran. The great fascines were released and cast into the bottom of the trench. The snouts of the tanks stretched out and out over the wide trenches until the point of balance was reached, then dipped down and down until they seemed to be standing on their heads. Then, when they touched the far side, up and up they reared until their tails rested on the fascines, and their

THROUGH THE HINDENBURG LINE

tracks being able to get a firm grip, their huge bodies clambered back on to the level again.

Thus was the famous Hindenburg Line, the much boomed bulwark of the German Army, crossed as easily as a boy jumps over a small stream.

In a dug-out in this line was discovered a message which had been rudely interrupted by the arrival of the tanks. It read: " Keep sharp look-out. Issue armour-piercing bullets. Attack expected by——" Further documents were found which showed that, on first being examined, the British prisoners captured in the raid of the 18th had informed the enemy that a raid was soon to take place. In consequence the Germans moved reserve machine guns up to the line. At a later examination at German Headquarters, however, the prisoners had given away much more valuable information, for an urgent wire was sent to the front line. It arrived too late, for this was the message found in the signal dug-out.

The reserve line was soon overrun. Everywhere the enemy was streaming back in complete disorder. General Elles' flagship, *Hilda*, having reached its objective, the general returned on foot to his headquarters, where, seated in his office, by aid of telephone and telegraph, he continued to conduct operations in a manner more in accordance with Field Service Regulations.

In some places the tanks ran up against fierce resistance. At Lateau Wood there was a thrilling fight between a 5.9 howitzer and a tank. As the tank came round a corner it suddenly encountered the gun, which immediately fired at what was point-blank range. The shell struck the right-hand sponson with terrific force, shattering it and blowing most of it away. For a moment the tank paused, reeling under this mighty blow, but luckily the engine was still intact, and the driver, without hesitation, drove straight at the gun. Before the gunners had time to reload the tank was on top of them, and the gun crushed into a shapeless heap.

Other tanks in the meantime had gone over the ridge and were speeding down to Masnières, where a bridge spanned the canal. It was one of the important routes to the next ridge. The retreating Germans had half destroyed the bridge, but, nevertheless, the leading tank made for it and attempted to cross. Half-way over, the remains of the bridge bent and slowly collapsed, throwing the tank into the canal. The crew escaped through the manhole in the top, the tank commander being the last to leave the sinking machine.

There was only one casualty in this tank—the wig of one of the crew, who had it knocked off when climbing through the manhole. To make up for his enforced baldness he put in a claim for compensation. Reams of correspondence followed. The authorities were puzzled; they could not decide under what heading a wig came. Was it " Loss of a Limb," " Field Equipment," " Medical Comfort," " Clothing," " Personal Effects," or " Special Tank Stores " ? In the end, tired of fruitless discussions, they solved the problem by awarding the owner a suitable amount of cash.

At Marcoing the tanks had better luck, but the bridge was only saved in the nick of time. The leading tank reached the main railway bridge just as the demolition party was about to blow it up. An engineer was actually running forward with a wire to connect up the electric batteries to the demolition charges. Realizing the urgency of the situation, the tank commander dashed from his tank and ran forward, revolver in hand. He shot the man when he was within a few feet of the bridge. Immediately a party of the enemy made a furious counter-attack, but the tank held the bridge and drove them back again.

CAPTAIN WAIN'S HEROISM

It was near this same village that a section commander, Captain R. W. Wain of A Battalion, performed a wonderful feat. He had gone into action in the tank of one of his lieutenants. When nearing the Hindenburg Support Line he spotted an enemy strong point which was holding up the advance of our infantry, and made straight for it. When almost on top a shell hit the tank and knocked it out completely. After the smoke and fumes had cleared away Captain Wain found that of the whole crew only one other man was alive, and he was in a terrible condition.

Though seriously wounded himself, Captain Wain crawled to the sponson door and looked out. The infantry was still held up.

"I'll get them yet," he murmured to himself, grabbed a Lewis gun, and clambered out. Clenching his teeth, he pulled himself together by a tremendous effort, dashed from behind the tank, and rushed straight at the strong point, firing away as he ran. The sight of this bloodbespattered apparition charging down on them was too much for the garrison: they wavered and broke. The next minute Captain Wain was on top of them, firing furiously. Half of the garrison surrendered, the others fell back, but he had not yet completed his task. Although his strength was fast ebbing, he still had a few minutes to live. He picked up a rifle and fired at the retiring enemy until he himself was hit in the head by a bullet.

The infantry had now come forward, and the stretcher-bearers hastened to his aid. There was no hope for him, his life blood was streaming from his wounds, but he refused to be bound up. His iron will-power kept him at his task, and he continued to assist in clearing the strong point. When his duty was done, and the last German had been killed or had fled, he collapsed and was carried gently away to die.

TANK WARFARE

For this superhuman display of courage and resolution he was awarded the V.C. In the words of the official report, "it was due to this most gallant act by this officer that the infantry was able to advance."

At Flesquières the tanks seem to have got ahead of the infantry of the 51st Division, which was using an attack formation of its own. As the tanks came up over the crest they were caught at point-blank range by the German artillery, and many were knocked out.

One gun at the west end of the village, which could see every tank outlined against the sky as it topped the ridge, did great damage. It was generously mentioned in Sir Douglas Haig's dispatch: "Many of the hits upon our tanks at Flesquières were obtained by a German artillery officer who, remaining alone at his battery, served a field gun single-handed until killed at his gun. The great bravery of this officer aroused the admiration of all ranks."

Some of the tank crews had miraculous escapes. One tank was pierced in the front by a shell which knocked off the driver's head, flung it on the knees of the officer sitting beside him, killed the two gunners in the right-hand sponson, and then went clean through the back without bursting.

Whilst attacking nests of machine guns near Flesquières, tank *Edward II.*, commanded by Lieutenant Bion, received a direct hit from a German field howitzer, which put it out of action. The tank commander gave the order to abandon ship. The sponson door, on the side away from the enemy, was jammed tight, and to evacuate by the other door meant being exposed to heavy machine-gun fire. Private Richardson, however, did not hesitate. Seizing his Lewis gun, he courageously jumped out of the door and, flopping to the ground amid a hailstorm of bullets, got his gun into action, whilst the

AT FLESQUIÈRES

remainder of the crew clambered speedily out and found refuge in a communication trench.

Lieutenant Bion then reopened fire with his Lewis gun from this trench, where his little garrison was, not long after, strengthened by the arrival of ten men of the 5th Gordons. One enemy machine gun, in a hidden position, annoyed him so persistently that Bion crawled out of the trench with a Lewis gun, climbed up to the top of the tank and, sheltering behind the huge fascine, blazed away until the nuisance had abated.

Seeing that there was only a handful of men in the trench, the Germans emerged from the village and attacked the position with about 200 men, but Bion's guns, firing in rapid bursts, soon nipped this attempt in the bud. Unfortunately this encounter exhausted all his ammunition, and if another attack took place his tiny garrison would be overwhelmed. But Lieutenant Bion was a man of resource. He searched round in the trench and found a German machine-gun with ammunition. He switched this gun round and kept the Boche at bay until, a few hours later, welcome reinforcements arrived in the shape of a company of Seaforth Highlanders.

Whilst discussing the position with Bion, the company commander was shot through the head. Once more Lieutenant Bion stepped into the breach by taking command of the company, and remained in charge until another lieutenant of the Seaforths arrived.

For thus saving the situation at a very critical moment this combined tank officer, German machine-gunner, and infantry commander received a well-earned D.S.O.

Although the attack was held up at Flesquières, the tanks on the immediate left went forward like an irresistible tidal wave. The infantry, following them, advanced to a depth of $4\frac{1}{2}$ miles, capturing Havrincourt and Graincourt. In the latter village the Germans had their headquarters below the vaults of a church, whence they had built a regular rabbit warren of underground galleries and chambers which were all heavily mined. The following incident is an extract from a tank officer's letter home :

"Graincourt had been taken by surprise and had changed hands so quickly that we had taken over these very eligible headquarters as a going concern 'ready furnished for immediate occupation.'

So sudden, indeed, had been the change of tenancy that the two Boche engineers whose job it was to run the electric lighting plant had been captured in their own subterranean engine-room, and were even now stolidly carrying on their old duties, seemingly but little concerned by the fact that they were now 'under entirely new management.'

"As it turned out, it was very well for us that we did capture and retain this precious pair, for when they found that they were going to be kept on to run the lighting as before they quite shamelessly said :

"'Well, if that's the case, there's just one little point we ought to warn you about, and that is, if any one moves what looks like the main switch—as any one would who didn't know when starting up the plant—the demolition charges would be blown. If you would like these removed in case of accidents, we can show you where to dig for them—we know exactly where to find them, as it was our job to lay them.'

"Even whilst I was there I saw these ruffians superintending the removal of case after case of high explosive from cunningly concealed chambers behind the timber linings and under floors." *

* From *The Tank Corps*, by C. and A. Williams-Ellis.

A TANK ON FIRE

From this village several tanks went on into Bourlon Wood, which they found practically empty. The infantry was too tired to follow, and the much-expected cavalry failed to appear on the scene, so the tanks withdrew again. A fresh brigade of infantry could easily have occupied this wood, which a few days later was to be the scene of desperate fighting.

When a tank is disabled by a direct hit, the crew are generally forced to leave it to escape being burnt alive. Naturally enough the Germans, whom they have fiercely attacked, are not inclined to mercy, and try their utmost to shoot and bomb them as they clamber out, and also to capture the derelict tank. Knowing this, tank crews put up a desperate fight when surrounded, and neither expect nor give quarter.

An incident of this kind happened to a tank at Havrincourt. It had just captured two strongly held shell craters when it caught fire. At the same moment about a hundred Germans appeared all round it. To escape the flames two of the crew jumped out of a door. They were shot down immediately. The remainder clambered out of the door on the other side into a shell hole, where bombs were thrown at them, one man being killed, the others wounded.

Meanwhile the tank commander, Lieutenant McElroy, had remained in the tank, fighting the flames, and had managed to subdue them with the fire extinguishers. Then, in spite of the fumes, he opened fire with his Lewis gun and killed many of the enemy.

He then noticed that they were creeping towards the shell hole where the four wounded survivors lay hidden. They had almost surrounded it when he opened a loophole and, firing rapidly with his revolver, shot eight of them dead.

Infuriated, the Germans tried to capture the tank by

rushes, but he held them at bay single-handed for over an hour, when our infantry arrived. He gained the D.S.O. for this heroic stand.

Whilst the fighting tanks were driving the enemy back in confused disorder, the supply tanks followed up with supplies, and the wireless signal tanks were busy transmitting messages. One wirelessed back the capture of Marcoing ten minutes after the infantry entered the village. The wire clearers, too, got to work at once, and by the aid of grapnels cleared three broad tracks for the cavalry, who indeed moved forward, but so hesitatingly that they never appeared where they were wanted.

By 4 p.m. on 20th November the battle from the Tank Corps point of view was won and finished. On a front of 13,000 yards the infantry had been enabled to advance 10,000 yards in ten hours. Eight thousand prisoners and 100 guns were captured, in addition to numerous stores, canteens, field post offices, hospitals, and even cinemas.

The British casualties had not been more than 1,500.

At the Third Battle of Ypres a similar advance took three months, and cost nearly 400,000 casualties.

The Tank Corps, numbering a little over 4,000 men, had that day changed the face of warfare.

The tactics outlined by the far-seeing Colonel Swinton in February 1916, seven months before the first tank went into action, had at last triumphed. If only the Higher Command had carried out his ideas earlier, what lives would have been saved, what victories would have been gained !

Mr. Winston Churchill, another early champion of tanks, in his book on *The World Crisis*, points the obvious moral : " Accusing as I do without exception all the great Ally offensives of 1915, 1916, and 1917 as needless and wrongly conceived operations of infinite cost, I am bound to reply to the question, 'What else could be done?' And I answer it, pointing to the Battle of Cambrai, '*This* could have been done.' This in many variants, this in larger and better forms, ought to have been done, and would have been done if only the generals had not been content to fight machine-gun bullets with the breasts of gallant men and think that was waging war."

The amazing victory roused England to great enthusiasm. Bells were rung in all churches. Little knowing what disasters were ahead, people talked of the end being in sight; they were mistaken, and yet their instinct was right, for that day the eyes of the generals had been suddenly opened, and a weapon placed in their hesitating hands which was destined to cleave the way to victory.

CHAPTER 12

The extra hand—A gearsman sees red—Desperate fighting at Fontaine—A tank to the rescue—Shaking off the Boche—How Private Smith died.

THE spirit displayed by all men of the Tank Corps on 20th November was truly amazing. They were intent only on victory, a victory which would prove their worth and justify their existence.

Even the non-fighting ranks were imbued with this invincible spirit. Lieutenant Parsons, a workshop officer, followed up his company on foot in order to be able to adjust any mechanical breakdown without delay. Just ahead of him a tank caught fire. Four of the crew were burnt and overcome by fumes. The tank commander and driver were courageously fighting the flames. Parsons raced up, jumped on board, and with his assistance the fire was subdued.

With four men out of action the tank commander was in a quandary, when up spoke Parsons: "If you want to go on, I'll act as a gearsman for you."

The offer was accepted, and the tank went forward. Shortly afterwards it ran across the line of fire of a battery of artillery, and with startling suddenness it was hit no less than three times. The interior became a shambles; every man was killed or wounded except the driver and the "extra hand."

The tank now being at a complete standstill, Lieutenant Parsons was in his element. His engineering instinct came to the fore, and eagerly he worked away

STORIES OF CAMBRAI

until he managed to start up the engine once more. Then, assisted by the driver, he succeeded in bringing the tank, with its cargo of dead and wounded, back to the rallying-point.

. . . . . .

To be in action inside a tank is to be like an ostrich with its head in the sand. Except for the officer, who must take risks if he wants to direct his tank efficiently, the crew get only fleeting glimpses of the outside world over their gun sights. This poor visibility, coupled with the thumping of the engine and the muffled roar of the guns, which is absolutely deafening, cuts the crew off almost completely from the hideous sights and sounds of the battlefield. They really cannot see the dangers they are running. Nor can they hear clearly the vicious roar of exploding shells—and sound is the greatest disseminator of fear. The protection given to them by the bullet-proof armour also adds to their confidence and courage.

Being therefore almost fear-proof, the tank man could generally be depended on to be cool and resourceful when in a tight corner.

In the Mark IV. tank the secondary gears were the cause of much bad language and much ill temper, especially when they refused to work. Private Summers of A Battalion thought they were the clumsiest contrivances ever invented. He was a gunner, and had just spotted a nest of three German machine guns. The tank commander gave the order to turn, so that Summers could get on to his targets. In great excitement he ran his eye along the sights of his Lewis gun and waited with hand on trigger, but the secondary gears refused to budge; the tank could not turn.

Extremely exasperated, Private Summers gripped his gun, opened the door, jumped outside, and dashing forward, engaged the enemy guns on his own account.

TANK WARFARE

Bullets whizzed round his head from all sides, but so accurate was his shooting that the crews of the three guns, who were only fifty yards away, scattered immediately. As they fled he toppled them over like ninepins. That was the kind of thing that happened when a good tank gunner was baulked by the misbehaviour of pestilential gears!

Gearsmen, too, had their savage moments. Gunner Hoult, sitting at the back of his tank and attending to the clumsy gears, had no very high opinion of a battle. There he was in semi-darkness, watching the gunners ram shells into the breech, and swerve their guns round; watching the swift recoil and the empty shells dropping on the floor; or else staring at the driver's back and waiting for signals.

He could see nothing of the outside world, and owing to the frightful noise he could hear next to nothing. Occasionally he caught the sound of a sharp rapping against the side of the tank, as if a storm of lead was beating against it, but that was all. He yawned heavily; he had always understood that fighting was highly dangerous.

The next moment there was a terrific crash, the tank shuddered, a stream of light rushed in through a large hole in the cab, the interior became full of smoke and fumes, the engine stopped abruptly, and Gunner Hoult was suddenly covered with something wet and slimy.

He put his hands to his face and looked at them. It was blood! He felt himself all over. He was not hit. Then from the floor he heard a low moaning. Peering through the smoke, he saw his officer crouched on his seat motionless, and to his horror the officer had no top to his head. Then the gunner understood what had drenched him. His wounded comrades lay groaning at his feet. He bound up their wounds, and then went to the sponson,

A GEARSMAN SEES RED

opened a loophole, and looked out. A group of Germans were advancing towards the tank. What should he do? He was unwounded, and he knew that he could not expect any mercy.

He opened another loophole and glanced towards the rear. There, 300 yards back, our infantry were slowly coming forward. Gunner Hoult made up his mind immediately. He was not going to let the Tank Corps down; neither his tank nor his comrades should be captured! He opened the door and crept out, revolver in hand, to advance alone and on foot towards the enemy, firing rapidly as he went.

Amazed at this sudden stream of bullets, the Germans thought that they were being attacked by a large party and came to a halt. Thus did the gearsman win his own little private battle, for in the words of the official report granting him a D.C.M., " By this action he stopped the enemy from advancing. This gunner showed great determination and a total disregard of his personal safety."

The huge fascines carried by the tanks on 20th November were often the cause of much trouble, for they sometimes slipped forward and wedged in the nose of the tank, completely obstructing the view of both the tank commander and driver, and bringing the machine to a standstill. To release them it was necessary for a man to climb out on the top of the tank, fully exposed to the enemy's fire, and then hack away with an axe until the fascine fell clear, which was done without hesitation, although it was often suicidal.

From one tank, ditched in this manner, two men in succession climbed out and endeavoured to fix the fascine in position, only to be killed by machine-gun fire. In spite of this a third man, Private Sykes, calmly got out and carried on with the task. Having already killed two men at the same spot, the Boche machine gunners had the position taped to a nicety, and a regular devil's tattoo beat against the cumbersome fascine.

Where two had failed, the third succeeded. Private Sykes fastened the fascine properly and climbed down again, untouched. The tank then unditched and went forward to fight. It was all in the day's work.

As the Tank Corps had no reserves, and the crews were thoroughly tired out after their strenuous efforts, it was not expected that they would be called on again, but the Higher Command was so astonished and delighted at the unexpected success of the attack that they decided to carry on with the battle, and they actually informed the French force that its assistance would not be required.

So on the 21st forty-nine tanks were scraped together and sent into action again. They assisted in the capture of Cantang and Fontaine-Notre-Dame, the latter being taken by four tanks and held until the infantry arrived half an hour later.

The latter village was recaptured by the Germans next day, and on the 23rd we attacked it again, using twenty-four tanks. The enemy reserves had now come up, determined to hold the village at all costs, and fully prepared for tanks. Most desperate fighting followed, and the village was taken by the tanks no less than eight times, our infantry being always too weak to hold it, until the tanks eventually retired at dusk, leaving eleven disabled machines behind. A photograph of one of these, in the hands of the Germans, appears opposite page 196.

Village fighting is the worst type of fighting for tanks, because in narrow streets the range of vision is extremely limited. At Fontaine-Notre-Dame the enemy gathered in the upper storeys of houses and showered down bombs and bullets. Field guns were hidden in doorways, whilst the infantry were instructed to let the tanks pass and then fire at them from the rear, at close range, with rifles and machine guns, sometimes so successfully that the petrol tank at the back was set on fire, and the whole tank burst into flames.

The tank 6-pounders blazed away at houses a few yards off, often smothering themselves with falling bricks and plaster. Many machines used up every round of ammunition; some had every gun smashed. Loopholes and flaps were opened, and revolvers emptied time after time. It was naked savagery.

One tank which had been obliged to stop through engine trouble, was immediately surrounded, the enemy bombing it heavily, firing at point-blank range through the gun mountings and loopholes and wounding several of the crew. Fierce voices shouted, " Surrender." The situation was desperate. Wounded in the arms, the gunners used their left hands and fired furiously, but with little effect ; the Germans were too near to be seen. For three-quarters of an hour the tank commander wrestled with the engine, whilst his men fought like tigers ; then he managed to start the machine again, and the attackers melted away.

The Germans themselves tell of a tank which climbed a steep orchard, knocking over all the trees in its path, battered its way through well-built garden walls five feet high, and in turning, with a contemptuous flick of its tail, knocked down the corner of a house.

With the fighting everywhere so bitter and murderous the tank crews could rely only on each other for assistance, for prisoners were not encouraged in Fontaine-Notre-Dame on 23rd November.

A tank being set on fire in the middle of the main street by a direct hit, the crew were forced into the open. Luckily another tank saw its plight and came to the rescue, drawing up alongside. The officer superintended the transfer of his crew to the new arrival under heavy fire, but was hit, and fell to the ground seriously wounded. Packed with men, the new tank started off again, when a voice suddenly exclaimed, " Why, where is your officer ? "

A gunner peeped out, and to his horror saw the officer still lying in the street in a pool of blood, forgotten in the hurry and confusion. Without the slightest hesitation the brave gunner climbed out of the door and made for the wounded officer. Snipers potted at him from the housetops, machine gunners blazed away from windowsills, but he reached the tank commander and, with a great effort, carried him back to the overcrowded tank.

There were now sixteen people crammed into a narrow, overheated space that was hardly big enough to hold the normal crew of eight. Eleven of the sixteen were wounded, and in their crowded midst lay one dead man.

The machine was suffering from mechanical defects, the radiator boiled over, filling the interior with steam. Herded on top of their guns the unwounded gunners worked their 6-pounders like men possessed. The air was foul with cordite fumes, and a vile stench of blood and petrol pervaded the interior. The whole tank was alive with deadly sparks, the splinters of armour-piercing bullets fired from doorways not ten yards away. The men tried to cover their eyes with their arms to escape this shower of stinging lead. Grimy faces became sore and bloodstained, but there was nowhere to take shelter : sixteen men cannot lie flat on a narrow tank floor. The wounded moaned in agony, gasping and choking for want of a breath of clean, pure air. The dead man, his sorrows and agonies for ever laid away, stared placidly at the roof with unseeing eyes.

The lives of these human sardines depended on one man now, the driver. He kept his head and cautiously drove on. Every round of 6-pounder ammunition had been expended, the tank was limping slowly to our lines,

A TANK BESIEGED

safety was near at hand, when, with the roar of a mocking fiend, a shell crashed through the roof and exploded in their midst.

. . . . .

At the end of this day, when darkness came, another tank was surrounded by a large number of the enemy. They swarmed over the top of the machine, tried to throw bombs down the exhaust pipe, fired through every crevice and slit they could discover, and, worming their way against the side of the tank, pulled down the machine guns.

In the darkness the tank crew was blind and helpless. They could not fire their guns, and could see nothing through the chinks and loopholes. They dare not switch on any lights for fear of revealing themselves too clearly to the men outside, or open a flap lest a bomb should be thrown in. They could hear the scraping of many feet on the roof. It was a nightmare.

Suddenly the officer had an inspiration. He spoke to the driver, who leant back and passed the word down to the right-hand gearsman, " Get her in neutral." Quickly the gear was in place, and then, pulling hard on the handbrake, the officer swung the tank round and round. There were terrible shrieks as the swinging machine swept off the raiders like flies, to be crushed under the merciless tracks, and the tank moved on.

It was one of the unwritten laws of the Tank Corps that the men never let their comrades down. When they were obliged to " abandon ship " they took their wounded with them. When the battered tank could crawl, the dead were always religiously brought back inside ; living and dead helped to bring the ship home.

Among the records of the Tank Corps of those who were faithful to the last, who thought more of the safety of others than of themselves, who earnestly and patiently

"They swarmed over the machine."

HEROISM OF PRIVATE SMITH

performed their allotted tasks and then quietly slipped away without fuss or murmur of complaint, there is nobody who merits more honour than plain Private T. Smith of E Battalion. He did nothing startling or sensational, he accomplished no superhuman deeds, but the manner in which he performed his duty, the total forgetfulness of self that he displayed, marks him out as the true embodiment of soldierly virtue. If members of the present Tank Corps want a tradition to follow, they will find no finer example than that set by this humble private.

When in action at Mœuvres he was wounded by bullet splash inside the tank, but remained at his post, steadily firing his gun. Half an hour later that dreaded thing happened which every tank man fears—a direct hit. He was wounded again, this time severely. The tank caught fire, and the crew had to get out quickly. They were only thirty yards from the enemy's trenches; the ground was flat as a pancake; if they had attempted to go back there would only have been one end—certain death for them all.

Luckily there was a small shell hole near at hand, into which they all dropped. They could not see the enemy, although they could hear him, but he saw them clearly and opened a heavy fire on that unsheltered spot. They squeezed themselves flat on the ground, but streams of bullets searched them out. In a short time two of the crew were killed, and three more wounded. The others kept absolutely still, pretending to be dead, and presently the Germans ceased firing; they thought they had wiped out the whole of the tank crew.

Then began the long agony of Private Smith. He was very badly wounded and suffering extreme pain, but he clenched his teeth, dug his nails into his hands and uttered not a sound. He knew that the enemy, twenty yards away, would be able to hear the least groan, and that if once German suspicions were aroused another storm of deadly bullets would sweep down on them. His two wounds had given him so much pain that he no longer cared whether he lived or died, but he remembered his comrades; so he fought with his pain, put his hand over his mouth and kept silent.

For five hours his trial continued, five hours of martyrdom, in which that noble spirit stifled the cries of the tortured flesh. Every long second, every weary minute, seemed an endless battle with the forces of intolerable pain. Sweat rolled from his brow, he almost bit his arm in the frenzy of his efforts, but no sound escaped from his lips.

His sacrifice availed. He saved his comrades' lives. When darkness came at length the officer crawled back and obtained assistance from the infantry, who carried in the wounded men. Private Smith was free to groan at last, free to writhe and twist as the pain racked his poor body, but he was too weary now, too feeble even to utter a sound, and soon afterwards, without stir or murmur, the brave spirit quitted that mangled body. Plain Private Smith had done his duty. In his award of a Military Medal are these words, which should have been written in letters of gold: " His conduct throughout showed that he had more consideration for the safety of his crew than for his own personal suffering." What epitaph could be finer?

The fighting at Cambrai ended in another tragic failure. The great success of 20th November had so far exceeded the expectations of G.H.Q. that not sufficient troops were held in readiness to exploit it, the cavalry were soon held up by barbed wire and machine guns, and no further gains were made.

On 30th November the Germans delivered a powerful counter-attack, and took 10,000 prisoners and 200 guns.

A TRAGIC ENDING

The tank crews, wearied out with continual fighting, were being withdrawn to a rest area. The tanks were just about to be entrained, not a single machine was filled up with petrol or ammunition, when, at 10 a.m., an urgent call came for them.

With great speed the crews got to work, by 12.40 twenty-two tanks had started for the battle, they were soon followed by fourteen more, and by 2 p.m. another twenty were able to go forward. By four o'clock in the afternoon seventy-three tanks had been launched against the enemy, and had helped to stem the German attacks— a remarkable instance of the Tank Corps' efficiency.

Next day tanks again fought, pushing back the Boche with the aid of the Guards and dismounted cavalry, until the counter-attack was stemmed. Then, exhausted by this unexpected fight, they went back to their winter rest.

CHAPTER 13

The Great Retreat—Repairing a breakdown—Attacked by aeroplanes—A rearguard action—The mad sergeant—Holding the gap—A bold raider.

ONE of the immediate results of the Battle of Cambrai was that the expansion of the Tank Corps from nine to eighteen battalions, which had been held in abeyance since July, was now approved.

During December 1917 and January 1918 all the battalions were in rest areas for winter training, and many officers and men were sent also to the new base at Treport. In this camp, pleasantly situated on downs overlooking the English Channel, tank commanders learnt the intricacies of the big naval compass. They returned once more to the school desk, and dabbled in logarithms. Strange formulæ were hurled at their unoffending heads, and their puzzled brains wrestled hard with sines and cosines.

Owing to the large amount of iron in a tank any kind of compass will naturally be deflected, so that to ensure correct readings adjustment is necessary. A large octagon was marked out on the ground with white tape, and the tank was driven alongside until the tracks were absolutely parallel with one of its sides. This was a difficult task, which required much delicate handling of the throttle. When the tank was in position, a reading of the compass was made and noted on a card. Each side of the octagon represented a point of the compass, and

ON THE SOMME

eight readings were thus made. The readings were tabulated and kept in the tank for the use of the driver. Supposing the tank wanted to go due north, the driver would perhaps have to steer N.N.E., and so on for all the other points of the compass.

Another method was to try to adjust the compass by inserting small magnets, about the size of the lead in a lead pencil, underneath the floating chamber. This, however, was not very satisfactory, as it was very difficult to calculate the right length of magnet to ensure an absolutely correct reading.

The training courses continued until February, when all tank battalions were moved up behind the line in anticipation of a German attack. Russia having collapsed, Germany had been able to transport 1,000,000 men and 3,000 guns from the eastern to the western front, and as the Americans were beginning to land in France, it was obvious that the Germans, with their added strength, would get in a blow before troops arrived from the United States of America in force.

The system of defence on the British front included a forward zone, intended to delay and break up the enemy, and the battle zone, in which it was thought that the main fight would take place. The depth of the defence system was about four miles, and no retirement was contemplated beyond this distance.

Behind the line for many miles stretched the bleak and barren wilderness of the Somme, a region of battered villages, shell-scarred ground, and dilapidated trenches. It was a melancholy land, haunted by ghosts and reeking with decay, strewn with rusted wire and rotting equipment.

The Tank Corps itself had requested to be allowed to concentrate at one spot, Bray, so that it could rush large bodies of machines to any particular area; but G.H.Q., although impressed by Cambrai, were still doubtful about the real use of tanks, and ordered that they were to be distributed along a front of sixty miles. This meant only one tank to every 300 yards of front line, for only 320 heavy tanks and 50 whippets were fit for action.

The whippets were a new type. Their tracks were nearly as long as those of the heavy tanks, but did not go all over the machine, only round the chassis. The

A Whippet Tank.

engine space was in front, under an armoured bonnet, whilst the fighting cab was perched at the rear. Each carried a crew of three men, and was equipped with three Hotchkiss machine guns. It weighed 14 tons, was 20 feet long, 9 feet high, and 8 feet 7 inches wide, and could reach a speed of 8 miles per hour. Its average speed was 5 miles per hour, and it could cross a trench about 7 feet wide.

THE STORM BURSTS

Each machine was fitted with two 45 h.p. four-cylinder Tylor engines, and called for great skill in driving. Steering was accomplished by varying the speed of either engine.

.   .   .   .   .   .

On March 20, 1918, everything was quiet on the Fifth Army front. Parties of tank officers were being taken round the various lines of defence, so that they would know where they might expect to fight. Occasionally a gun fired or an aeroplane droned sleepily overhead, otherwise silence reigned.

The sun was shining, spring was in the air, the youthful officers frisked about like schoolboys on holiday. They went over all the lines in turn—the red line, the green line, and the blue line. The last line of all, called the purple line, existed on the map only because it was never imagined that the Germans would ever get so far.

In the rear, members of the labour battalions were toiling away filling up holes in the roads. In one ruined village a couple of old soldiers were building up a strong point with bricks. It was only half finished, but they were in no hurry; trowel in hand they smoked and chatted.

"Ah lad! it's a great war!" they said.

At dawn next day, 21st March, 6,000 German guns opened out on a front of forty miles in a perfect fury of destruction. Gas shells rained down on headquarters and artillery positions. The air was alive with them, shrieking and whining, and under this barrage, hidden by a thick mist, the German hosts advanced to the attack.

It was the mightiest assault in the history of the world. More than three-quarters of a million Germans were flung unseen against the British line, held by only three hundred thousand men, and wherever they encountered weak spots especially chosen storm-troops pushed through and widened the gaps. Flares were then sent up to indicate to the main body where to advance. Swarms of infantry and artillery hurried through and thrust straight ahead.

Where our infantry put up a stout resistance no further attacks were made, but soon they found the Germans in their rear. The great flood had burst through the front at several points and left behind many firm islands high and dry. But unless the defenders of these islands retreated, the force of the flood soon overwhelmed them altogether.

When the mist cleared, our startled artillery found the Germans only a few yards away and all round them, and before they could withdraw their guns, gunners and drivers were shot down.

By the evening of the 21st, in some parts of the front the blue line had gone, the red line had gone, the green line had gone, and even the famous purple line, which was not yet dug, had been overrun. The half-completed strong points were never finished, and the roads so carefully built up by the toiling labour battalions were taken over for use by the advancing Germans.

Tanks came into action in many places, but they were too few in numbers and too scattered to stem the advancing hordes. It was like trying to hit an opponent with an open hand instead of a closed fist.

On the 22nd March thirty tanks of the 2nd Battalion delivered a straight left at the Germans, who had broken through near Vaux. They charged the oncoming mass alone, and severely upset its equilibrium. A field battery was put out of action, and the tanks, after straddling the trenches in which the Boche infantry had taken refuge, swept them with machine-gun fire. They considerably reduced the enemy in numbers, and upset his plans of

THE GREAT RETREAT BEGINS

advance, but being entirely unsupported, they paid a heavy price. Seventeen were knocked out, and seventy per cent. of the crews were killed or wounded.

As the British line crumbled and the survivors retreated to avoid being cut off, the scattered tanks fell back with them trying to cover their retreat, but after a few days' hard " trekking " a thirty-ton tank begins to show signs of wear. Many machines broke down, supplies of petrol, grease, and oil ran short, tanks had to be set alight and abandoned.

The following episode, which is true in every detail, is representative of what happened to many tanks.

It was 22nd March, the second day of the German advance. A batch of tanks which had been held in reserve were slowly crawling back. The sun was shining brightly. There was no sign of any infantry, though guns were booming not far away, and the war seemed a distant thing.

With a clattering of wheels and a jingle of harness a gun team rattled by, then turning right, suddenly halted. The 18-pounder gun was placed in position, and two of the artillery men went forward a hundred yards to the summit of a small mound. The tank men watched them idly. "What's the game?" they asked each other.

The tank company commander ambled casually along on horseback, a riding stock in hand, two magnificent Irish wolfhounds trotting at his heels. They might have been going for a day's hunting.

On the mound the two observers were lying flat on the ground, peering through field glasses. There was a flash, and the solitary gun fired

" What does it all mean ? "

Suddenly a loud crump was heard, and a shell burst right on the mound. The two observers retired hastily. The tank men looked on in surprise.

TANK WARFARE

"They must be under direct observation," said a tank driver, after a pause. Then another man spoke. He uttered aloud what everybody else had been thinking.

"Blimey! Jerry can't be far away."

Nobody said another word. The tanks continued on their route; the major trotted on unconcernedly, the glossy coat of his horse gleaming in the sun, the lithe and beautiful bodies of the wolfhounds gliding easily over the turf beside him. It was a picture of youth in full springtime vigour, overflowing with the joy of life and the rhythm of movement.

In the distance could be heard a sullen sound which grew ever nearer, but none of the tank men knew that it was the roaring of that great tidal wave which had practically swamped the whole of the Fifth Army and was hourly creeping nearer.

The tanks, mostly old machines which had seen much fighting in the Battle of Cambrai, were beginning to show signs of distress. From one tank came loud knocking noises. The battalion engineer officer rode up and made an investigation. "The cylinders have seized," he declared. "She won't go much farther. You had better take her to that village down there and we'll see what we can do."

Clanking away like an old steam roller, the tank went down the hillside. The crew passed a group of American engineers working on a light railway, and asked for news.

"Something funny is happening up the line. Our trucks are still going forward, but they don't come back again. It's kind of queer." The speaker shook his head doubtfully.

As food was running low the tank men asked if it were possible to buy provisions anywhere.

"Not a cent's worth. We have closed our canteen and sent all the supplies back. We have just got our

FITTING A NEW ENGINE

day's issue and that's all. Sorry, you fellas." They went steadily on with their work, calmly chewing gum as if the Germans were a hundred miles away.

The tank stopped outside Moislains, not far from Peronne, and after a complete overhaul the engineer officer made his decision.

"It's no use. We might as well set fire to her and leave her behind." He reflected for a few seconds. "Wait a minute, though; there is one hope—an entirely new engine. I tell you what, I'll get one and bring it here by lorry to-morrow morning. Do you think you could get the engine unscrewed and ready for hauling out by then?"

The tank officer looked at his crew; the sergeant conferred with them and announced the result. "It will mean working all night, sir, but we are ready to do it if there is a chance of getting the bus away."

The engineer nodded his head in approval. "Right-o, you can rely on me to have a new engine here in the morning." He mounted his motor bicycle and sped swiftly away.

Throughout the night the crew worked steadily. It was no light task to remove several iron plates from the roof of the tank and gradually to unscrew the heavy six-cylinder engine from its bed, but they had volunteered to do it, and they were determined to finish the job.

Not far away an abandoned aerodrome blazed furiously, casting strange flickering shadows among the ruins of the village.

Morning came, and true to his word the engineer officer appeared with a "box body" containing a new engine, which he had conjured up from some mysterious source.

He also brought with him a repair tank, a machine with a huge crane projecting from its head. It waddled alongside, waiting to haul out the defective engine. The crew were still toiling away at their task of loosening the engine. It would not be long now.

Suddenly, in the village behind them, shells began to fall. A few splinters rattled ominously against the sergeant's steel helmet, and he looked inquiringly at the tank commander. " We shall have to get a move on, sergeant," said the officer. The crew redoubled their efforts until, at last, they managed to fix the tackle round the engine.

A car, driven by a staff officer, drove up to them; he shouted in a loud voice :

" If I were you I should clear. The Germans are only a thousand yards away. They will be here in half an hour ! " Then the car turned and drove swiftly back.

The tank commander gazed through his field-glasses at the main road leading to Peronne. It was black with marching troops. He rubbed the glasses with his handkerchief and looked again. There was no mistake about it. By the peculiarly shaped steel helmets he could see at once that they were Germans !

He informed the crew and told them to stop working; but they pleaded for a little more time.

" Give us a few more minutes, sir, and we'll get her away before Jerry arrives. We have worked hard all night, and we don't want to throw up the sponge at the last minute."

So they carried on, working feverishly. The shelling behind them had grown in intensity, and some of the shells were dropping unpleasantly near.

Inch by inch the engine was being hauled up. Slowly and gradually it rose through the hole in the roof, higher and ever higher. Soon it would swing clear. . . .

A runner dashed up with a message from the section commander.

"THE GERMANS ARE HERE!"

"Abandon work at once and retire in repair tank. Bridge is being blown up in five minutes."

A sharp order was given. The disappointed men ceased work, the crane slackened its chains and dropped the engine back in its bed once more. Quickly the telescopic sights and breech-blocks were taken from the 6-pounder guns and removed to the repair tank. The Lewis guns, small arm ammunition, and 6-pounder shells were also transferred; the broken-down tank was set alight, and the non-combatant machine, with its crew of fighting men, crawled slowly and preposterously through the ruins to the bridge over the Tortille. The box body carrying the new engine sped quickly past—only just in time. A few hundred yards away the advance guards of the enemy had come into sight.

Near the bridge stood a sapper of the Royal Engineers, anxiously waiting. He looked apprehensively at the huge crane, thrust heavenwards from the tank like a vast horn, and asked the officer in a trembling voice, "Are you the last to come over, sir?" The tank commander nodded, and the machine lumbered over the narrow bridge. The sapper connected some wires, and going back a little way bent down. The next second there was a vivid flash, then a great roar, and in a cloud of smoke and dust, fragments of the bridge were hurled skywards.

Fifty yards from the bridgehead a white puff of smoke blossomed from the ground, then another twenty-five yards nearer, preceded by a vindictive roar. The tank crept slowly up the slope like some monstrous toad, whilst overhead, aeroplanes, with the iron cross on their underwings, wheeled round and round like vultures. Every second bombs blew great holes in the earth on every side of the machine.

Then came a jarring, grating sound. The tank stopped. The officer emerged with his crew and found

TANK WARFARE

the differential gear had gone wrong beyond hope of repair.

An aeroplane came sweeping down, the iron cross growing bigger and bigger.

"Get a gun out," snapped the officer, and swiftly a Lewis gun was mounted on top.

The 'plane came lower and lower, firing spasmodically with its forward gun as it dived down on the motionless tank. The gun on the roof barked in reply, and the pilot, suddenly scenting danger, waved his hand in a gesture of defiance, and the 'plane shot swiftly heavenwards.

Weary-looking groups of infantry trudged past the broken-down tank. Hollow-eyed with lack of sleep, heavy with over-fatigue, their faces black with a three days' growth of beard, they seemed like ghosts of men drifting through a nightmare. They were the hard-pressed survivors of a South African brigade, many in kilts. They were just fighting and falling back, fighting and falling back, again and again, until now they no longer cared if they went on or died where they stood. The artillery had vanished utterly, no friendly aeroplanes traversed the sky, only swarms of enemy machines which harried them mercilessly day and night. Black despair and discouragement had joined their thin ranks.

And always the field-grey flood swept down on them relentlessly. Fighting it was like trying to stop a plague of locusts with a butterfly net.

The young tank officer surveyed the handful of men that went by, looking for the officer in charge. His heart sank within him at the thought of what was yet to come.

"Where are you going?" he asked a dejected looking corporal.

A hoarse whisper answered, "Back to the next ridge, sir."

"Where are your officers?"

REAR-GUARD ACTIONS

The corporal, eyes half closed, shrugged his shoulders. " All gone, sir."

For a second the officer gazed at the oncoming tide of grey, then turning quickly he ordered two Lewis guns with ammunition to be taken from the tank, and was just taking aim with his revolver when a shout made him pause and wheel.

Up the slope came a sergeant waving his hand violently. With him was a private soldier leading a cart horse. The sergeant ran forward and saluted. He was a thick-set man of medium height, his black eyes were blazing with excitement, and his voice husky with emotion.

" Give me a gun, sir ! Give me a gun ! " he panted.

The officer looked at him curiously.

" Where is your battalion, sergeant ? "

" Swallowed up, sir. The last went this morning. I'm sick to death of going back ! For God's sake give me a gun, sir ! I want to do some fighting—not running ! " He was almost hysterical.

" You are just the man I've been looking for. You can join my crew. You know how to handle a Lewis gun ? "

" Give me one and I'll show you, sir. Only let me get at the blighters ! "

Another machine gun was taken from the tank, and the little group waited whilst the officer fired at the carburettor. As the petrol began to trickle out he threw in a lighted match and ran. The next second, with a roar, flames enveloped the tank.

On the summit of the ridge the retreating troops rallied for yet another stand; the tank officer, with his Lewis guns, taking up a position slightly in front of them. The newly found sergeant was posted some thirty yards from him, out of sight, on a point overlooking the battered remains of the village in the valley.

TANK WARFARE

The patient horse, so strangely saved from destruction, was grazing peacefully not far away. The abandoned tank still blazed furiously, and at intervals dull explosions could be heard as the flames set light to 6-pounder shells.

The field-grey tide crept steadily forward. Wave after wave appeared, marching as if on a parade ground. Behind rode officers on horseback. Against the sky-line, between the long row of trees on the highroad, surged the endless trail of human ants, the main forces advancing on Peronne. The ruined houses in the valley had been subjected to a final bombardment. Now the shelling ceased; the first waves swirled up and trickled into the village. Already the sky was thick with low-flying aeroplanes dropping Very lights here and there.

In a few minutes he knew the enemy artillery would begin to range. Already the advance scouts must be crossing the river. They could not be more than a few hundred yards away now. Soon they would be swarming up the slope. What could three puny machine guns and two hundred exhausted men do against four thousand fresh troops? He looked through his glasses far away to the left, but there were no men there, only a wilderness.

The sun shone brightly. Larks, undisturbed by droning aeroplanes, rose heavenwards in full song. Violets peeped from the grass at his feet, and clumps of yellow primroses flaunted their beauty on the slope. The thrill of spring was in the air, yet here in the hearts of men only hatred reigned.

In the trench behind him men had fallen asleep where they stood. One had found a tin of jam which he opened, tasted, and passed solemnly round. His comrades seized it eagerly, seriously, dipped in their grimy fingers regardless of flies, ate ravenously, and passed the tin on.

A staff officer had appeared from nowhere, and was

THE MAD SERGEANT

walking up and down on the parapet prodding the sleeping men with a stick, repeating wearily in a monotonous voice, " Wake up ! The enemy are going to attack ! "

Zip ! Zip ! Something whizzed into the ground near the machine guns.

" Heads down ! " the tank officer cried. " There is a sniper about ! "

He put his cap on a rifle and held it over the edge of the small trench.

Zip ! came another bullet, rending the khaki material asunder.

" Wait a minute ! We'll get the blighter ! "

Rat-tat-tat ! Rat-tat-tat ! Rat-tat-tat ! barked the Lewis gun in the grass a little to the right. The sergeant had found a target at last !

Cautiously, revolver in hand, accompanied by a man with a rifle, the officer crawled out in search of the sniper. Slowly and with infinite caution he crept to the edge of a shell-hole. Ahead the grass moved slightly. The revolver spoke three times. The grass swayed, there was a very faint groan. Then silence.

Startled by the explosions the horse looked up in mild surprise, but it had grown accustomed to the din of warfare ; it proceeded to nibble the grass once more. Back at his post the officer watched the ground ahead warily through field-glasses. The private who had led the horse was sitting on the ground awaiting orders. He had opened his coat and was picking lice from his shirt. The officer sent him to his sergeant, with orders to retire on a signal.

A runner appeared from the rear. " The left flank has gone. Fall back as quickly as you can, or you will be cut off," ran the urgent message.

Grey forms were creeping up the slope from all directions. Nearer and nearer came the tide. The machine gunners lay low. " Wait," said the officer, " we'll let them have it right in the neck."

The tank gunners did not stir. Their hearts beat quickly.

" Now ! A full burst ! "

The two guns chattered and barked, grey forms stumbled and fell heavily, the remainder crouched hastily in the long grass.

" Where the devil is that infantry sergeant ? Why doesn't he come back ? " the officer muttered.

As he spoke a haggard-eyed man came stumbling through the long grass, followed by the hiss of pursuing bullets. " My God, sir, the slope is packed with them. He says he won't come back, sir ! "

Again the gun barked, and in reply shots were heard and guttural words of command.

" He says he's going to fight the whole German Army. He will never come back. Don't you realize, sir, he's mad ! "

The air was suddenly alive with bullets. There was no time to be wasted. The little party would be surrounded in a few minutes. A sharp order was issued, the tank crew with their officer and stray infantrymen fell back in short dashes, their guns blazing as they went.

From behind the knoll, where the mad sergeant was fighting single-handed, a terrific chattering ensued as though a gun were being worked at top speed. Then there came a yell, charged with agony and defiance. The tide had swept him away.

· · · · · ·

That same night the remaining tanks of the 1st Battalion were holding a gap in the line almost a mile wide, between the 21st Division and the remnants of the 9th Division. It was an anxious and perilous time. Two sentries, armed with revolvers, paced to and fro in

STILL FALLING BACK

front of each tank, for a distance of twenty-five yards, meeting each other at regular intervals. If they saw or heard anything in the darkness they were to challenge, and if there was no reply they were to shoot immediately.

Behind the tanks lay groups of officers and men waiting, revolvers in hand. At any moment the German scouts might creep up. Nobody knew how near they were, but everybody was aware of the danger of being outflanked or completely surrounded.

The night was black and still. Nothing could be heard but the soft swishing tread of the sentries through the grass. For three nights the crews had had practically no sleep, food had run out, and water was unobtainable except in very small quantities from petrol tins carried on the tanks, and with a vile taste of petrol which made empty stomachs revolt.

In spite of the danger, many a head began to nod drowsily and weary eyes to close. Suddenly the loud "chug-chug" of an engine sounded near at hand, and a motor bicycle drove up in the dark. It was the battalion reconnaissance officer, with an important message from headquarters in the rear.

"All you chaps are to start up the 'Willies' at once. We must all get back to the Somme line by dawn. If any of the machines break down, set fire to them right away. No time must be lost!"

The sleepy groups came slowly to life again, and the silent valley soon echoed with the roaring of engines as, one by one, the tanks crawled away in the darkness. Knowing their whereabouts, "Jerry" had not troubled to attack them, but had worked his way round their flanks; when dawn came they would have been completely surrounded.

The trek back over the old Somme battlefield was a nightmare journey. So pitch black was the night at first that it was difficult to follow the tank in front, but as several machines broke down and were set on fire, great flames lit up the countryside. Far away on the right a huge dump of petrol was blazing, and in the distance sparks and flames shot up from burning huts and aerodromes. Up and down swayed the tanks, over crumbling trenches and forgotten craters, through rusty wire and decaying dumps. Not a sign of life was encountered. For over eight miles they journeyed through an abandoned and ghost-ridden wilderness.

The British Army appeared to have completely vanished. Only flames, smoke, and desolation remained.

After dawn the battalion reached Maricourt, where they found a field hospital which had just been abandoned. In the wards blankets still lay on the deserted beds or scattered over the floors. Eagerly, famished men searched the buildings for food, but there was nothing to be found except a large tin half full of arrowroot. They shared it amongst them, each man having a portion poured into his hand; then solemnly they munched that dry, white powder as though it were manna from heaven.

But worse than the pangs of hunger was the thirst that tormented their parched throats. It was so insistent. But at last they found water, and for a time, as they drank greedily, war was forgotten.

Later on in the day the miracle happened; reserves arrived from the north, and for the first time since 21st March contact was established with the outside world. Neither officers nor men had the faintest idea what was happening on other parts of the line; they did not know whether the whole British front had collapsed or whether only the Fifth Army had been attacked. Now, with the fresh troops, strange rumours arrived. It appeared that we were only drawing the Germans into a great trap; the French were waiting on the flanks with a huge army,

THE EXPLOITS OF "SLIPPERY"

ready to strike at the enemy when he had advanced far enough! Stranger still, the Americans had landed at Ostend, and were attacking the Germans from the rear. Such was the inspiring news which put new life into the troops, although there was not an atom of truth in it.

That day, 24th March, a couple of tanks went out on a raiding expedition, to hold up the enemy in the neighbourhood of Curlu and Hem. One of them came back in the evening, but there was no sign of the other, commanded by a Lieutenant Oldham, who had been nicknamed "Slippery" for his daring and the many times he had slipped from the jaws of death, and it was feared that "Slippery" would never be seen again.

But on the following afternoon he turned up, with all his crew intact! He had been having the time of his life. His tank went through the enemy lines and crawled on for a distance of a mile and a half, chivvying and chasing parties of Germans. Then it broke down. Although in the heart of the enemy country, "Slippery" was determined not to surrender, so working hard all night, with constant interruption from over-curious Germans who were soon warned off the premises by machine-gun fire, he managed to get the tank going again.

In the morning he sallied forth to slay once more. Wonderful targets presented themselves, and German reinforcements hurrying forward were greatly perturbed when they suddenly found themselves under fire in a place which was supposed to be entirely cleared of British troops. The confusion grew, and traffic was held up as roads were blocked by a disorganized mass of supply wagons and troops who had come under the guns of this bold filibuster: urgent messages were sent back for reinforcements. S.O.S. flares shot skywards. The British were surrounding them!

TANK WARFARE

Meanwhile, the cause of all the trouble found that his petrol was running low, so he wisely turned the landship homewards. On and on he went, until at last the old tank collapsed; the petrol had run dry. Getting out with his crew and a couple of machine guns, " Slippery " discovered that our troops were still out of sight, but by bold and skilful advances the small party fought their way on foot through the startled enemy until at length they reached our outposts.

" Slippery " thought it was great fun. " You should have seen them running like rabbits. They were scared stiff—thought they were caught in a trap. The old ' Willie ' fairly purred with delight ! "

On 26th March the whippets came into action for the first time. Twelve of these small and fleet machines were ordered to investigate the position at Colincamps. They discovered the usual gap in the line, and went merrily down the main street of the village without meeting a single German.

Turning the corner they suddenly came upon several large groups of the enemy advancing on the village. At first the Germans halted in surprise; then they decided that the whippets were the new German tanks, and began to cheer heartily! Thereupon the whippets charged down upon them, firing vigorously, and the astonished Germans cheered no more but fled in disorder, pursued rapidly by the light destroyers.

This first encounter promised well, but for weary and desperate weeks the promise was unfulfilled. Of the 370 tanks which took part in that great retreat, 180 were abandoned without having fired a shot, worn out and broken down, and for a time the Tank Corps, as such, ceased to exist; it became a screen of machine gunners who remained behind to cover the withdrawal of the exhausted infantry.

THE NIGHTMARE ENDS AT LAST

Many highly trained tank men gave their lives, many brave deeds were accomplished in the fulfilment of this dangerous task, but it seemed as though nothing could stem the German advance. For nearly forty miles that tidal wave swept forward, submerging unit after unit of the British Army. Sixty thousand men were taken prisoners, over a thousand guns were captured, and still the wave swept on, threatening to drive our forces back to the sea.

Nobody but a survivor of that nightmare retreat can realize how near the Germans were to breaking through completely. Those of us who have lain out on lonely hillsides with a handful of weary machine gunners, hopelessly outnumbered yet strangely unconquered, with thirst racking our parched throats and black despair gnawing at our hearts, watching those field-grey swarms sweeping steadily forward, yet stubbornly opposing them without hope of help or escape, cannot understand even now why that mighty host failed in its colossal enterprise.

We can only assume that the age-old defect of the British soldier—his lack of imagination—proved a stumbling-block to the German plans. He never knew when he was defeated, in fact he could not imagine himself as being defeated, and so, though few in numbers, and weary unto death, he stubbornly fought on.

This, and the fact that the Germans had no cross-country mechanical transport to bring up supplies, caused the great drive to slow down and then stagnate. Soldiers without food, guns without shells are useless; an army that advances over a barren waste without supply tractors is like a desert caravan without camels—it will never reach the place of victory.

CHAPTER 14

Villers-Bretonneux—Tank meets tank—Whippets in full cry—
The turning of the tide.

AT the beginning of April, 1918, many of the tank units, which had been in practically continuous action since 21st March, were withdrawn and sent to the Tank Depot at Erin to refit. Here, after a brief spell of rest, they took over old tanks, overhauled and patched up for the occasion, and returned with them once more to the line, which had formed again as the German advance was checked.

" A " Company of the 1st Tank Battalion was hidden in the Bois l'Abbé, near Villers-Bretonneux. In this sector the Germans had advanced to within seven miles of Amiens, and threatened the capture of that city. If they succeeded, they would cut the Amiens–Paris railway, which was even then being used solely at night, and the solitary railroad left for the British Army would be through Abbéville, only ten miles from the coast.

To prevent this formidable disaster the French had placed their crack Moroccan division, the finest fighters in the French Army, at the danger spot.

In the Bois de Blangy, not far from the Bois l'Abbé, the Algerian and Moroccan troops had dug for themselves very deep and very narrow shelters. These were covered with branches of fir trees placed flat on the ground, so that it was exceedingly difficult to discover their presence, either from the air or from the ground level.

AT VILLERS-BRETONNEUX

The first tanks entering the wood in the dark ran straight into the undergrowth, and were considerably alarmed to hear weird yells and shrieks coming from the ground. Terrified black faces popped up on all sides, and the wood suddenly swarmed with strange figures, who had bolted out of their holes like startled rabbits.

Next day, when the machines had been covered with tarpaulins, camouflage nets, and branches, the Moroccans were still not too trustful, and would creep up and gingerly touch the tanks with their fingers—as if to make sure that they were real—and then slink away again.

In the same wood were also detachments of the renowned Foreign Legion, including a company of Russians; and Australian troops, in their picturesque slouch hats, added to the variety of the scene, whilst away in front, for almost a quarter of a mile, stretched an unbroken line of French 75's (the famous quick-firing field gun), mingled with batteries of British 18-pounders.

On the 17th April the enemy shelled the Bois l'Abbé with mustard gas, causing heavy casualties in the forward sections of tanks, whose crews returned with eyes swollen and weeping, and faces and bare knees heavily blistered.

As the German attack was daily expected, a new section of tanks, consisting of a male and two females, was sent to the Bois d'Aquenne, immediately behind Villers-Bretonneux. The wood was drenched with gas, and had been evacuated by the infantry. Dead horses, swollen to enormous size, and birds with bulging eyes and stiffened claws lay everywhere. In the tree-tops the half-stifled crows were hoarsely croaking. The gas hung about the bushes and undergrowth, and clung to the tarpaulins.

On the night of the 23rd April the shelling had made

the spot almost unbearable. The crews had worn their masks during the greater part of the day, and their eyes were sore, their throats dry.

Then two enemy 'planes appeared, flying slowly over the tree-tops, and dropped Very lights that fell right in the glade where the tanks were hidden. As the lights slowly flared up we flattened ourselves rigidly against the tree-trunks, not a man daring to move; but it was in vain, for the bulky outlines of the tanks showed up in vivid relief.

We were discovered!

An hour later, when clouds hid the moon, three huge toad-like forms, grunting and snorting, crept out of the wood to a spot some hundred yards in the rear.

Just before dawn on 24th April a tremendous deluge of shells swept down upon the wood, and I was aroused in the dark by some one shaking me violently.

"Gas, sir! Gas!"

I struggled up, half awake, inhaled a foul odour, and quickly slipped on my mask. My eyes were running, I could not see, my breath came with difficulty. I could hear the trees crashing to the ground near me. For a moment I was stricken with panic, and confused thoughts chased wildly through my mind; but, pulling myself together, I discovered to my great relief that I had omitted to attach my nose-clip!

My section commander and I and the orderly who had aroused us groped our way, hand in hand, to the open. It was pitch dark, save where, away on the edge of the wood, the rising sun showed blood red, and as we stumbled forward tree-trunks, unseen in that infernal gloom, separated our joined hands, and bushes and brambles tripped us.

Suddenly a hoarse cry came from the orderly: "My mouthpiece is broken, sir!"

"GAS, SIR! GAS!"

"Run like mad for the open!" shouted the section commander.

There was a gasp, and then we heard the man crashing away through the undergrowth like a hunted beast.

Soon I found my tank, covered with its tarpaulin. The small oblong doors were open, but the interior was empty. In the wrappings of the tarpaulins, however, I felt something warm and fleshy, and found that it was one of the crew lying full length on the ground, wearing his mask but dazed by gas. The rest of my crew I discovered in a reserve line of trenches on the edge of the wood, and the crews of the other two tanks, as we found later on, were sheltering inside their machines, with doors and flaps shut tight.

Behind the trenches a battery of artillery was blazing away, the gunners in their gas masks feverishly loading and unloading like creatures of a nightmare.

The major in charge of the battery informed us that he had had no news from his F.O.O. (Forward Observing Officer) for some time, the telephone wires having been blown up. If the Boche infantry came on, would our tanks immediately attack them whilst his 18-pounders engaged them over open sights? Our captain agreed to this desperate measure, and grimly we waited.

Meanwhile, as the shelling grew in intensity, a few wounded men and some stragglers came into sight. Their report was depressing: Villers-Bretonneux had been captured, and with it many of our own men. The Boche had almost broken through.

By this time two of my crew had developed nasty gas symptoms, spitting, coughing, and getting purple in the face. They were led away to the rear, one sprawling limply in a wheel-barrow found in the wood. A little later an infantry brigadier appeared on the scene with two orderlies. He also was unaware of the exact position ahead, and, accompanied by Captain J. C. Brown, M.C., and the runners, he went forward to investigate. In ten minutes one of the runners came back, limping badly, hit in the leg. In another ten minutes the second returned, his left arm torn by shrapnel. Twenty minutes after that, walking unhurt and serene through the barrage, came the brigadier and our captain.

The news was grave. We had suffered heavy losses and lost ground, and if our infantry were driven out of the switch-line between Cachy and Villers-Bretonneux, the Germans would obtain possession of the high ground dominating Amiens. They would then perhaps force us to evacuate that city and drive a wedge between the French and British armies.

A serious consultation was held, and the order came: " Proceed to the Cachy switch-line and hold it at all costs."

We put on our masks once more and plunged, like divers, into the gas-laden wood. As we struggled to crank up, one of the three men collapsed. We put him against a tree, gave him some tablets of ammonia to sniff, and then, as he did not seem to be coming round, we left him, for time was pressing. Out of a crew of seven there remained only four men, with red-rimmed, bulging eyes, while my driver, the second reserve driver, had had only a fortnight's driving experience. Fortunately one gearsman was loaned to me from another tank.

The three tanks, one male, armed with two 6-pounder guns and machine guns, and two females, armed with machine guns only, crawled out of the wood and set off over the open ground towards Cachy, Captain Brown coming in my tank.

Ahead loomed the German barrage, a menacing wall of fire in our path. There was no break in it anywhere.

TANK MEETS TANK

Should I go straight ahead and trust to luck? It seemed impossible that we could pass through that deadly area unhit. I decided to attempt a zigzag course, as somehow it seemed safer.

Luck was with us. At top speed we went safely through the danger zone and soon reached the Cachy lines; but there was no sign of our infantry.

Suddenly, out of the ground ten yards away, an infantryman rose, waving his rifle furiously. We stopped. He ran forward and shouted through the flap, " Look out ! Jerry tanks about ! " Swiftly he disappeared into the trench again, and Captain Brown immediately got out and ran across the heavily shelled ground to warn the female tanks.

I informed the crew, and a great thrill ran through us all. Opening a loophole, I looked out. There, some three hundred yards away, a round, squat-looking monster was advancing; behind it came waves of infantry, and farther away to the left and right crawled two more of these armed tortoises.

So we had met our rivals at last ! For the first time in history tank was encountering tank !

The 6-pounder gunners crouching on the floor, their backs against the engine cover, loaded their guns expectantly.

We still kept on a zigzag course, threading the gaps between the lines of hastily dug trenches, and coming near the small protecting belt of wire we turned left, and the right gunner, peering through his narrow slit, made a sighting shot. The shell burst some distance beyond the leading enemy tank. No reply came. A second shot boomed out, landing just to the right, but again there was no reply. More shots followed.

Suddenly a hurricane of hail pattered against our steel wall, filling the interior with myriads of sparks and flying splinters. Something rattled against the steel helmet of the driver sitting next to me, and my face was stung with minute fragments of steel. The crew flung themselves flat on the floor. The driver ducked his head and drove straight on.

Above the roar of our engine sounded the staccato rat-tat-tat-tat of machine guns, and another furious jet of bullets sprayed our steel side, the splinters clanging against the engine cover. The Jerry tank had treated us to a broadside of armour-piercing bullets!

Taking advantage of a dip in the ground, we got beyond range, and then turning, we manœuvred to get the left gunner on to the moving target. Owing to our gas casualties the gunner was working single-handed, and his right eye being swollen with gas, he aimed with the left. Moreover, as the ground was heavily scarred with shell holes, we kept going up and down like a ship in a heavy sea, which made accurate shooting difficult. His first shot fell some fifteen yards in front, the next went beyond, and then I saw the shells bursting all round the tank. He fired shot after shot in rapid succession every time it came into view.

Nearing the village of Cachy, I noticed to my astonishment that the two females were slowly limping away to the rear. Almost immediately on their arrival they had both been hit by shells which tore great holes in their sides, leaving them defenceless against machine-gun bullets, and as their Lewis guns were useless against the heavy armour-plate of the enemy they could do nothing but withdraw.

Now the battle was to us, with our infantry in their trenches tensely watching the duel, like spectators in the pit of a theatre. For a moment they became uncomfortably more than spectators. As we turned and twisted to dodge the enemy's shells I looked down to find that we

THE END OF THE DUEL

were going straight into a trench full of British soldiers, who were huddled together and yelling at the tops of their voices to attract our attention. A quick signal to the gearsman seated in the rear of the tank and we turned swiftly, avoiding catastrophe by a second.

Then came our first casualty. Another raking broadside from the German tank, and the rear Lewis gunner was wounded in both legs by an armour-piercing bullet which tore through our steel plate. We had no time to put on more than a temporary dressing, and he lay on the floor, bleeding and groaning, whilst the 6-pounder boomed over his head and the empty shell cases clattered all round him.

The roar of our engine, the nerve-racking rat-tat-tat of our machine guns blazing at the Boche infantry, and the thunderous boom of the 6-pounders, all bottled up in that narrow space, filled our ears with tumult, while the fumes of petrol and cordite half stifled us. We turned again and proceeded at a slower pace. The left gunner, registering carefully, began to hit the ground right in front of the Jerry tank. I took a risk and stopped the tank for a moment. The pause was justified; a well-aimed shot hit the enemy's conning tower, bringing him to a standstill. Another roar and yet another white puff at the front of the tank denoted a second hit! Peering with swollen eyes through his narrow slit, the gunner shouted words of triumph that were drowned by the roar of the engine. Then once more he aimed with great deliberation and hit for the third time. Through a loophole I saw the tank heel over to one side; then a door opened, and out ran the crew. We had knocked the monster out!

Quickly I signed to the machine gunner, and he poured volley after volley into the retreating figures.

My nearest enemy being now out of action, I turned to look at the other two, who were coming forward slowly, while our 6-pounder gunners spread havoc in the ranks of the advancing German infantry with round after round of case-shot, which scattered like the charge of a shot gun.

Now, I thought, we shall not last very long. The two great tanks were creeping relentlessly forward; if they both concentrated their fire on us at once we would be finished. We fired rapidly at the nearest tank, and to my intense joy and amazement I saw it slowly back away. Its companion also did not appear to relish a fight, for it turned and followed its mate, and in a few minutes they had both disappeared, leaving our tank the sole possessor of the field.

This situation, however gratifying, soon displayed numerous disadvantages. We were now the only thing above ground, and naturally the German artillery made savage efforts to wipe us off the map. Up and down we went, followed by a trail of bursting shells. I was afraid that at any minute a shell would penetrate the roof and set the petrol alight, making the tank a roaring furnace before we could escape.

Then I saw an aeroplane flying overhead not more than a hundred feet up. A great black cross was on each underwing, and as it crossed over us I could see clearly the figures of the pilot and observer. Something round and black dropped from it. For a fraction of a second I watched it, horrified: the front of the tank suddenly bounded up into the air, and the whole machine seemed to stand on end. Everything shook, rattled, jarred with an earthquaking shock. We fell back with a mighty crash, and then continued on our journey unhurt. Our steel walls had held nobly, but how much more would they endure?

A few minutes later, as we were turning, the driver failed to notice that we were on the edge of a steep shell

A DEADLY SILENCE

hole, and down we went with a crash, so suddenly that one of the gunners was thrown forward on top of me. In order to right the tank the driver jerked open the throttle to its fullest extent. We snorted up the opposite lip of the crater at full speed, but when just about to clamber over the edge the engine stopped. Our nose was pointing heavenwards, a lovely stationary target for the Boche artillery.

A deadly silence ensued. . . .

After the intolerable racket of the past few hours it seemed to us uncanny. Now we could hear the whining of shells, and the vicious crump as they exploded near at hand. Fear entered our hearts; we were inclined at such a steep angle that we found it impossible to crank up the engine again. Every second we expected to get a shell through the top. Almost lying on their sides, the crew strained and heaved at the starting handle, but to no effect.

Our nerves were on edge; there was but one thing left, to put the tank in reverse gear, release the rear brake, and run backwards down the shell hole under our own weight. Back we slid, and happily the engine began to splutter, then, carefully nursing the throttle, the driver changed gear, and we climbed out unhurt.

What sweet music was the roar of the engine in our ears now!

But the day was not yet over. As I peeped through my flap I noticed that the German infantry were forming up some distance away, preparing for an attack. Then my heart bounded with joy, for away on the right I saw seven small whippets, the newest and fastest type of tank, unleashed at last and racing into action. They came on at six to eight miles an hour, heading straight for the Germans, who scattered in all directions, fleeing terror-stricken from this whirlwind of death. The whippets plunged into the midst of them, ran over them, spitting fire into their retreating ranks.

Their work was soon over. Twenty-one men in seven small tanks overran some twelve hundred of the enemy and killed at least four hundred, nipping an attack in the bud. Three of the seven came back, their tracks dripping with blood; the other four were left burning out there in front, and their crews could not hope to be made prisoners after such slaughter. One broke down not far from Cachy, and I saw a man in overalls get out, and, with a machine gun under his arm, run to another whippet, which stopped to pick him up.

We continued to cruise to and fro in front of the Cachy switch-line, and presently a fourth German tank appeared, about eight hundred yards away. The left gunner opened fire immediately, and a few minutes later the reply came swift and sharp, three shells hitting the ground alongside of us. Pursuing the same tactics as before, we increased our speed and then turned, but the Jerry tank had disappeared; there was to be no second duel.

Later on, when turning again, we heard a tremendous crack, and the tank continued to go round in a circle. " What the blazes are you doing ? " I roared at the driver in exasperation. He looked at me in bewilderment and made another effort, but still we turned round and round. Peeping out, I saw one caterpillar track doubled high in the air. We had been hit by the Boche artillery at last, two of the track plates being blown clean away!

I decided to quit. The engine stopped. Defiantly we blazed away our last few rounds at the slopes near Villers-Bretonneux and then crept gingerly out of the tank, the wounded man riding on the back of a comrade.

We were making for the nearest trench when—rat-tat-tat-tat—the air became alive with bullets. We flopped to the ground, waiting breathlessly whilst the

ABANDONING SHIP

bullets threw up the dirt a few feet away. When the shooting ceased we got up again and ran forward. By a miracle nothing touched us, and we reached the parapet of a trench. Our faces were black with grime and smoke, and our eyes bloodshot. The astonished infantrymen gazed at us open-mouthed, as if we were apparitions from a ghostly land. " Get your bayonets out of the way," we yelled, and tumbled down into the trench.

It was now almost one o'clock, and we had been in action since 8.30 a.m., but, so intense had been the fighting, so fierce the unexpected duel, that it scarcely seemed half an hour since we had quitted the gas-laden wood.

We stayed in the narrow trench for a couple of hours, and as the enemy made no further attack, and the officer in charge of the infantry no longer required my services, I decided to return to Company Headquarters.

By this time I had procured a stretcher for the wounded man, and climbing over the parapet we made for home. To our great amazement machine guns immediately opened on us from the wood on our right, practically in the rear of the trench we were leaving. We fell to earth automatically. Breathless minutes passed. Then I gave the signal to go forward again, and in some mysterious manner we escaped untouched, even by the heavy shelling.

A hundred yards back we met a team of horses wildly dragging an 18-pounder across the open. The youthful officer on horseback addressed me excitedly.

" I say, old man, I've been sent forward to knock out a German tank. Is that the blighter over there ? " He pointed in the direction of my derelict.

" No," I replied, " you are a bit late ; the German tank is already knocked out, and——"

" What," he interrupted me, " already knocked out ?

Good enough!" and without another word he turned, gave a sharp command, and rode swiftly back, the gun team galloping furiously after him.

I felt immensely relieved to think that he had not been sent up earlier in the day, or my tank might have been heavily shelled from the rear! As it was, we all reached Company Headquarters in safety, and handed over the wounded gunner to a field dressing-station.

For his part in the tank duel my sergeant, a courageous and cool-headed Scot named McKenzie, was awarded a well-earned Military Medal. The official report contains the following interesting details:

"Although his eyes were affected by the enemy gas, and his face badly cut by armour-piercing bullets, in spite of his suffering this non-commissioned officer continued to serve his quick-firing gun for four hours, while his own tank, No. 4066, was engaged with large enemy tanks, one of which was eventually put out of action. Throughout, this N.C.O., by his conduct and coolness, set a splendid example to all the men in his crew."

A Military Cross was awarded to me.

That day was a notable one in Tank Corps history. For the first time the whippets had had the opportunity to prove their mettle to the full, and for the first time British and German tanks had met in battle. It seemed a fitting coincidence that the British machine should be No. 1 Tank of the 1st Section, A Company, 1st Tank Battalion, and that the defeated German should have been put out of action at the farthest point of their terrible advance. The attack upon Amiens had failed, and the field-grey tidal wave began to ebb at last.

. . . . .

The tank duel had more than one sequel. In the German report of the battle, written by Lieutenant

1. After the heavy fighting at Fontaine-Notre-Dame.

2. A captured German tank, the *Elfriede*.

BRINGING IN THE "ELFRIEDE"

Volckheim in a pamphlet called "Deutsche Kampfwagen im Angriff 1918," which has appeared since the war, it is definitely stated that one of the German tanks was hit three times by 6-pounder shells and completely knocked out. Although the machine was badly damaged the Germans managed, however, to remove it to the rear during the night.

Another tank, called the *Elfriede*, while trying to cross a shell-hole, tipped over on to its side and was abandoned. It lay in no-man's-land, some fifty yards from the front line, which was now occupied by the French colonial troops, and naturally the Higher Command were most anxious to examine it closely, especially as it was the first German specimen available.

The French considered various ways and means of dragging it back, but decided that owing to its weight (45 tons) at least four Mark IV. tanks, with eight towing ropes, coupling shackles, and a few dozen sacks would be necessary, that the job would take at least four or five hours, and, moreover, that it would be impossible except in daylight.

However, the tempting prize was there waiting to be claimed, and the 1st Battalion Tanks found the lure irresistible; so one dark night two tanks, equipped with tackle, crept up to the trenches and out into no-man's-land. Working without lights, and as silently as possible, with a low-flying aeroplane helping to drown the noise of their engines, they managed to haul the prize back to a place of safety without a single casualty, although they were liable at any minute to have a few score guns open on them. For this courageous and remarkable feat of engineering the officers and crews were awarded the Croix de Guerre by the general commanding the French Moroccan Division. (A photograph of this German tank appears opposite.)

TANK WARFARE

Next morning two German soldiers walked into the Australian front-line trench, which adjoined the French line, carrying two great canisters of steaming soup and rolls of bread. They had been in the habit of taking the broken-down German tank as a landmark, and, not knowing that it had disappeared, marched straight ahead. The Australians gave them a warm welcome, and enjoyed a good hot breakfast.

More than eighteen months later, when the war was over, I submitted a claim to the War Office for prize money for myself and crew. I pointed out that tanks, or rather landships, were first brought into existence by the Admiralty, that my landship had knocked out an enemy landship in action, and that under naval regulations a crew are entitled to prize money for sinking an enemy ship.

The claim was made more by way of a joke than in earnest. A considerable silence ensued, while my letter, the first of its kind received by the military authorities, apparently travelled round from one puzzled department to another, causing much delving into regulations and shaking of heads. Then I received a very courteous reply from the Financial Secretary of the War Office: " It is regretted that your claim for Prize Money for Officer and Crew of the Tank belonging to 'A' Company, 1st Tank Battalion, cannot be admitted, there being no funds available for the purpose of granting Prize Money in the Army."

CHAPTER 15

The Mark V. arrives—The German tanks—With the "Aussies" at Hamel—Brave Americans—A brilliant show—With the French at Moreuil.

AFTER the great German advances of March 1918, another blow was dealt to the Tank Corps. As reinforcements were so badly required by the infantry, the extension of the tanks to eighteen battalions was temporarily suspended; it was proposed that the number should be reduced to twelve, and one battalion was converted into an armoured-car battalion.

Owing to every available ship being required to rush troops to France, no tanks were sent out from England in April. The workers in the tank factories, who had been urged to speed up construction, saw the machines accumulating in the workyards, and began to ask questions. They were told that the losses of the tanks had been heavier than reported, and that whilst the battle was still raging it was impossible for the Tank Corps to take deliveries.

However, the appearance of the German tanks at Villers-Bretonneux, near the end of April, gave the Higher Command a distinct shock. The ban on shipping tanks to France was immediately removed, and the proposed reduction was cancelled. It was realized that even the best troops must fall back before a tank attack, and that the only way to stop such attacks was to have more tanks of our own.

During May tanks were arriving in France at the rate

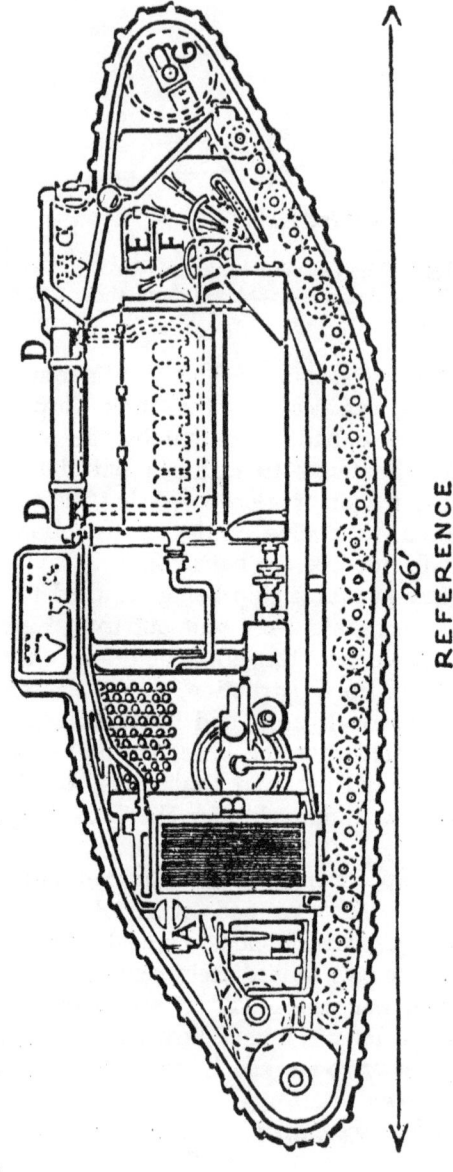

REFERENCE

A Oil Tank   D Silencer   G Idle Wheel
B Water Tank   E Revolver Case   H Petrol Tank
C Epicyclic Gear   F Water Tank   I Gear Box

Section of Mark V. Tank.

of sixty per week. They were all of the new, improved type called the Mark V., which was vastly superior to the Mark IV. It could reach a speed of almost five miles per hour, had a radius of action of twenty-five miles, could turn easily, and could change direction while mounting a slope. It was fitted with epicyclic gears and a 150-h.p. six-cylinder poppet-valve Ricardo engine.

The epicyclic gears were a tremendous improvement, for one man could now drive and steer the machine, releasing three men to attend to the guns, and the disappearance of the differential gear-case made much more room in the rear of the tank. An observation cab was fitted in the roof in place of the old manhole, thus giving excellent all-round vision, and allowing the unditching beam to be fitted from inside. Hotchkiss machine guns were introduced once more, and one was fitted in the rear wall. Furthermore, the seventy-five gallon petrol tank at the rear was divided into three compartments, so that if one was hit by a shell the tank could still keep going on petrol from the others.

The advent of this new tank was the cause of much brain fag amongst the officers and men of the corps. New courses had to be taken to wrestle with the intricacies of the epicyclic gear, and whilst every one voted the driving to be child's play compared with that of the Mark IV., yet the attempts to understand the workings of this complicated gear almost drove some to suicide.

It was gratefully realized, however, that Mark V. would prove a far more efficient machine than Mark IV., not only in action against infantry and emplacements, but in the duels with German tanks which seemed forthcoming, and it was very interesting to have some details of these enemy machines.

The German tank of the earliest type was 24 feet long, 10 feet 6 inches wide, 11 feet high, and weighed 32 tons.

TANK WARFARE

The walls were of very thick steel, capable of resisting armour-piercing bullets, but the roof was only lightly protected, and the flaps in the conning-tower, the gun-shield, the machine-gun apertures, and the joints between the thick plates were very vulnerable to splash of rifle and machine-gun bullets. The engines were two 100-h.p. Daimlers, each driving one track, and the tracks were sprung—a great innovation which has since been adopted in the British tank.

The machine could not cross large shell holes or trenches over eight feet wide, and the fact that the armour-plating covered the tracks made it very clumsy; but on fairly level ground it could reach a speed of eight miles an hour, twice that of the British heavy tank.

The officer in command directed operations from the conning-tower. There was a crew of nineteen, consisting of two mechanics as drivers, artillery men to work the guns, and infantrymen for the machine guns; and as they had apparently not been trained to work together they were continually squabbling among themselves, the infantry blaming the gunners for not backing them up, and vice versa. The armament was one 5.7 cm. gun and six machine guns. Every member of the crew received the Iron Cross.

The machine was sometimes called a *Schutzengrabenvernichtungsautomobil*, and the corps was named *Sturmpanzerkraftwagenabteilung*, which must have been rather a strain on a cap badge.

. . . .

Now that several battalions had been fitted out with the new Mark V. tanks, General Elles was anxious that they should be given a trial run. He knew that General Headquarters still regarded tanks as rather a failure, for though they acknowledged that Cambrai had been a wonderful tank success, they did not believe it could be repeated.

MAKING FRIENDS WITH THE "DIGGERS"

The Australians, who were straining at the leash in front of Villers-Bretonneux, were chosen as companions in this preliminary canter, and the first task was to overcome their prejudices, for ever since the battle at Bullecourt, in 1917, the cry of the Australian soldiers had been "Tanks are no good. We don't want tanks." When General Rawlinson, the Commander of the Fourth Army, proposed a tank attack to the Australian generals, the latter were not at all keen; but Rawlinson insisted, and so the Australian infantry were taken down to the Tank Training School at Vaux to see and play with the new tanks and meet the crews.

The "Diggers" were received with open arms. The workings of the tanks were explained to them, they were allowed to examine the interior and clamber all over the machines, many were taken for joy rides, and some even permitted to try their hands at driving. The tank officers, mingling freely with the Australian platoon and company officers, argued out the pros and cons of tank fighting.

The Australians were then asked to construct the strongest lines of trench defences possible, and the thickest wire entanglements; and having done so, they assembled to watch the downfall of the tanks. Much to their surprise, however, a batch of Mark V.'s waded easily through the wire and crossed every trench. To make the affair more realistic, the infantry fired off real rifle-grenades to indicate to the tanks the strong points to be attacked, and what delighted the Australians more than anything else was the rapidity with which the tanks swung right and left to flatten out these machine-gun emplacements.

From that moment the fame of their wonderful exploits ran like wildfire through the Australian Corps, and the "Diggers" took the tanks completely to their hearts. They were allotted to the machines with which they were to fight, and were thus able to rehearse over and over again every detail of the attack. Each batch of infantry gave a nickname to its own particular tank, which was scrawled in chalk on the steel sides.

Two American divisions, the 33rd and the 82nd, were at that time attached to the Australian Corps, and it was arranged that two battalions of their infantry should take part in the action. As this was the first time that American troops would fight with the British, General Rawlinson, as a compliment to them, selected 4th July, the American Day of Independence, as the day of attack. But when General Pershing, the American Commander-in-Chief, heard of the proposed battle, he sent orders that only half the number of the American infantry chosen were to be used, and the day before the attack further orders arrived that no Americans were on any account to take part in the action.

General Rawlinson was much perturbed. The withdrawal of troops when they were actually moving up to their positions might upset the whole plan of battle, and would certainly be a great blow to the American soldiers, who were very keen and very proud of the chance of fighting with the tanks and the Australians.

So, like Nelson, General Rawlinson turned the " blind eye " on Pershing's orders, and four companies of American infantry went forward unofficially with the Australians, who were so impressed by their dash and ardour that after the battle they remarked tersely, " We're mighty glad they're on our side ! "

The Australian staff work was very thorough, and their plans, coupled with the wonderful organization of the tank staff under Colonel Fuller, had provided for the smallest details of the fighting, which were definitely fixed three days before the fight, and were not to be altered in any way whatever—a great point.

THE TANKS TRIUMPH AT HAMEL

One order was that no tanks were to approach the line across tilled fields, which experience had shown to be a very necessary precaution. At the beginning of April 1918 a batch of tanks of the 1st Battalion hid themselves in a wood after a cross-country trek. An hour later a Jerry aeroplane flew over, circled round the wood, and disappeared, and half an hour afterwards, as the officers were sitting in the open eating their lunch, a couple of shells landed a few yards away with startling suddenness, killing a cook and a mess waiter. At first nobody could understand how Jerry had found out the tanks' hiding-place, because every machine was most carefully camouflaged and invisible from the air. Then it dawned on us that the aeroplane had taken a photograph which plainly showed tank tracks leading across the fields to the wood.

Sixty tanks were to take part in the attack, which was designed to capture the village of Hamel and Vaire Wood. Aeroplanes kept flying over the enemy's lines for two hours before dawn in order to drown the noise of the approaching tanks. At 3.10 down came a rolling barrage, then a smoke barrage, and behind this wall of smoke and flames the bold Australians advanced to the attack, followed by the tanks, which very soon, however, passed them and forged ahead to their objectives.

Everywhere on the three-mile front the Germans were surprised, and the infantry surrendered or retired. The machine gunners put up an obstinate resistance, and would have caused much trouble, but the tanks made straight for them and, passing by their nests, suddenly swerved, crushing both guns and gunners into the ground, while the Australians whooped with joy. No less than two hundred machine guns were destroyed or captured, and then the tanks were called upon to deal with snipers hidden in cornfields, who were taking heavy toll of the

"Suddenly swerved, crushing both guns and gunners into the ground."

SNIPERS IN THE CORN

"Diggers." As the great machines plunged into that unbroken sea of waving corn, the effect was startling. On all sides steel helmets bobbed up, and terrified Germans scurried through the crops like rats from a hayrick, to be shot down by the waiting guns as they ran out into the open.

Moreover, it was not only by their terrible destructive powers that the tanks proved their value. Every fighting tank carried ammunition and water for the infantry, and four supply tanks took forward loads of stores, including pickets and wire weighing ten tons, which were delivered within half an hour of the capture of the final objectives. It is worth noting, too, that in this battle aeroplanes were used to drop ammunition by parachute to the leading lines of infantry, no less than one hundred thousand rounds being delivered in this way.

The Tank Corps had remarkably few casualties. Only sixteen men were wounded, there were no mechanical breakdowns, and though five machines were damaged, all these were salved later—a point of great importance, for if a single one of the new Mark V.'s had fallen into enemy hands their secret would have been betrayed.

Tank commanders kept a sharp look-out for any machines which had broken down, or had been hit. One tank was thus disabled within three hundred yards of the enemy, who shelled it vigorously; but in good time another arrived on the scene, and the officer, jumping out, calmly fixed up a steel towing-rope by which the "lame duck" was dragged out of the danger zone.

Early in the battle a tank was heavily bombed from the rear by the German infantry, and the splinters which came through at the back of the cab gave the driver slight concussion. Undaunted he stuck to his post, and as the enemy began to clamber up behind, he suddenly reversed his engine and, driving backwards, ran over and crushed them. This swift running in reverse would have been impossible with the old Mark IV. tank.

The Tank Field (Salvage) Companies performed remarkable feats of repair on this day. Determined that no machine should fall into the hands of the Germans, they followed up the fighting tanks closely, and immediately one was put out of action they hastened forward with their tools to get it going again.

In Hamel a tank was hit and had one track completely ripped off. A salvage corporal and a couple of fitters came on the scene within a very short time, and set to work to repair the damage. Putting a track on a tank, however, is a very heavy task, requiring a gang of workmen, and as the day was hot, the corporal and his two mates laboured with difficulty.

If only they could have got some assistance they would soon have had the tracks on again. But a fatigue party cannot be conjured up from thin air on a battlefield, with fighting taking place only a few hundred yards away.

At length a salvage sergeant arrived on the scene, and realizing the impossibility of getting the disabled machine away without further assistance, pondered hard. Suddenly he had an inspiration. He went to the village of Hamel, which had just been captured, rounded up fifteen German prisoners and marched them to the broken-down tank. This novel fatigue party worked with great zest, not because they loved their task, but because their compatriots were every now and again sending over friendly little streams of machine-gun bullets. When the job was finished, after four hours' work, the corporal solemnly marched his squad of prisoners back to the village and handed them over to the Australians again. Then he drove the repaired tank back to the rallying-point.

SALVING WRECKED TANKS

The finest feat accomplished by the Tank Field Company was undoubtedly in Hamel itself. A section, consisting of an officer and ten men, following on the heels of the advancing infantry, had started to repair a disabled tank on the morning of 4th July. The village was being heavily shelled and gassed, but the salvage men, working in gas masks, stuck to their arduous task throughout the day and night. On 5th July the officer and two men had to retire from the effects of gas, and later in the day six more men were obliged to go back for medical treatment. Only a sergeant and one man were now left, but doggedly they worked on, and after toiling through a second night, they brought back the salvaged tank in triumph on 6th July.

It was by such perseverance and resource, and utter disregard of danger, that the salvage men succeeded in clearing the battlefield of all the broken-down machines, and thus preserving the secret of the Mark V. tanks.

In the matter of co-operation between infantry, aeroplanes, and tanks, the battle of Hamel was a model of efficient organization. Everything had gone without a hitch, all the objectives had been captured with few losses, and the Australians had been converted to complete faith in the tanks, which had returned carrying loads of their wounded on top as a final seal of friendship. For the first time the Higher Command nodded their august heads in approval of the Tank Corps, and plans for a battle on a much larger scale were begun at once: the day of the tank had definitely arrived.

One early result was a unique honour for the 9th Tank Battalion. Impressed by the news of the brilliant miniature action at Hamel, and the obvious superiority of the new machine, the French asked, on 17th July, that

Mark V. tanks might be sent to assist them in an attack near Moreuil.

A battalion from the 5th Tank Brigade was selected, but difficulties arose. This brigade was attached to the Australians, who objected to having a battalion of their very own tanks, blood-brothers of the battlefield, taken away from them; and in the end an extra battalion, the 9th, was allotted to the 5th Brigade and detailed to fight with the French.

The action was fixed for 23rd July, so there was only a week in which to make all arrangements, and the forty-two machines of the 9th Battalion had to cover no less than twenty-five miles before they reached their jumping-off points, which imposed a great strain. Nevertheless thirty-five machines reached the French line fit to fight.

Unfortunately, at ten o'clock on the night before the battle, zero hour was changed from dawn to 5.30 a.m., which meant attacking in broad daylight, and as a result the casualties among both the tank crews and the French infantrymen were rather high. Fifteen tanks were knocked out, and fifty-four officers and men killed or wounded.

The French were very pleased, however, for no less than 1,800 prisoners were taken and 275 machine guns captured, in addition to field guns and trench mortars, and in a Special Order of the day General Debeney, of the First French Army, praised the tanks in no uncertain terms:

"They have given to the Division the finest example of bravery, of energy, of comradeship in action, and of training for war carried to the highest degree of perfection. Their assistance has enabled the infantry to gain a brilliant victory in which they themselves share largely."

As a sign of its appreciation, the 3rd French Division

A UNIQUE HONOUR

(La Grenadière) presented its badge to the 9th Tank Battalion, to be worn by every member of the battalion for all time. This badge, a grenade enclosed in a belt with the motto " Qui s'y forte s'y brûle," is now proudly worn on the left sleeve of every man in the 3rd Tank Battalion (the present descendants of the 9th Battalion), an honour unique in the British Army.

CHAPTER 16

How a battle is planned—Mark V. Star tanks—Bluff—Detraining at night—Spying out the land—Battle orders—The approach march—The hi-hi bird.

WHEN a large tank battle is contemplated much work has to be done by the Headquarters Staff. Battalions of tanks which are stationed at various points of the line have to be assembled in the battle area, which means that special trucks have to be obtained to carry the tanks by rail, special ramps constructed for entrainment and detrainment, and a separate railhead and date of detrainment allotted to each battalion to prevent any clashing. Sites have also to be chosen for dumps of petrol, grease, and ammunition.

When all the tanks have arrived at their railheads, the battalion reconnaissance officers have to find routes from the place of assembly, near the railhead, to the jumping-off points. The journey along these routes is known as the Approach March. The jumping-off point, or starting-point, is the spot just behind the front line, where the tanks lie hidden until they sally into battle.

Naturally the main object in all these movements is to preserve profound secrecy, and all rail journeys and cross-country trekking take place at night.

In addition to reconnoitring the district near the line, it is essential to procure as much information as possible concerning the ground to be attacked. This is obtained from ;

PLANNING A TANK BATTLE

1. Maps and reports issued by the Intelligence Department, which show the strength of the enemy, the position of his machine-gun emplacements, artillery batteries, trenches, battalion headquarters, etc., and the nearest point from which reserves can be rushed up to the area attacked.

2. Aeroplane photographs, which give a very good idea of the nature of the ground and its condition: whether it is swampy, for example, or well wooded, or has been heavily shelled. (See page 216.)

3. Personal reconnaissance by the battalion reconnaissance officers and section commanders, who work from specially selected points of observation which give good views of the enemy's sector. (See pages 220–21.)

After a careful study of the information gathered from all these sources, the routes of the tanks to their objectives are carefully mapped out, and a chart is made of prominent landmarks that will come into view, to enable every tank to keep direction.

Then, immediately before the battle, each tank commander is given a copy of the battle orders, showing the plan of attack, a map of the sector on which the route to his objective is marked in green ink, and an artillery barrage map. On his map is also indicated the rallying-point where the tanks of each company assemble after the fight is over.

To illustrate all these preparations for a big battle, I shall now endeavour to describe the movements of the 1st Tank Battalion before the battle of 8th August.

In July this battalion was situated behind the line to the south of Arras. After the fretful and exhausting days of March and April 1918, it had gone for a period of rest and training to the little seaside *plage* of Merlimont, where reinforcements were received and training was given in the Hotchkiss machine gun and the 6-pounder, the tanks ambling over a large area of deserted sand-dunes among which guns could be fired with perfect safety.

I remember most distinctly one rather exciting incident. I was training one of my crew in the use of the 6-pounder gun. After blazing away several rounds, he took careful aim once more and pulled the trigger. To his great surprise there was no report. Turning slightly pale he looked back at me and said, " Nothing's happened, sir. It's a misfire." At any moment I expected the shell to explode in the breech, but, trying to keep as cool as possible, I waited the regulation two minutes (an endless time !) and gave the order, " Open the breech." Then I gingerly seized the offending shell, took it in my arms, and flung it quickly through the space at the bottom of the sponson door. And how relieved I was to get rid of the loathsome thing !

After leaving Merlimont the battalion was trained in the handling of the new Mark V. tank, and then issued with a special type of tank known as the Mark V. Star, which was $32\frac{1}{2}$ feet long and weighed 33 tons. It could span a trench 14 feet wide, and carry 20 men in addition to the ordinary crew.

With these monsters the battalion took up its position in reserve near Arras. On first arriving at the wood in which they were to be hidden, the heavy machines showed a tendency to slip their tracks and also to slide backwards if resting on a slight incline, and owing to this slipping about, their great length and weight, and their quickness in turning, they wrought much havoc, knocking down and crushing many a slender tree, until it looked as if a herd of clumsy elephants had stampeded through the wood, tearing up and trampling down everything in their path. The count who was the landowner was furious ; he complained bitterly to the colonel, claiming huge

THE GAME OF BLUFF

damages and refusing to allow any more of his property to be used as a park for those " sacrés tancques."

Towards the end of July rumours began to circulate about a forthcoming battle. Parties of officers were taken up by motor lorry daily to observation points, where they would stand, map in hand, peering through their field-glasses at the German positions, whilst a reconnaissance officer explained the features of the countryside at great length. I was somewhat surprised to find this spying-out of the land being done so openly.

Numerous tanks began to appear in the neighbourhood, nestling under the shelter of banks, covered only by their tarpaulins. It seemed strange that they could not have been hidden in the woods which were plentiful in this district.

Then came definite news of a move; we were going farther south near Gommecourt. The reconnaissance officers set off on their motor bicycles, thoroughly explored the new region, and mapped out routes from the new railhead.

At the eleventh hour, however, the plans were suddenly changed once more, and the tanks moved across country to a different railhead. Nobody could find out where we were going; the colonel had secret instructions which he had orders not to open until after the train had started on its mysterious journey. All the tank commanders and their crews were greatly excited. Was it to be north or south this time? They discussed imaginary battlefields.

"Do you know, I discovered a funny thing yesterday," said one. "I was passing near one of those 'Willies' lying by itself under the shelter of a bank. There was not a soul about, so I went up to the old 'bus' and pulled the tarpaulin on one side. What do you think I found?"

TANK WARFARE

"A canteen in disguise, I suppose?" chirped a facetious young man.

"Not exactly, but it was made of wood. It was only a dummy!"

At first everybody was incredulous. Then gradually it dawned on them that they had been the innocent instruments of a gigantic bluff. The countryside had been strewn with dummy tanks placed in positions where they could be spotted from the air. Those large observation parties, taking notes in full view of the enemy, the orders to move up to Gommecourt, were all part of a clever scheme to mislead the Germans.

Meanwhile, in the dead of night, the mystery train, with its load of tanks, was steaming southwards. It passed near a large town, where the dim outline of a cathedral could be seen in the darkness.

"Why, that's Amiens!" said somebody.

On and on the train went, still heading south; then slowly it came to a halt.

"All tanks to be detrained immediately," came the order. Engines were started up, and the delicate business of getting the tanks off the train began.

The first few machines ran right off the trucks and down the ramp on to the ground without difficulty, but for the others it was a slow and weary job. As there was only a space of six inches on either side of the truck, the driver could not afford to make mistakes, and each commander had to guide his tank by means of a torch, covered with a khaki handkerchief to dim its brightness. He flashed the light on one edge of the truck and stepped slowly backwards, the driver following the light inch by inch, and knowing that if he made any mistake the tank would go over the side, taking him with it. The most weary task of all fell to the man on the last tank, who had to drive his huge 33-ton machine over thirty-

An aerial photograph of the German front near Dodo Wood.
(Royal Air Force official—Crown copyright reserved.)

A COW IN TROUBLE

five trucks. As he could only crawl inch by inch, and had to peer down continuously through the darkness at the dimly lighted edge, his eyes and his temper were much strained by the time his " bus " reached the ramp.

All the tanks now being assembled near the station, hot tea was served out, and then the battalion set out across the new countryside in complete darkness, following their guide over fields and ditches, through hedges, up and down grassy banks, and across lanes to the large wood which was to be their hiding-place.

They moved in single file, snorting and puffing as they went, with the tank commander, torch in hand, walking in front of each. Everybody was very drowsy and tired. At intervals the column rested, to prevent the engines overheating, and no sooner did the machines stop than the crews fell asleep in their seats, overcome by the heat and the fume-laden atmosphere.

As I was walking in front of a tank I heard a strange noise immediately ahead, and suddenly a huge form charged down on me out of the night. As I recoiled, it rushed past me, missing me by inches, and then pulled up abruptly, heaving and panting. Greatly startled, I flashed my torch in its direction, and discovered that it was a poor inoffensive cow, shuddering with fear! Hastily I rushed to the driver's flap, yelling to him to stop, and he pulled up just in time. The cow was tethered to a peg in the ground, and the rope, becoming entangled in the track, had dragged the terrified animal nearer and nearer, in spite of its frantic efforts to escape.

At length the dim outlines of the wood came into sight, and the tanks, like huge toads, crawled into the undergrowth to find hiding-places. To enter the pitch-black depths of a wood at night is a weird experience. Branches are cracking and snapping on every side, occasionally a young tree falls heavily to the ground, startled birds flutter by squawking and crying, the muffled light of a torch sweeps to and fro revealing great trunks standing like pillars in the night.

At last the nose of the tank is manœuvred between a group of trees. "Stop!" the tank commander yells through the flap. The grunting machine becomes silent. Shadowy figures creep out of the sponson doors. More little figures of light pierce the gloom. Horn covers are put over the nose (or horns) of the tank to disguise its shape, a tarpaulin is flung over the clumsy body, and then, after much climbing and clambering, the four corners of the camouflage net are tied to tree trunks and the net spread out taut above the tank, which is now secure from observation from the air. Some of the crew settle down under the tail, covered by the tarpaulin, whilst the remainder stretch themselves out over the seats in the warm interior. Gradually the wood returns to its former profound silence.

Next day the reconnaissance officers and the section commanders were given an O.P. (observation post) chart and sent up to the front line, about nine miles away, to examine the ground over which the tanks would operate.

As strict secrecy was still the order of the day all tank cap-badges and buttons were removed, and the white tank worn on the arm was taken off, together with the battalion distinguishing mark—a red ribbon sewn on the shoulder-straps—the cap-badges and buttons being replaced by those of a noncommittal General Service pattern. Everybody was warned not to say a word to a soul about a forthcoming battle, even if they were asked direct questions by senior officers.

The first part of the line we visited near Moreuil was occupied by French troops. It was a very quiet sector of the front, in which hardly a shell was being fired, though there were occasional sharp reports as though somebody was indulging in a little bird-shooting.

The sun was shining brightly as we walked merrily down the main road to Moreuil.

"Just look at that froggy over there," remarked a captain.

A French soldier was scurrying along near the road, crouching low. Suddenly he disappeared into a trench, and the next minute we heard agitated shouting, and saw a French officer in the trench waving excitedly to us.

"I'll go over and see what's the matter. You fellows stay here; I shan't be long," said the battalion reconnaissance officer.

A minute later he was back at the double, gasping. "If you don't want to be soon kicking up the daisies, for heaven's sake clear off this road. It is under direct observation by Jerry. He has a little machine-gun practice on it every day !!"

We did not stop to argue, but plunged into the safety of the nearest trench. Thereafter we were more careful. We passed groups of French soldiers who eyed us curiously, wondering no doubt what brought us to their trenches, and at length we came to a signpost which was marked on one side "ARMÉE BRITANNIQUE," and on the other "FRENCH ARMY." Proudly we straddled the parapet, one foot in the French sector, the other in the British.

We reached our observation post and searched the enemy's country through glasses. There was no sign of life to be seen. The reconnaissance officer held forth.

"Do you see that large wood ahead there on the right of the Amiens-Roye road? That's Dodo Wood. If you look carefully you can see a patch of white where Dodo Wood meets the road. That's where the ground has been

O. P. CHART.

	Location.	View.
No. I	Road running through U.7.a. & U.1.b.	Good View of Marcelcave. Morgemont Wood & intervening Ground.
No. II	U.3.a. — S. Edge of Bois d'Aquenne.	Do.
No. III	Salamander Alley U.25.a.	Bois Dodo. Bois de Moreuil Hill 102 Villers aux Erables Moreuil Road.

Note — Leave car or bicycle at valley in T.22.a. Proceed along road & up valley B.6.a. & T.30.a. & c. Turn right at head & enter Salamander Alley.

No. IV	Trench in U.25.a. & c.	Very Good General View.

4th Tank Brigade "I"

Prominent Landmarks

1 For Units Operating in Northern Sector.

(a)	Marcelcave Village.
(b)	Water Tower in V.9.d.
(c)	Row of trees along road in V.15.b. & 16.a.
(d)	Tree Stumps round Monument.
(e)	Morgemont Wood.

2 For Units Operating in Centre Sector.

(a)	Poplar Trees along road in U.23.c. N. of Hangard Copse.
(b)	Trees along S. edge of Hangard Wood.
(c)	Morgemont Wood.
(d)	Dodo Wood.

3 For Units Operating in Southern Sector.

(a)	Moreuil Wood (Thennes Mill in Foreground).
(b)	Dodo Wood.
(c)	Main Roye Road trees.
	White Patch of Shelled Ground where road meets Dodo Wood.

Note — Hangard Wood consists entirely of Scrub except isolated trees such as in 2 (b).

heavily shelled. Take a good note of it. It will be a landmark for tank commanders."

Other landmarks were also pointed out and duly noted, and every feature of the countryside was well scanned.

Immediately behind the observation post stood an orchard full of apples. When we had completed our survey we fell to the temptation and raided the apple trees, and after eating our fill bombarded each other at short range. Two days later, when looking back from the edge of the captured Dodo Wood, I discovered to my amazement that the Germans must have seen every movement we made in that orchard. Obviously they could not have taken our appearance seriously. How could the stolid Teuton imagine that a party of officers playing about like schoolboys in an orchard were in reality planning his destruction?

Next day the tanks were filled up with petrol, ammunition, and grease, and extra tins of Shell A petrol were placed inside each tank; while in the company office, a small shelter made of branches covered by a tarpaulin, the major sat on a wooden box and detailed the plan of battle to his section commanders.

"We shall be attacking to-morrow with a Canadian division. To-night we move up to the 'jumping-off point' at Gentelles Wood, where each tank will pick up two Canadian Lewis-gun and two Vickers-gun teams, who will be carried into action. We attack from the green line at four hours after zero, namely 8.25 a.m. All tanks will proceed over Domart bridge and down the main Amiens-Roye road. Just beyond Vignette Wood Nos. 3 and 4 Sections will turn to the left, work round Valley Wood, and pass to the left of Beaucourt. No. 3 Section will then turn right and, wheeling round, attack Beaucourt from the rear. No. 4 Section will carry right

PREPARING THE ATTACK

on through Le Quesnel to the blue dotted line, where it will drop its infantry machine-gunners and patrol until they have consolidated.

"Meanwhile, Nos. 1 and 2 Sections will continue down the main road. At the Maison Blanche No. 2 Section will swerve in and pass Beaucourt on its left, mopping up any machine-gun nests it can see, and firing at Beaucourt. It will then go right ahead and fight its way down the main street of Le Quesnel and so on to the blue dotted line. No. 1 Section will follow a route parallel to the main Amiens-Roye road until it also reaches the blue dotted line and drops its infantry. Whilst the machine gunners are consolidating, half the tanks will patrol in front of them; the other half will return to assist the advance of the Canadian infantry.

"All tanks will rally at D.17.b,6.7.

"The French are attacking to the right of the main road."

Then various details were discussed, and maps, intelligence reports, aeroplane photographs, and barrage maps were issued.

"Is there any point on which any one would like further information?" asked the major.

The youngest officer present spoke up.

"Supposing the French are held up on our right, we shall be exposed to the Boche fire from that direction. Is the flank being protected in any way, sir?"

"We don't expect that any hitch whatever will occur. In any case, the corps have made full arrangements for that sort of thing," replied the major.

The conference was at an end; the captains returned to their sections and explained the plans fully to the tank commanders, who pored eagerly over the maps with the thin green lines which denoted the routes to be followed by their machines. They searched for valleys, noted the high ground (which was coloured yellow), and scanned every square inch for machine-gun nests and battery positions—the latter carefully marked, for the field gun is the most dangerous opponent of the tank. Objectives had to be carefully noted also. The first, wriggled across the map, was a thick green line; the second, more curved, was the red line; and the final objective, the end of a perfect day's fighting, lay almost on the edge of the map, an elusive dotted blue line. (See page 225.)

They then carefully examined the aeroplane photographs of all the main places to be attacked, picking out the landmarks, such as heavily shelled patches on the road, clumps of tall trees or ruined houses, and gazed hard at the shadows, noting banks that were likely to be very steep or valleys that were too narrow and therefore dangerous (see page 216). All the aeroplane photographs had, in addition, been combined into a large one as big as a map, which was spread out over a few petrol tins and closely pondered.

Next they studied intently the map issued by the Canadian Intelligence, showing the enemy organization, a wonderful plan which gave clearly and accurately everything that could possibly be discovered about the German side of the line—where their Headquarters were situated, the location of support troops and reserves, the position of dumps, hospitals, aerodromes, rest billets, railways, and artillery batteries.

Another map showed the enemy's lines of defence, and notes issued with it gave details of the battalions occupying it, their names and their strength. Apparently the Germans had done very little towards constructing strong defences, because they did not expect in the least that we would attack them on a large scale. In addition, information was given as to where the German reserve battalions would take up their positions when the front

SECRET BARRAGE MAP.—Zones of fire for heavy artillery bombardment.
brought *west* of any line after hour indicated. All fire to cease at zero plus six
where stated. *Official instruction on map.*

Zero hour is the time at which an attack begins. It is not divulged to batt

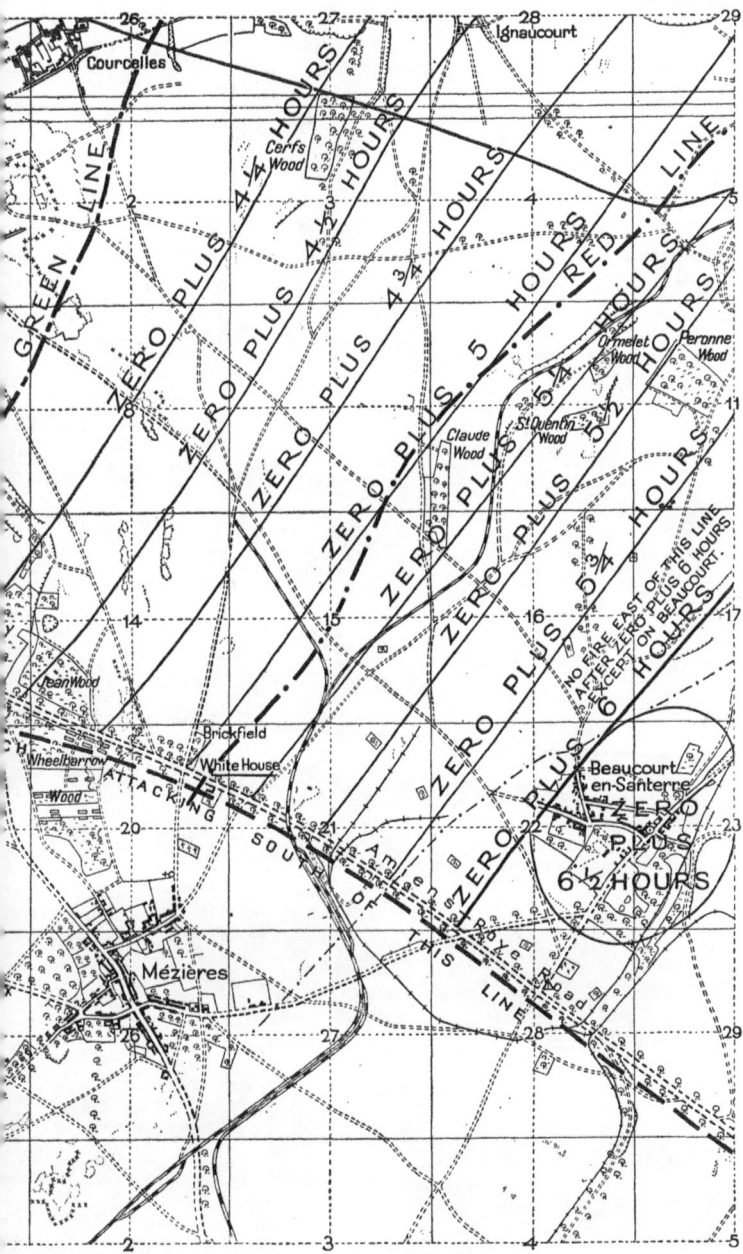

ew hours before the battle. In this instance zero hour was 4.25 a.m. The second
attack left the Green Line at four hours after zero—*i.e.* 8.25 a.m.—and the barrage
l of fire) lifted and jumped forward at zero plus 4¼ hours—*i.e.* 8.40 a.m.—and
d to move forward at intervals of a quarter of an hour as indicated on the map.

STUDYING THE MAPS

line fell. A further diagram showed the complete strength of the four German Army Groups in France, the numbers of fresh, tired, and weak divisions and their positions with reference to the line. It was pointed out how far away the nearest reserve divisions were, and how long it would take for them to get to the battlefield.

All this wonderful mass of information had been collected by our Intelligence from spies, prisoners, captured documents, and repatriated civilians.

The last map, perhaps the most important of all, was the Artillery Barrage Map, which showed the times at which the barrage lifted and crept forward. It advanced at intervals of quarter of an hour, and after zero plus 6 hours (10.25 a.m.) concentrated on villages. This map had to be carefully watched by a tank commander to see that his tank was not going ahead too quickly and running into the barrage.

All these maps were divided into large squares bearing large letters A, B, C, etc. These squares were subdivided into small squares numbered 1 to 30, or 1 to 36, the size of which varied according to the scale of the map. The small squares were again subdivided into four minor squares marked a, b, c, d; the sides of which were divided into ten by small ticks.

Supposing one was given the map reference C.29.b,6.7, one found the large square C, then the small square numbered 29, then the subdivision b, and finally counted six ticks along the base from west to east, and seven ticks up the side from south to north. Where these two lines intersected was the exact spot required.

That same evening the tanks crept out of the wood and began their long trek to the jumping-off points. The first part of their journey was across country and then along a main road. It was packed with troops, limbers, cavalry, and artillery, all moving forward under

TANK WARFARE

cover of the night. Progress was slow, for the marching troops, the last batches of Canadians who had foot-slogged it all the way from Vimy Ridge, were dog-tired.

The Canadian Corps, which belonged to Foch's Reserve Army, had been undergoing a special course of training, and had not been in the line for some time. They were nicknamed " Foch's pets " on this account. During the week preceding 8th August they had tramped southwards under sealed orders. Tremendous secrecy enveloped their movements, which took place at night time only; during the day they lay hidden in woods. Only senior officers were given a list of the names of the villages through which they would pass, and before dawn they were off the road and the lists were burnt. As a final precaution against leakage of information, orders were given the day before the long march that the Army Post Office would not accept any more letters from the troops.

In order to deceive the Germans, parties of Canadians and Australians were sent to the north, and a Canadian casualty clearing station was erected near Kemmel. These troops purposely took part in a series of raids, in order that they could be identified by the enemy, and as a further piece of bluff Canadian maple leaf badges and Australian slouch hats were served out to British soldiers in the Kemmel and Ypres sectors. All the wireless sets of the four Canadian divisions had been sent to Flanders with instructions to use the Canadian code as much as possible, so that the German stations would get the idea that the Canadian Corps were about to attack in that region. There had also been a huge concentration of tanks in the St. Pol area, and on very fine days, when enemy aeroplanes were about, Canadian troops practised continually and ostentatiously with the tanks.

All this camouflage succeeded admirably. Every

THE CANADIANS

one in the region was firmly convinced that the British were staging a vast attack near Kemmel, and the rumours grew so strong that King Albert, in command of the Belgian Army on the left of the British, visited the Army Commander and indignantly asked him why the Belgians had not been informed of this great offensive, and why they were not taking part in it; while the Canadian Headquarters in London complained to the War Office that the Canadian forces were being divided and sent to different parts of the line, without their consent !

In the meantime the Canadian artillery had moved into secret positions very near the line, guns, gun-pits, and ammunition dumps being heavily camouflaged. Not a single gun had fired ; they were waiting for the dawn of 8th August to open out together in one vast hurricane of destruction.

Every German gun position was well marked. Some of their batteries had been shifted, but although we knew this quite well, our guns in the line continued to fire on the deserted positions in order to give the enemy the impression that we were half asleep, and thus lull him to a false sense of security.

Now the long preparations were nearly finished, and zero hour was approaching rapidly as the huge tanks nosed their way along the crowded road. They had to go delicately, for with the new one-man drive they could turn and swerve very quickly, and in the darkness it was the easiest thing in the world for a flick of their mighty tails to knock over a wagon or crush a party of weary soldiers.

I saw one tank turn slightly to the left in order to give more room on the road. Its tail just touched a motor lorry that had suddenly come up behind. The chassis crumpled up like an egg-shell, and the lorry was left stranded right across the middle of the road, blocking all traffic. Soon great confusion prevailed, neither limbers nor lorries could move forward, and the congested mass of vehicles effectively stopped the plodding infantry. Everybody was in a desperate hurry to be under cover before dawn. Angry voices filled the darkness, bitterly cursing the tanks.

The commander of the offending machine decided that it was time to act, and act quickly; the carcass must be shifted at once. A steel towing-rope was brought down from the roof, hitched on to the great hook at the back of the tank, and then attached to the front of the broken-down lorry. A few grunts and snorts, and the tank drove off the road, lightly pulling the lorry with it. Limbers and lorries, cavalry and infantry, surged forward once more, then the tank crept down to the road again and quietly joined the great stream that was flowing forward.

During this long trek I walked for part of the time with a young lieutenant, a mere boy, who had just joined the battalion. He was a quiet, earnest lad, somewhat gentle and shy, who felt rather bewildered by the strangeness and excitement of the approach march. He asked many questions, and was very grateful for anything I could tell him. As it was very dark I could not see his face, but he told me his name—Lieutenant Cassels, and I promised to meet him when his tank had reached its objective.

In order to prevent damage the field telephone wires along the road had been raised to a height of ten feet, just sufficient to clear the roof of a tank. On one machine the company cook was dozing on top of the tarpaulins, when one of these wires caught him round the waist. Feeling a distinctly nasty pain in his stomach he awoke with a start, found himself slipping, and grabbed frantically at the nearest part of the roof. He let go at once with a mighty yell. He had touched the almost red-hot

THE HI-HI BIRD

exhaust pipe! Meanwhile, as the tank went steadily forward, the pressure on the wire had increased, until it had become as arched as the string of a bow. When the unlucky man released his grip on the tank the wire suddenly straightened out again and shot him clean through the air like a stone from a catapult. Luckily he landed in the middle of a hedge, and except for a few scratches he was unhurt, but he was vastly scared!

As the tanks neared their lying-up places the heavens became full of a loud droning. A flight of low-flying aeroplanes with very noisy engines had been sent up to drown the noise of their approach.

On reaching the wood which was to hide them until the hour of attack, the three companies split up; the machines nosed their way into the undergrowth at their allotted places, engines were switched off, tarpaulins and camouflage nets were draped over the bulky forms. The Canadian machine-gun officers, who had been waiting for us, were introduced to the tank commanders; all the officers lay down to rest beneath a large tarpaulin shelter made of branches, and soon they and the crews had settled down for a couple of hours' sleep before the battle.

I sank at once into a deep sleep, but a moment later, as it seemed, I was aroused by the deafening noise of an engine almost overhead, and an agonized voice yelling, "Hi! hi!"

It was a tank coming right on top of us!

Half asleep, I made a dive for the opening. Something struck me heavily on the shoulder. The track of the tank! To escape being crushed to death I plunged madly forward, and then opened my eyes with a start. In the dim light I saw a strange sight. I was some ten yards from the shelter, with my blanket still clinging to me. Several other figures were near by, staring round with startled looks on their faces. Two yards away another officer was hanging on to the branch of a small tree by one hand, but before I could open my lips he swayed and fell fainting to the ground. The entrance to the shelter was littered with blankets. Every one, though fast asleep, had heard that strange engine and that warning voice, and, half awake, had darted out in panic to avoid being crushed to death.

But no engine was running, the nearest tank was twenty yards away, and every machine was silent and still. Nobody had shouted. What could it have been? We discussed the strange affair excitedly, but could come to no conclusion. There was something sinister about those mysterious noises. Was it an omen? Some one broke the silence by a bright remark. "It must have been the hi-hi bird." We laughed in a slightly forced manner. A cold breeze swept through the wood, the darkness was slipping away, a voice said excitedly, " Listen ! "

We heard a low growl, which deepened to a roar and then burst into furious thunder. The air trembled with pity. The battle had begun; even now the first line of tanks was sweeping forward to the attack.

CHAPTER 17

The exploded dump—Zero hour—A receipt for a village—Tiny and Co.—The great cruise of Musical Box—Thrilling raid of armoured cars—Flotsam.

AFTER the triumphant rehearsal at Hamel, General Rawlinson of the Fourth Army had accepted the model of a tank battle, and had planned to attack on a front of eleven miles. No less than four hundred and twenty fighting tanks were lying hidden in the woods behind the line. Every valley, every wood was packed with guns and troops waiting for zero hour. Australian, Canadian, and British infantry were to follow the tanks, and after them field batteries were to move forward. The cavalry were appointed to race through the gaps and dash ahead into the blue.

Farther south the French were attacking, but as they had but few tanks their advance was fixed three-quarters of an hour after the British, so that their artillery bombardment should not destroy the element of surprise. Every effort had been made to keep the Germans in absolute ignorance of the Allies' plans, apparently with complete success, and then on the evening before the battle, August 7, 1918, a terrible misadventure occurred.

A company of supply tanks, loaded up with explosives, gun cotton, trench mortars and bombs, in addition to two fills of petrol each, was lying hidden in an orchard behind Villers-Bretonneux, when a chance shell set one of the tanks on fire. At once it blazed up furiously.

TANK WARFARE

The enemy artillery, their curiosity aroused, began to shell the orchard with great thoroughness. One by one the tanks caught alight, and terrific explosions rent the air, and though a rescue party plunged into the heart of the blaze their heroic efforts resulted in no more than two of the tanks getting away.

Had the enemy's suspicions been awakened? Did he think it was just an ordinary dump he had set alight, or did he know of that vast concentration of tanks and troops? Was he just waiting to forestall the attack by a tremendous bombardment of the packed woods and valleys?

Nobody could tell. All we could do was to wait anxiously until the fateful dawn. At 3 a.m. our worst suspicions seemed about to be confirmed. The enemy batteries suddenly came to life and began intense shelling, sweeping positions that they had not previously touched. He seemed to know our plans in spite of all our efforts at secrecy. Then abruptly, and without reason, the shelling died away, and all was silent again. Was it just a show of nervousness on the part of the Germans, and were we so keyed up that we unconsciously exaggerated the importance of a few stray shells?

At 4 a.m. a dense mist covered the ground. The first wave of attacking tanks were waiting now in no-man's-land. Behind the front line the new batteries had thrown aside their camouflage and were preparing for action.

Voices called dramatically through the fog, " Fifteen minutes to go." . . . " Ten minutes to go." . . . " Five minutes to go." The misty air was tense with excitement ; the gunners crouched over their guns expectantly. The last minute drew agonizingly near, the announcing voices trembled a little. " Thirty seconds to go, twenty, ten—five—Let her rip ! ! "

ZERO HOUR

Whistles blew piercingly, and the next second the guns let loose a shrieking tornado of shells on the unsuspecting Germans.

Simultaneously, with a great whirring roar, the mighty fleet of tanks started up their engines, all doors were bolted, all flaps securely shut, and with a fearsome clanking noise the irresistible wave of iron landships swept into action, steering by compass through the blinding mist.

The great wall of fire moved slowly forward, the tanks followed two hundred yards behind, and then came lines of sunburnt men in skirmishing order, lean and eager Australians, grim Canadians, determined British. Overhead aeroplanes raced to the attack, bombing the enemy's headquarters and reserve lines.

Everywhere the Germans were completely surprised. Our bluff had absolutely fooled them. In the north they had made elaborate preparations to meet an attack, but here in some places they had not even troubled to construct regular lines of defence. The sudden, fierce bombardment had thoroughly dazed the German infantry, and before they had time to recover their wits swarms of tanks rushed down on them out of the fog, killing and crushing relentlessly.

In less than two hours 16,000 prisoners and more than 200 guns were taken by our forces. The new Mark V. tanks, with their increased speed and power of manœuvre, literally brushed aside any opposition. If machine-gun nests became troublesome the tanks simply ran over them, flattening out both crews and guns; but most of the German machine gunners did not wait for such a ghastly fate: they turned and fled.

A squadron of aeroplanes worked with the tanks, dropping news of progress at the Advanced Tank Headquarters. The first message received read as follows:

TANK WARFARE

" To Advanced H.Q. Tank Corps
(per aeroplane).
" W.4.8th.

" Machine landed 8.30 a.m. reports AAA 6.15 a.m. 4 tanks seen in action on a line 500 yards west of road through C.17.b, C.11.d, C.12.a AAA 7.15 a.m. 4 tanks seen together heading E. on road beyond Hourges at C.11 central AAA 3 tanks seen together in C.6.d uncertain AAA 7.20 a.m. Green Line taken, tanks rallying to move off again AAA Foregoing report applies to 5th Tank Battalion Sector AAA 7.45 a.m. 4 tanks on road leading north out of Demuin V.25, c.4.8 AAA 1 tank at D.1.c central AAA 4 tanks at C.11.d.3.8 heading east AAA 7.45 a.m. French infantry seen in large numbers on western outskirts of Moreuil wood and French barrage on a line C.17.c, C.23.a, and C.29.a and 28.D AAA Motor transport probably armoured cars seen on road in U.26 near Domart AAA German balloon observed up just east of Caix about 8 a.m. at 1,200 feet AAA Bombs dropped in W.22.d south of Harbonnieres, target guns AAA Addressed 22nd Wing 3rd, 4th, and 5th Tank Bde. Advanced Hqrs. AAA

" Sent by aeroplane to dropping ground Advanced H.Q. Tank Corps.

" Note added.

" Cavalry and tanks in large numbers proceeding east at 8 a.m. south of Bois d'Aquenne.

" INTELLIGENCE OFFICER,
" 8th Squadron, R.A.F.
" 8.50 a.m."

With the Australians everything went like clockwork. Having had previous experience of fighting with tanks, the " Aussies " detailed selected sharpshooters to follow the tanks closely and pick off the gunners of enemy

A RECEIPT FOR A VILLAGE

field batteries which were menacing the advance. This plan was a great success, and saved many tanks from being knocked out by direct hits.

The commander of one tank battalion followed his machines on foot as far as their final objective, managing to reach the village of Harbonnieres at the same time as his leading machines. He triumphantly ran up the Australian flag in a prominent position, as a gesture of victory.

At Marcelcave the enemy put up a stiff fight, but a tank commanded by Lieutenant Percy-Eade came to the rescue and, blazing its way down the main street, crushed six machine guns and killed their crews. Having taken many prisoners and captured the village single-handed, the tank commander handed his prizes over to the infantry, but not before he had completed the transaction in a business-like manner. He made the infantry sign a receipt somewhat in this style :

"Received from Lieutenant Percy-Eade, 2nd Battalion Tank Corps, the village of Marcelcave, in fairly good condition, together with remains of garrison."

Having thus settled beyond all doubt the question of the capture of the village, Lieutenant Percy-Eade went on to tackle three field guns, which had already knocked out several tanks and were firing furiously at his own at very short range.

By clever manœuvring he managed to get his guns on to the enemy gunners, and going full speed ahead, ran straight over one of the field guns. The German artillerymen of the other two did not wait for a like fate, but scattered in terror. Next he ran boldly into the village of Bayonvillers, and by his whirlwind tactics so scared the Boche that his tank rounded up about forty prisoners.

TANK WARFARE

For one tank, with a crew of eight men, this was not a bad day's work. A couple of villages, a battery of field guns, and numerous prisoners! A year before it would have been considered a fine bag for a division of infantry.

The second phase of the attack, which began four hours after zero (8.20 a.m.), was not such a walk-over. The sun was now up, the mist had cleared, the enemy's artillery had a clear view of the attackers, and his resistance began to stiffen.

As I was that day assisting the company reconnaissance officer, I did not take a tank into action but followed on foot, and I caught up the tanks of A Company just before they were due to leave the Green Line. The enemy on this sector had had no protection beyond a few machine-gun posts, which had mostly been stamped into the ground by the tracks of the tanks, and in some places the crushed and mangled bodies of the machine gunners were lying near at hand.

The tank and section commanders were in good humour. The sun was now shining brightly, and Jerry was falling back. It seemed as if their task would be an easy one. It was true that they would not have the protection of a creeping barrage, for by this time the guns were concentrating on the villages, but it was not expected that they would meet with much resistance.

Captain Brown, called " Tiny " because he stood over six feet high, was explaining various points of the attack to his tank commanders. There was a slightly serious look on his kindly face. He was Irish, a shy and modest man with a passion for fishing. He had brought his fishing rods to France with him, and wherever he found a pond, stream, or river which might possibly contain a fish, he angled eagerly and with tremendous patience. His talk was of shooting and hunting, and of the wonderful fish he had caught on the Blackwater. He had been my section commander at Villers-Bretonneux, and this morning, as he talked, I remembered vividly an incident in that earlier battle.

Captain Brown had been running in the open, from tank to tank, under heavy machine-gun fire, and at last he had been obliged to take refuge in a trench with the infantry. Just then there came a lull in the German attack, and Tiny, who was gazing anxiously over the parapet through field-glasses, was amazed and delighted to see two brown forms creeping along through the grass in no-man's-land.

He bobbed down, excitedly called the sergeant of the infantry platoon, and thrust the glasses into his hand. " Look out there, man, and tell me what you see ! " he commanded eagerly.

Very cautiously the sergeant peeped over the top. " Why, it's only a couple of birds, sir," he said in surprise.

" Yes, my boy, two fine partridges ! What a stroke of luck ! " Tiny's face lit up with joy ; he had forgotten all about the war. He borrowed a rifle, and then made a sporting offer to the sergeant.

" Now, sergeant, we'll both take shots at the partridges, shooting alternately. I bet you five francs I get them first."

The sergeant was naturally taken aback ; he hardly expected that kind of shooting in the front line, especially when the Germans might attack at any moment. No doubt he considered this excited tank officer utterly mad, but nevertheless he thought it wiser to accept the offer.

The curious contest lasted some time, for a third party entered into the game—German machine gunners in a wood almost behind them. Every time a steel helmet showed above the parapet, machine guns opened out in disapproval, so the rivals were forced to be very wary; but eventually the birds rose into the air, and thereupon Tiny brought them both down.

Another section commander, Captain Keogh, also an Irishman, was a dapper little fellow, very quiet and conscientious, who always dressed very neatly. No matter where he was, his buttons always shone beautifully, his puttees were precisely wound, and there was never a speck of mud or a stain on his uniform. They nicknamed him "the perfect little gentleman." On this occasion he was as spick and span as if he was just going on parade, instead of into battle. He smiled broadly when somebody chipped him: "You can't beat it, Keogh, always the perfect little gentleman. No flymarks on this child, what!"

A third section commander, Captain Grove, was another tall, good-natured man, who had previously been a reconnaissance officer. He had a profusion of sandy hair and a bristling moustache. Everybody called him affectionately "Sandbags."

As we stood there talking on the sunlit hillside the order came to go forward. I wished them all good luck, the Canadian machine gunners clambered on board, and the line of tanks, their engines roaring ominously, sped on to the attack.

Success was in the air. The Australian infantry, full of daring and enterprise, never missed an opportunity presented to them by the tanks. Field batteries were overrun, canteens full of wines and light beer were taken intact, officers and men were cut off and made prisoners in their messes and billets, an entire divisional staff was captured, and a train loaded with troops was surrounded and the passengers forced to surrender.

Many tanks were fired at by machine guns hidden in

THE VOYAGE OF "MUSICAL BOX"

the standing corn, but they soon trampled through the crops and crushed their opponents. Near one village a machine-gun nest in an isolated building was causing much trouble. A tank treated the building to a heavy dose of fire, but still the machine guns chattered. The tank commander lost patience and, racing his engine at top speed, deliberately rammed the building. Three times he charged, until the walls tottered and collapsed on top of the German machine gunners, and nothing remained but a pile of bricks and rubble.

The small whippets, ninety-six in number, did useful work, but were unable to take full advantage of all their wonderful opportunities, because the cavalry, to which they were attached, were often held up by solitary machine guns. So the light and speedy whippets were forced to mark time. Instead of forging ahead five to ten miles in front of the infantry and thoroughly scaring and demoralizing the enemy, they were tied to the heels of the unarmoured horsemen, who every time serious machine-gun fire was met were forced to retire to avoid extermination.

When they were able to get going on their own initiative, the whippets accomplished remarkable feats, their outstanding exploit being the thrilling voyage of the famous whippet *Musical Box*, commanded by Lieutenant Arnold.

This machine, which belonged to B Company, 6th Battalion, started out at 4.20 a.m., and catching up with the first line of advancing Mark V.'s and infantry, came under heavy fire from a four-gun field battery. Two of the Mark V.'s were knocked out, so Arnold, greatly daring, ran diagonally across the front of the battery at full speed, firing heavily with both Hotchkiss guns. Reaching the shelter of some trees, he turned sharply to the right and descended on the battery from the rear.

Utterly surprised, the gunners bolted, but the whippet's guns soon laid them low.

Musical Box then went forward again, passing through two of our cavalry patrols and rooting out snipers from the corn. A party of Germans were firing from the parapet of a bridge at the cavalry, but the bold whippet ran up on the bridge and killed most of them with one burst of its forward gun. Lieutenant Arnold then raced into a valley of huts, surprised the Germans as they were packing up, and cleared the entire valley. Although they were now a long way ahead of our troops, a gunner actually got out of the tank and calmly counted the casualties, which amounted to over sixty.

From this time the lonely whippet, with its bold crew of only three men, carried on a war of its own. It shot down retiring infantry, attacked horse and motor transport, and regularly terrorized the bewildered Boche, although petrol from the spare tins carried on the roof began to run down inside, and this, with the great heat, obliged the crew to breathe through the mouthpieces of their respirators.

At last they were surrounded and under tremendous fire from all sides. A revolver port cover was shot away, leaving a gaping hole. Arnold acted at once. Withdrawing his forward gun, he locked the ball-mounting and held the body of the gun against the danger spot. So for a few minutes longer they fought back the enemy. Then *Musical Box* was hit by a shell and burst into flames. The driver and gunner collapsed, but Lieutenant Arnold dragged them out on to the ground. They were all on fire, and the ground near them was one big pool of flaming petrol. They got up to run from the blaze. One man was shot and killed, Lieutenant Arnold and the other man rolled over and over on the ground desperately trying to extinguish the flames.

ARMOURED CARS

Angry Germans surrounded them. Arnold was bayoneted in the arm and knocked down by a rifle butt, both were severely kicked, and finally they were marched away, their captors striking Arnold in the face because he refused to answer any questions.

For eleven hours *Musical Box* had skirmished and fought, entirely unsupported, and this frail little craft, with its crew of three daring men, caused more panic and destruction behind the German lines than any squadron of cavalry.

The armoured cars belonging to the 17th Battalion Tank Corps plunged into the thick of the fray and had some exciting adventures.

The day before the battle they were a hundred miles away, working with the French Army. At 9 a.m. they received orders to report to the Australian Corps, and, speeding along unfrequented byways, they arrived at Amiens the same evening. They were ordered to wait until the Australians had made a break in the German line and then to race through, search for all German headquarters, seize every document they could find, and shoot every German at sight.

They were towed across no-man's-land for a distance of two and a half miles by heavy tanks, and then, getting on a main road, pushed rapidly forward. Near Warfusee-Abancourt several large trees, knocked down by shell-fire, lay across the road, barring the way. Again their heavy brethren came to their assistance and hauled away the obstacles. The road being then clear and free from shell holes, the armoured cars went full speed ahead, ran past our attacking troops, and, greatly daring, raced through our barrage.

They were now well behind the enemy's lines, and their appearance created great consternation and panic. The infantry scattered before them, and they chased car loads of highly excited German staff officers through the village of Foucaucourt.

At Proyart their visit was so unexpected that they found the German soldiers at dinner in their billets. They shot through the windows of the houses, killing and wounding the alarmed troops, who fled in all directions. The road ahead became so blocked with the vehicles of the retreating enemy that the cars could advance no farther, but a few of our aeroplanes, flying low over the congested roadway, sprayed the unhappy transport drivers with machine-gun fire, causing indescribable confusion.

Going back in reverse, the armoured cars spied large groups of German infantry who were retiring before the vigorous Australian advance. As these men were coming in their direction, the cars hid in the outskirts of the village. When the Germans were about one hundred yards away, they emerged from their hiding-place and, racing forward, shot them down by the score. Thereupon the bewildered Jerries, absolutely astounded at being attacked from the rear, fled hastily across country to Chuignolles, only to encounter more armoured cars that fired at them mercilessly. Near this village one car indulged in " running practice " against a lorry-load of German soldiers, keeping up its fire until the lorry ran into a ditch.

Some of the cars crept up quietly behind German transport vehicles, absolutely unsuspected until they opened fire at point-blank range.

By noon one section had penetrated as far as Framerville, nine miles from our front line. They had shot their way through batches of retreating Germans, who were by this time completely disorganized, and made for the German Corps Headquarters, situated in an old farmhouse.

There they found all the horse transport and many

lorries drawn up in the road ready to move off. Frightened out of their wits by this sudden appearance of British cars, the leading drivers fled in one direction and the tail of the column in another, blocking the road and causing complete confusion. Shooting rapidly, our cars killed or scattered the lot. From the leading car a bold officer then jumped out, revolver in hand, and darting up the steps of the farmhouse dashed into the front room. It was empty. He saw another door, strode over to it quickly and flung it open. The room was full of papers; he had found what he wanted—the office of the Corps Headquarters! Rapidly seizing every document he could find, he stuffed them into sandbags and dashed out to his car again.

Meanwhile four German staff officers on horseback had come round the corner of the road, but the car outside, with a single burst of its forward gun, toppled them all off their horses.

From the car the enterprising raider took an Australian flag, which had been brought for the purpose, and pulling down the German flag, hauled up the Australian one in its place. Then quickly scribbling out a message, he fastened it to the leg of a pigeon and sent the bird speeding home. In a few minutes the news of the raid was known to the Armoured Car Headquarters, ten miles away.

This wonderful day's work, by a handful of daring men, had a strange sequel. The valuable documents captured from the Corps Headquarters included plans in minute detail of the Hindenburg Line, and it was these plans which enabled us to break through the enormously strong defences of that famous Line, thus forcing the Germans to retreat into open country, and bringing the war to an end a little over three months later.

For his brave coup the armoured-car commander,

Lieutenant Rollings, was awarded a bar to the Military Cross which he had won earlier in the war, and thirteen years later he received another and much more surprising award. In November 1931, to his complete astonishment, he was hailed by the Press as the "Man who won the War," on account of his capture of the vital plans. He stated modestly that he had never known the importance of the documents he had seized, he had merely done his duty as ordered; but a tremendous surprise was in store for him, perhaps an even greater surprise than that which was inflicted on the German Headquarters Staff, for he was publicly presented with a sum of £5,000 by the generous Lady Houston, in commemoration of his daring raid.

. . . . . .

The great attack, so long and carefully planned, had succeeded beyond our utmost expectation. Indeed, success was so swift, and the casualties of the infantry so light, that it seemed hard to believe we had dealt the Germans a deadly blow. But deadly it was. General Ludendorff, the German Commander-in-Chief, called the 8th August the "black day of the German Army."

Those of us who had seen the British troops reel back under the mighty attacks of the German armies in March and April never imagined for a moment that a few months later we, in turn, should be smashing through the German lines and driving them to defeat.

In the spring we had lost nearly 300,000 men, and been forced to retreat as much as forty miles. The huge gaps in our armies had been filled by reinforcements, many of them mere boys under military age, who had been rushed out from England in a desperate effort to stem the tide. When eventually the great German advance slowed down, and some sort of line had been formed, we only hoped to be able to keep the field-grey hordes at bay until the spring of 1919, when the Americans would have arrived in force.

Yet here we were, four months afterwards, attacking with confidence. It seemed too good to be true.

Following up the advancing tanks on foot, across practically open country, is a strange experience. At one moment one is walking through an apparently peaceful countryside; a few minutes later, round the corner of a wood, one is suddenly plunged into the heart of a battle. And on this great day the air of unreality about the whole business was even stronger than usual. The sun was hot, the fields were yellow with ripening corn, and the leafy woods offered their cool shade invitingly. Groups of Canadian soldiers were trudging by. They belonged to a British Columbian regiment, and were a strangely mixed crowd. Some were obviously of Japanese descent, whilst others had the proud, motionless features of the Red Indian. The latter were carrying their packs by a strap round the forehead, a method supposed to be much easier and more comfortable than having the whole weight resting on the back.

I came to a German field dressing station, built underground, and, revolver in hand, went down the steps. It was apparently deserted, but from one corner I heard a low moaning. I walked over and pulled aside a blanket. A young flaxen-haired German was lying there, gazing straight up at me, but there was neither fear nor recognition in that agonized stare. Two other Germans were lying in bunks near him. They were all twisting with pain and groaning horribly. The battalion doctor was with me; he glanced at them with a calm, professional gaze. "Shot in the stomach. They won't last long," he said, and turning away searched for lint and bandages which would be useful to him later on.

TANK WARFARE

In some of the dug-outs, scooped out of the side of a valley, the rough tables were laid for breakfast, the plates were half full of a kind of porridge, and half-eaten pieces of bread lay near by. An overturned cup of coffee showed only too clearly that the breakfast party had been suddenly interrupted and had fled in haste.

In another dug-out, which was evidently an office, a pad of message forms was lying on the table, an unfinished message on top. " Very urgent," it ran. " Send Under-officer Schwartz up at once with two wagons. We have just time to . . ." and there the message came to an abrupt end.

Here and there on the grass were lifeless bodies in field-grey uniforms. Their waxen faces gazed at the bright sun with a stolid, unblinking stare. Equipment, rifles, cartridges, strewn all over the fields, marked the path of the retreating enemy.

A little distance away from this abandoned valley I saw a rifle sticking up from the ground, and an arm waving excitedly. I went over and found a Canadian soldier lying on the ground, wounded in the leg. He was a funny-looking little man, and he shouted to me in a shrill, squeaky voice :

" Mind your step, sir. There's a sniper in the tree-tops in that wood over there. He got me a minute ago."

Then we knew that fighting was taking place near at hand. We came to the top of a small hill, and spotted a tank some two hundred yards away. As we gazed through our field-glasses we could see the tank nosing this way and that, and the Canadian soldiers following warily with bayonets fixed. Beyond the tank little black figures were scampering along, making for a wood. Some fell to the ground and did not rise again.

Suddenly the tank was enveloped in a cloud of mist.

FOLLOWING TANKS ON FOOT

"They are throwing out smoke bombs," said my companion.

We went on to the rallying-point and waited for the return of the tanks. Twilight descended, but only one had appeared. Its sides were covered with bullet marks. It had reached Le Quesnel, but the German machine-gun fire had been much too heavy to allow the Canadian machine gunners to be dropped, so back they had come.

They staggered from the machine in a semi-asphyxiated condition; some had been vomiting, and others were on the point of fainting. The extremely hot and close atmosphere of a tank interior on a sunny August day, combined with the cordite and petrol fumes, had soon bowled them over, and as they slowly came round, they swore forcibly and repeatedly that never again would they travel in tanks, not for all the generals in creation!

For the first time the infantry had realized that going into action behind the armoured walls of a tank was not exactly "roses all the way."

CHAPTER 18

The faithful servant—The man of peace—" Slippery " in a tight corner—The perfect little gentleman—Buried alive—Fruits of victory.

HOUR after hour we waited at the rallying-point, but no more tanks returned. Uneasy forebodings of disaster grew upon us, and the sultry night became oppressive with gloom. What could have happened? When darkness came German aeroplanes bombed the valley incessantly, and we sat in a captured dug-out despondently listening to the crash of bombs outside.

At dawn we went forward to find our lost comrades. Not one of the four section commanders had returned, and ten tank commanders and their crews were still missing.

Captain Brown's batman had preceded us. He worshipped his master. At Cambrai, when Tiny failed to return, Private Boyson went forward the next morning and found him with the infantry in the trenches, where he had been forced to shelter. During the March retreat he rarely left his master's side, and a bullet hole through his sleeve gave evidence of his devotion. At Villers-Bretonneux he was badly gassed, but after being given an emetic by the French, recovered enough to return alone across the heavily shelled battlefield to search for his captain. Again he found him in the front line trench. Now, once more, before anybody else was astir, he had gone out on his lonely quest.

A MAN OF PEACE

We saw a couple of men slowly coming towards us, carrying a stretcher. As they drew nearer I recognized one of them as Private Boyson. The faithful servant was bringing home his master for the last time. His face was the picture of grief; he could not speak for sorrow, but shook his head slowly as if to forestall any painful questions. I understood, and without saying a word walked to the stretcher and lifted up the ground-sheet.

Tiny lay there motionless. His jaw was hanging loose. They had found him in front of a knocked-out tank, an ash stick in his hand. Unarmed he had walked ahead of his tanks to certain death. I covered up that body from which a great soul had fled, and the stretcher bearers went sadly on their way.

As I silently watched them go my thoughts sped back to that day, a few months before, when he had asked me to accompany him through a gas-drenched wood to an infantry brigade headquarters. In the deserted glades, foul with decay and poisonous fumes, he opened his heart to me. "I asked you to come because I was afraid to go alone," he said. "I hate war like poison. Some fellows seem to revel in it; but every time I go into action I want to turn round and run away. I am really a coward. But it's no use, we have got to go through with it to the end." The brave and noble words were the confession of a man big enough to admit his fear, a man of peace, who had already won the Military Cross and bar for bravery in action, but was haunted by fears of being afraid.

Living up to his sense of duty, and fighting down his fear, he had walked forward alone, ahead of his tanks, to guide them on to their objectives, with no other weapon in his hand than a stick. The German machine gunners must have watched him with amazement and then ruthlessly riddled him with a storm of bullets. Thus perished the bravest man I ever knew.

TANK WARFARE

We were not long now in discovering why the tanks had failed to return. Their huge carcasses were strewn all over the countryside. As they climbed the slope beyond Beaucourt they came on to a piece of land as flat as a billiard table. The French had not advanced as quickly as the Canadians, and so on the right flank the German guns were intact. The Corps had *not* foreseen this eventuality, and field guns hidden in a copse near Le Quesnel caught the monsters one by one at point-blank range.

The gunners could not miss such targets. One after another the shells tore through their walls, the loose tins of petrol inside flared up immediately, and the packed cargoes of humanity were either burnt alive or shot down mercilessly as they tried to escape through the sponson doors.

Lieutenant Oldham lived up to his nickname of Slippery. Captain Grove (Sandbags) was in his tank when it was suddenly hit and set on fire. This was the tank I had seen from the distance enveloped in smoke, which I thought came from smoke bombs. The machine flamed up with one great roar, and in a few seconds the interior was a furnace.

Slippery and Sandbags made for a sponson door and somehow scrambled through, dragging with them a man who was on fire. Directly they got outside the door the German machine gunners blazed away at them. They took shelter beneath the tail of the tank, lying flat on the ground. They managed to extinguish the flames on the burning man, but in doing so Sandbags raised his head and was caught by a stream of bullets. He screamed like a rabbit and died. Slippery, stretched out flat on the ground, dared not make a movement. Just above his head the burning tank flamed and roared. The heat was intense. The burnt man groaned in agony at his side, whilst deadly machine-gun bullets kicked up the ground a few feet away.

It was the tightest corner Slippery had ever been in. He lay there waiting for death, for at any moment the tank, which carried a charge of guncotton and many bombs, might be blown sky high. But luckily the Canadian infantry were not far behind. They came to the rescue. Slippery escaped with burns and a grazed skin—a bullet actually went through the seat of his riding breeches—but his thirst for adventure was never again so keen.

Nearly every tank had been gutted by fire. We did our best to identify the dead, but it was a heart-breaking task. Sometimes all that we found was a few steel helmets on the floor, and underneath each helmet a charred pile of bones. The day before they were young and strong, exulting in life; now nothing remained of that proud flesh but a handful of ashes. They had utterly vanished into the lists of " missing, believed killed."

I found Captain Keogh a few yards in front of a tank. He, too, had walked to death, another victim of the Robertson tradition. He was lying on his back, his eyes wide open, and there was no obvious wound on him; but for his complete stillness you would have said that he was resting. He did not see me, but stared fixedly over my shoulder at the bright sky beyond. His thoughts were far, far away in another world. Behind him there was a great hole in the cab of the tank where a shell had ploughed through. It must have passed within an inch of him. We discovered a small bullet wound below one knee. Either the shock of the hurtling shell had killed him immediately, or else he had slowly bled to death.

Even death is not sacred on the battlefield, for the brutes had stripped him of his Military Cross ribbon and ransacked his pockets. The " perfect little gentleman "

TANK WARFARE

lay there rumpled and untidy, but on his face there was a look of quiet happiness.

When the tank he was guiding had been hit and set on fire, the crew and the Canadian machine gunners had made desperate attempts to escape from the burning machine. Men had run out in all directions, but it was hopeless. Being completely surrounded, they were shot down like rats. One man was lying at full length with his hands above his head; another, crouching behind a dead horse, had been shot through the head from the rear.

Of all the cruel deaths provided by war none can be quite so agonizing as some the tank crews met that day. One man had just escaped out of the sponson door, when a bullet hit him and he was unable to move another inch. He leant in agony against the side of the tank, and the hungry flames, leaping out of the door, had licked his defenceless flesh and slowly roasted him alive. His back was like a lump of well-done steak.

One driver had been blown right into the engine, and we could not extricate his remains. The tank commander, Lieutenant F——, whom I knew very well, was not to be seen, but on his seat lay a skull and a couple of bones, and as the skull looked very much like his, which was prominent owing to his baldness, we placed it in a sack and buried it under his name.

When on leave in London, a month later, I met a friend of his from another company. We talked about the death of F——, and he told me a surprising thing. "I wrote a letter of condolence to his parents," he said, "and to my astonishment they wrote back saying that they had heard he was not dead but wounded and in hospital." "You can take it from me," I replied, "that he is dead. I buried him. But if you get any further news let me know."

A few weeks later I had a letter to say the parents

A DEAD MAN COMES TO LIFE

had discovered that the Lieutenant F―― in hospital, although bearing the same initials as their son, belonged to a different battalion; they had heard from another source that he was wounded and a prisoner. I thought it wiser not to destroy their hopes.

A year afterwards, when the war was over, I attended a battalion reunion dinner in London. A friend came to me smiling. "There is some one over here who wants to see you. He says that he has an account to settle with you." I walked over, and a familiar voice said, "I have a bone to pick with you. You buried me! What are you going to do about it?" I stared in amazement; there, standing before me in the flesh, was Lieutenant F――. He roared with laughter, and then told me what had happened. When the tank was hit he was wounded and lost consciousness. When he opened his eyes he heard the flames roaring angrily, and the sounds of moaning and groaning all round him. Through his mind there ran one thought: "I must get to the door or I shall be burnt alive." He dragged himself painfully along the floor, the flames leaping above him, and, after what seemed an eternity, managed to reach the door and pull himself up. As he did so a German helmet appeared in the doorway and the cold muzzle of a revolver was thrust against his temples. He fainted away again, and remembered no more until he woke up next day in a German field dressing station.

I was immensely pleased that he was alive and well, but I could not keep my eyes off his bald head for the rest of that evening.

The Mark V. Star tanks had one sensible feature: a trapdoor in the cab, immediately above the seats in front. This enabled men to escape who would otherwise have been completely trapped.

TANK WARFARE

One officer, whose tank had been hit several times and the driver killed, set the machine going straight for a wood near by. Then he and his crew jumped out on the side away from the enemy, and ran beside the tank, completely protected until they reached the shelter of the wood. The huge driverless machine lumbered on, knocking down trees and bushes, until it came to a standstill against a clump of trees of heavy girth.

As we proceeded on our melancholy task, sorting out the dead, we realized only too well what a mistake had been made in employing these extra-large tanks on the flank of the battle, and in making them carry loose tins of petrol inside. The German artillerymen, safe from attack, could not have wished for easier targets. The Canadian infantry were fully justified in their opinion that the machines were death-traps, and never again were they used for the purpose of carrying troops.

We could not help also recalling to our minds the strange episode of the "hi-hi bird." It seemed to have been a mysterious warning, for no less than three-quarters of the officers sleeping beneath that shelter were dead within twenty-four hours, and nine out of eleven tanks knocked out by the Boche artillery.

The last tank we approached was far ahead of the others, headed straight for a copse near Le Quesnel. It had discovered the field guns that were causing so much destruction, and had bravely raced straight at them. When only a hundred yards away it had been hit by a shell with such force that the officer's head was blown right off and his body hurled clean out of the tank. I had to search his pockets to identify him, and I found a letter addressed to Lieutenant Cassels.

The name seemed very familiar. Then I remembered that quiet and eager boy with whom I had walked for part of the approach march; it was his first time in

A RENDEZVOUS WITH DEATH

action, and I had promised to meet him at the rallying-point. Now here we were. I glanced at his poor headless body. I had never seen his face by daylight and now it was too late, but the memory of his keen and gentle voice rings in my ears for ever.

Shells began to drop plentifully near at hand, but we were too numbed by our terrible task to heed them. For me nothing existed but roasted flesh, charred bones, and mutilated bodies. Was victory worth such a terrible price?

"Look," said the padre, and touched my arm. Two hundred yards away, on the other side of the Amiens–Roye road, scores of figures were running forward, bayonets to the fore; the French were attacking. We watched them indifferently.

The padre looked inside the tank and closed the door, shuddering.

"I can't stick any more of this," he said; "I have had enough. Let us get back."

We walked slowly back over the field, and came to a copse. To our surprise it was full of Canadians, crouching on the grass in expectant attitudes. An officer was seated on a tree-trunk, whistle in hand, gazing intently at a watch. He started when he saw us. "Where on earth have you sprung from, Padre?" he asked in an amazed tone. We told him. He pointed out over the field in the direction from which we had just come. "Do you see that wall over there? That's the cemetery of Le Quesnel. The Boche are behind there. We are attacking in five minutes."

Unwittingly we had been walking about no-man's-land.

We returned to bury our comrades in one long pit, with blankets for their shrouds. Even as the padre was reading the burial service, we heard the fierce rat-tat-tat-

tat of machine guns. . . . The Canadians were launching their attack.

At that same moment the newspaper boys were racing and shouting down Fleet Street and the Strand. Excited people eagerly grabbed a paper and read the unbelievable news. The shouting spread to the City and the West End.

" Great British victory ! Piper ! "

" Triumph of tanks ! Piper ! "

London thrilled with joy. The end was in sight at last. . . . We looked down at the row of still forms, and wondered what it all meant.

" Ashes to ashes . . . Dust to dust . . ."

" Great British victory ! Piper ! "

CHAPTER 19

Tank crews sorely tried—A lame tank—A one-man tank—Never say die!

THE Battle of Amiens lasted for another three days, during which every available tank was used to the utmost, and the attack penetrated more than seven miles ; but by the third day, 10th August, when only sixty-seven tanks were still fit to go into action, the British troops had reached the edge of the old Somme battlefield, which was plentifully pitted with shell holes, and the enemy's resistance hardened.

By this time some tank crews had been continuously in action for three days, and the whole Corps was becoming thoroughly exhausted by its tremendous efforts, for the scorching sun outside, and the terrific temperature inside, made the Mark V. tank almost unbearable after three hours in action. The ventilation was bad, the fumes of petrol and cordite soon impregnated the close atmosphere, drivers collapsed on their seats, gunners fainted at their guns ; many vomited and grew delirious. Often the heat and fumes became so overpowering that the crew were forced to get out and take cover underneath. Headaches and giddiness attacked the uncomplaining men, and many had alarming palpitations of the heart, but doggedly they stuck to their task ; if tanks were wanted by the infantry, all who could go into action went without a murmur of protest.

On the fourth day a mere handful of surviving machines was employed with the Australians, and shortly afterwards all the tanks were withdrawn to refit.

TANK WARFARE

During those four days 688 machines had been in action, and of the survivors no less than 480 had to be handed over to salvage, whilst all the remainder required a complete overhaul.

They had accomplished marvels. British generals suddenly became loud in their praises, whilst the astonished Ludendorff issued reams of excuses to account for the unexpected German defeat: " Troops allowed themselves to be surprised by a mass attack of tanks, and lost all cohesion when the tanks suddenly appeared behind them, having broken through under cover of a natural and artificial mist." He went on to criticize the woefully inadequate anti-tank defences, and recommended numerous remedies.

A German divisional order was more frank: "Counter-attacks against hostile infantry, supported by tanks, do not offer any chances of success, and demand unnecessary sacrifices; they must therefore be launched only if the tanks have been put out of action."

But the German soldier was already fully aware of this. His feeling of confidence in his leaders had received a tremendous shock. After the great attacks of March, April, and May, in which the irresistible German Army had gone from one success to another, he had been promised a final victory that would destroy for ever the weakened forces of Britain and France. Instead, he suddenly found himself vigorously attacked and driven back in confusion by these same enfeebled armies, led by a fleet of tanks against which he was practically powerless.

Strange incidents occurred during this fighting. One tank was hit by a shell and the driver wounded in the knee, but he continued to drive until a second shell hit the front of the tank with such force that it blew the driver and the tank commander backwards off their seats. Suddenly bereft of its guiding hand, the machine lurched heavily down a gully, completely out of control, and turned right over. A fire broke out immediately, but in spite of the awkward angle at which they were placed, the crew managed to put out the flames. Then, though heavily shelled, they toiled and sweated until the tank was righted, when they succeeded in bringing her safely back.

A tank of the 2nd Battalion had an adventurous trip on 9th August, under the command of Sergeant W. E. Smith, who had been in action throughout the whole of the previous day. Near Rosières a shell hit the left sponson, disabling the gun and wounding two men, who were sent back to the dressing station. Sergeant Smith then prowled into the railway yard, knocked out a machine gun and proceeded to clean up the station. He suddenly noticed a 9.2-inch gun on a ramp with Germans all round it, and charged it at top speed, but the gun crew did not wait ; they fled in terror.

The tank then came under heavy enemy fire, receiving four more direct hits, one of which damaged the left epicyclic gear so much that it was now impossible to turn to the left. As the battered "bus" still went forward an even more serious defect developed, for it refused to run straight, and insisted on going off to the right.

Sergeant Smith scratched his head in bewilderment; but whilst there was life in the old "bus" he was determined to keep in action. Finally, by a little skilful manœuvring, he discovered a novel method of going forward. Putting the machine in top gear he let it race ahead. Immediately it began to curve to the right. He waited until it had completed a wide curve, then clapping on the foot-brake, he swung round to the right in a circle. He then repeated the performance, and thus continued to advance, though in a very slow and peculiar fashion.

After a time he found that in spite of all his efforts

he could not keep up with the infantry, so he made for the rallying-point. Misfortune dogged him, for no sooner had he turned than a shell hit the right track, blowing off a plate and one of the links, yet by some strange freak of fortune the track still held fast, so the much-damaged landship was able to keep crawling slowly on. A few minutes later a further direct hit caught the left rear horn right on top of the driving sprocket. By a miracle this final disaster did not completely interrupt the transmission. The courageous sergeant was determined not to abandon vessel, so very slowly and ponderously the gallant " bus," battered and bruised and broken, but still moving, clawed and curved its uncertain way back to the rallying-point.

For thus bringing his landship home after a perilous voyage, in which it had been hit no less than seven times, Sergeant Smith was awarded a well-earned D.C.M.

A striking aspect of the Battle of Amiens was the intense determination of the tank crews to carry on when they could easily have retired from action as casualties. They were intent on not letting the infantry down, and to achieve that object they often fought to the last man and the last round of ammunition.

One tank was nearing its objective when a shell exploded a dump of gas shells near at hand, and the whole crew were gassed except two men, who contrived to carry on. The driver collapsed at his post, but the two dragged him from his seat and drove the tank out of the gassed area. Opening the doors, they then carried out the unconscious men, one by one, and by means of the first-aid ammonia phials pulled them round again, meanwhile mounting a Hotchkiss gun near by to defend themselves against attack.

The crew responded to the treatment after a time, and without hesitation they all returned to the tank and went

A BRAVE DRIVER

on into action. They had not gone far when the two rescuers fainted from exhaustion, but they, too, recovered eventually and, though feeling very weak and dizzy, manned their guns once more. They did not wait for orders, for whilst it was physically possible they were determined to pull their weight. The tank attained all its objectives. With such a crew it could hardly do otherwise.

A brave driver saved another tank from destruction. The "bus" was approaching an enemy battery of machine guns. All its guns were firing at top speed, the tank had been in action for several hours and the heat was intense; the German machine guns skilfully succeeded in knocking out every Hotchkiss gun in the tank. A perfect fury of armour-piercing bullets swept the tank's sides, the interior rained with splinters, and under this terrific fire and the tremendous heat the crew, one by one, collapsed. In a fainting condition the driver put the engine into fourth gear and charged down upon the machine-gun battery. At top speed the heavy tank, with its crew of unconscious men, crashed through barbed wire and ruthlessly flattened out the troublesome nest—only just in time, for the driver, his task accomplished, fell from his seat unconscious.

When tank crews who could fight no longer were lucky enough to be taken prisoners they did not always receive the best of treatment, for the Germans saw in the merciless monsters of iron the instruments of their defeat. One tank, which had been hit several times, was at last completely knocked out in the midst of the enemy, and three of the crew who escaped alive, though wounded, were captured at once. The Boche stripped the defenceless men of their clothes, took away all water and food, and left them shivering in a shell hole.

They had not, however, reckoned with the tank

spirit. One of the men, Private Vernon, was only slightly wounded in the arm, and could easily have made his way back alone to our lines, but such a thought never entered his head. When darkness came, he cautiously crept out to seek for food and water and something to cover up the nakedness of his seriously wounded comrades. For forty-eight hours he tended them, foraging nightly for scraps of bread to keep them alive, and sacks to prevent them dying of exposure. At the end of that time they were rescued by a party of advancing Canadians, who were amazed to find the wounded men still alive after undergoing such hardships, and were emphatic in their praise of the selfless conduct of Private Vernon. He earned the Military Medal and the lifelong gratitude of his two comrades.

Hardly had the tanks been withdrawn from the Amiens front than they were called on to fight farther north, and there was no time for thorough repairs, for rehearsal with the infantry, or for reconnoitring the ground. Luckily many of the officers knew the region from having fought over it in the spring.

In the Battle of Bapaume, on 21st August, old Mark IV. tanks, Mark V.'s, and whippets worked together. In all, one hundred and ninety tanks attacked, with remarkable effect, for large parties of the Germans surrendered immediately the machines raced towards them. On the other hand, the German artillery concentrated on the advancing machines, and though this enabled the infantry to go forward with few casualties, the unwelcome attention by no means pleased the tank crews.

On the following days the area of the battle spread to the south and the north, until the First, Third, and Fourth British Armies were all attacking. Everywhere the Germans fell back, until the fury of the fighting

THROUGH THE WIRE

reached a climax when the immensely strong Drocourt-Queant line was pierced on 2nd September.

The tanks easily ploughed a way for the infantry through the great belts of wire, and met with no great opposition. The German machine gunners appeared to have no stomach for fighting tanks, and surrendered freely, one company of tanks alone destroying seventy machine guns. What this meant to the infantry is well shown by the following description of the battlefield after the attack, which is given by Mr. Winston Churchill in *The World Crisis.—Part II.* :

" I walked over the Drocourt–Queant line, and went on up to the extreme high-water mark of our attack. I noticed several remarkable things. The Drocourt–Queant trench was strongly held with Germans, and it was a very fine, strong, deep trench. In front of it was a belt of wire, nearly one hundred yards broad. This wire was practically uncut, and had only little passages through it, all presumably swept by machine guns. Yet the troops walked over these terrific obstacles, without the wire being cut, with very little loss, killed many Germans, took thousands of prisoners and hundreds of machine guns. Three or four hundred yards behind these lines was a second line, almost as strong and more deceptive. Over this also they walked with apparently no difficulty and little loss. Behind that again, perhaps a mile farther on, were just a few little pits and holes into which German machine guns and riflemen threw themselves to stop the rout. Here our heaviest losses occurred. The troops had got beyond the support of the tanks, and the bare, open ground gave no shelter. In one small space of about three hundred yards wide nearly four hundred Canadian dead had just been buried, and only a few score of Germans. . . . You would have been shocked to see the tragic spectacle of the ground where our attack for the time being withered away. It was just like a line of seaweed and jetsam which is left by a great wave as it recoils."

The passages through the wire which enabled the infantry to advance easily were, of course, made by the tanks.

Throughout this period, from 21st August to 2nd September, many tanks were hit by the German anti-tank rifle, a cumbersome weapon mounted on a tripod and firing large armour-piercing bullets; it was $5\frac{1}{2}$ feet long and weighed 36 lbs., and its "kick" was so great that the German troops were very chary of using it. Iron stockades, concrete walls, carts full of stones, and buried mines were also encountered, but these obstacles were much less feared by the tank crews than the terrific heat, which rendered the badly ventilated tank more like a furnace than a fighting machine.

After an hour's running on a sweltering day the exhaust pipes became white-hot and the joints began to warp, thus releasing quantities of carbon gas into the already fume-laden interior. Men became delirious and then fainted, and when they eventually recovered consciousness they suffered for a time from complete loss of memory and utter exhaustion. In the small whippets the heat, being more highly concentrated, actually caused the ammunition to swell so much that the guns were jammed, and many rounds exploded inside the machine. Often the machine guns became too hot to hold, and sometimes the steering-wheels scorched the drivers' hands. Altogether, during those August days of blazing sun the tanks well earned the name given them by a Canadian soldier who once had the misfortune to go into action as a passenger. His phrase was brief but very expressive: "A regular pocket-hell."

A ONE-MAN TANK

At Bihucourt, on 23rd August, Private Bussey, belonging to a whippet battalion, set a wonderful example of grit and determination. His tank had not long been in action when the tank commander and the sergeant were wounded. He carefully carried them out of the machine and placed them in a safe shell hole, where they could easily be found by stretcher-bearers. As a whippet has only a crew of three, Private Bussey was now alone. "What shall I do?" he thought. The other whippets were racing ahead into the fight, and the sight of them decided him. He jumped in, started up the engine, and drove full speed towards the enemy. In a few minutes he was in the thick of the fighting. Locking his back axle, he left the tank to steer itself whilst he blazed away with both guns. He was truly a man of infinite resource, for, single-handed, he drove the machine and fired the Hotchkiss guns alternately for four hours. Then proudly he brought his whippet home. His great feat shows what powerful weapons one-man tanks would be if the guns and the driving were electrically controlled.

As the infantry advanced, the approach marches of the tanks became longer and longer, and the fatigue of the crews was proportionately increased, but their resolution was unshaken.

On 24th August Lieutenant Walsh took a tank into action in the morning, reached his objective, and returned to the rallying-point thoroughly worn out, after covering a distance of over twelve miles. Four hours later he was ordered into action again. Uncomplaining, the crew started up the engine and, going at top speed, reached the new point of attack in an hour and a half. Briskly the tank set to work and mopped up many nasty machine-gun nests, but when dusk came the infantry was held up.

TANK WARFARE

Whilst crossing a sunken road in the twilight, the engine gave out, and the tank was stranded two hundred yards in front of our lines. Immediately the enemy surrounded it and deluged it with phosphorous bombs. All the kit inside caught fire, and the poisonous fumes made the atmosphere unbearable. Lieutenant Walsh ordered the crew, except one man, to evacuate.

The undaunted pair then fought down the fire, and managing to start the engine up again, turned the "bus" for home, but by this time the fumes made it impossible to stay inside, so putting the tank in bottom speed, they clambered out and walked in front between the horns. Lieutenant Walsh was on the point of collapse, but stalwart Gunner Perry held him up and urged him forward. The enemy followed them, but the desperate pair kept them at bay by shooting right and left with their revolvers. Looming close behind them the empty tank blundered slowly forward; all around in the dusk hostile forms clustered; there was the sharp crack of rifle fire, the staccato rat-tat-tat-tat of machine guns as a hail of bullets beat against the steel horns, just above their heads.

The weary men, one supporting the other, staggered slowly on, fighting every inch of the way. Every second there was a loud report as a revolver flashed in the semi-darkness. Gradually the enemy closed in on them, and the dauntless two were forced to climb into the tank again. Luckily the fumes had slightly cleared, and they were able to drive the "bus" safely home, after fighting in two actions and covering twenty miles in one day. For this great feat of endurance and dogged resistance Lieutenant Walsh was awarded the D.S.O., and the faithful Gunner Perry the D.C.M.

CHAPTER 20

Crossing the Canal du Nord—The attack of the wooden tanks—
Peace at last—The flag reaches Cologne.

AFTER 2nd September the weary tank battalions were withdrawn to rest and refit; but they came into action again a fortnight later, and from this time until the end of the war they assisted in all vital attacks, though in ever-dwindling numbers.

The casualty lists grew daily. In many battalions N.C.O.'s were given charge of tanks because there were not enough officers available, and General Elles had to inform the Minister of Munitions that the machines possessed by the Tank Corps would see out the men in 1918. It was only too true. The tank men, he said, were killed and wounded in considerable numbers, and the permanent wastage of personnel was high. A smashed-up tank could be repaired and sent into action again, but a dead man was dead for ever.

The niggardly policy of the War Office was bearing full fruit. After the brilliant victory of 8th August the authorities, suddenly shaken from their stupor, hastily decided that the Tank Corps should be increased at once, but it was too late: a tank battalion requires at least four months' training, and by the time new battalions were ready the war was over. There was nothing for it but that the survivors of the existing battalions should plod doggedly on, watching their chances of coming out alive grow fewer and fewer, but never shrinking from their duty.

TANK WARFARE

Meanwhile the great forward movement which Foch had begun so brilliantly on 18th July continued almost unceasingly, and by the end of September 1918 the Allies were hammering against the great Hindenburg Line—with the plans of it in their possession. This powerfully fortified line was many miles long, and in some places ten miles deep, and a whole series of attacks had to be launched against it, by the Americans between Verdun and the Argonne, by the French between the Argonne and Rheims, and by the British to the north.

The British had to attack along the Canal du Nord, where every possible step had been taken to meet them. The canal was a dry one, 15 feet deep and about 50 feet wide, with very steep brick sides, in which the Germans had cut vertical walls 9 feet deep, to prevent tanks from crossing. Thus there was a sheer drop of 9 feet, then a platform 8 feet wide, and finally a slope of 1 in 2 to the canal bed.

A plan had been formed for driving three worn-out tanks down into the bottom of the canal, and placing them side by side so that the fighting tanks could climb over them; but the decrepit veterans broke down long before they reached the canal. And the plan proved unnecessary, for the obstacles which Ludendorff himself had regarded as insuperable were surmounted by practically every tank. One battalion used sixteen Mark IV. machines, over a year old, and even these gallant old crocks scaled the steep banks without effort. In their wake came the infantry, sweeping forward to that victory which now began to dawn upon the dark horizon and to which the tanks steadily led the way, with many adventures.

A clever ruse enabled four tanks to cross the river Selle at a point where there was no bridge and all the fords were under direct artillery fire. The Germans were

CROSSING THE CANAL DU NORD

confident that the tanks could not cross. But in the dead of night, on 20th October, the Royal Engineers built a submerged sleeper-bridge which was not visible on the surface, and at dawn the tanks approached the river and calmly crawled across to the utter astonishment of the Germans. What would the British do next? Here were heavy machines swimming serenely across the water! Needless to say, the tanks sailed on to an easy victory.

As the fighting was now all in open country, the heavy "buses" were of tremendous help in crushing down hedges and fences, thus cleaving a passage for the infantry, and in night attacks the tanks' 6-pounders worked great havoc with bursts of case shot, which spread panic and death amongst the enemy. Indeed, such was the state of nerves of the German infantry as they gave way more and more rapidly before the Allied advance, that towards the end of the war the mere sight of advancing tanks created a panic in their ranks.

As tanks grew scarcer and scarcer, some of our divisions hit on the happy notion of using dummies. The Engineers made very good imitations out of canvas and wooden lathes, and strapped them on the backs of mules, which underwent a course of "tank training." Each mule was led by a man enclosed in the "tank," who had a good view from a slit in front, but no very safe position, for if his "machine" attracted shell fire he was quite unprotected.

The dummies presented a very comical spectacle near at hand, for under each machine showed two human legs, encased in field boots, and four mule's legs, but seen from a distance, in the faint light of dawn, they were most realistic. They went into action in one long line, just behind the infantry, and to make their movements more convincing light bridges were built across the trenches, so that from the distance they appeared to be climbing over the parapets.

On one occasion when they were used in large numbers, their mere appearance on the battlefield decided the day, for large numbers of Germans surrendered at once, and the remainder fled in haste. Meanwhile there had been a few very obstinate breakdowns among the "tanks," and all the skill of the drivers could not start the "mule engines" again. Some machines were seen to bound about violently, and strange noises issued from the interior. Obviously the engine was much overheated and was boiling over; or, in the words of the driver, "That —— mule did nothing else but buck the whole time."

In spite of these minor tragedies, the action was brilliantly successful, for the German report next day contained the following news: "The enemy, by using great masses of tanks, forced us to withdraw," etc.

Another little piece of bluff was brilliantly successful some days later. A section of three supply tanks, carrying bridging stores, were nearing the canal at Landrecies, when they found themselves in the midst of the fighting. The advance was held up by machine guns on the opposite bank, and one supply tank was knocked out, but the other two went boldly forward under heavy fire, followed by the infantry. Thoroughly convinced that they were fighting tanks, the German machine gunners surrendered, and our own troops were able to cross the canal.

But neither tanks nor infantry had to fight their way much farther, for on all fronts the enemy's power was rapidly crumbling. In the latter half of September the British, French, Greek, and Serbian troops of the Salonika Army had broken through the Bulgarian lines and forced the Bulgars to surrender, thus finally cutting

ARMISTICE

off the Germans from Turkey. By the end of October General Allenby's brilliant offensive in Palestine had crushed the power of the Turks, compelling them to ask for an armistice; the Italians had completely defeated the Austrians; and Austria-Hungary was in a state approaching civil war. Cut off from all help, half starved and terribly shaken, with revolution spreading in navy and army, the Germans soon realized that their position was hopeless.

The last tank action of the war was fought on 5th November, when eight whippets, the only machines the Tank Corps could get together, assisted the Guards in an attack near the forest of Mormal.

Then the Germans sued for peace, the Kaiser fled to Holland, and at 11 a.m. on November 11, 1918, the silence of the Armistice fell along the Western Front. That long nightmare of insane destruction, which had drained away the life-blood of victors and vanquished alike, was over at last, at the cost of eight million lives and fifty thousand million pounds, and the exhausted survivors could rest.

Since 8th August there had been practically one continuous battle, and 1,993 tanks and armoured cars had been engaged, of which 887 were disabled and handed over to salvage.

All these machines except fifteen, however, could be repaired. With the human element it was another tale. Some men of the Tank Corps were in action no less than sixteen times in the last three months of the offensive. During 1918, out of a fighting strength of under 10,000, 707 officers and 3,581 men had become casualties. No less than 212 officers and 1,107 men were killed during the war; these were all beyond repair.

On December 6, 1918, when the first British troops entered Cologne, they were led by the crews of armoured cars belonging to the 17th Battalion Tank Corps, and the Corps flag was the first to float proudly over the Rhine. It was particularly appropriate, for throughout the length and breadth of Germany the tank was known as " Deutschlands Tod "—the death of Germany. To the German citizens the Tank Corps colours were the real symbol of defeat.

CHAPTER 21

Tanks in Egypt—The French *chars d'assaut*—The U.S.A. Tank Corps

SO far our story has dealt only with British tanks on the Western Front, for in other armies and other theatres of war the new weapon played a very much smaller part, or did not appear at all; nevertheless there are a few more tales to tell before we can pause to ask what the tanks accomplished during the Great War.

In December 1916, at Colonel Swinton's suggestion, orders were given for twelve tanks to be sent to Egypt; but by one of these strange mistakes in which the military authorities seemed to specialize, eight old training machines, which had been in constant use for months, were shipped from Avonmouth, whilst the twelve new Mark II.'s destined for Egypt were sent instead to the training camp at Wool.

Weary as they must have been, however, the veterans were used in Palestine with a fair amount of success. At the second battle of Gaza in April 1917, owing to the Command's complete ignorance of tank tactics, the machines were given far too much to do, the eight operating on a five-mile front and having as many objectives as two battalions of tanks would have had in France. It says much for the crews' gallant behaviour, under most trying conditions, that they protected the infantry to a considerable extent; but each tank covered an average distance of forty miles across desert country, and 40 per cent. of the crews became casualties.

One tank was set on fire by a direct hit, but three men from another dashed up and managed to rescue from the flames the officer and four of the crew, whom they succeeded in carrying back to a trench two hundred yards behind. They were all three wounded by Turkish fire, yet even when their comrades were safe these stalwarts went back once more over the bullet-swept ground to save the guns from the blazing tank. For this wonderful exhibition of self-forgetfulness and devotion to duty, all three were awarded the D.C.M.

Later on, three Mark IV.'s were received as reinforcements, and eight tanks took part in the Third Battle of Gaza on November 1917.

The machines were assembled in a fig grove, some being painted white and sprinkled with sand, whilst others were covered with imitation cactus. Colonel Swinton's suggestion that warning texts from the Koran should be painted on their steel sides was not carried out !

They attacked at night, steering by compass, and though again they were given too much to do, six of them being allotted no less than twenty-nine objectives, they contributed notably to the British success. After this battle tanks were not used again in Palestine.

A representative of the Tank Corps was sent to Salonika, to report on the suitability of tanks for that theatre of war, and decided that the mountainous nature of the country, and the difficulties of supply, made it impracticable to use heavy tanks with advantage. The French, however, sent out one company of light Renault tanks, at the urgent request of the French General in Salonika, and these did good service.

It is a peculiar fact that the French evolved a tank

of their own, quite independently of the British. Colonel Estienne, who had seen Holt caterpillars hauling guns behind the British front, came to the conclusion that the weapon required to smash through the barbed wire and machine guns of the German line was an armoured caterpillar. He placed his ideas before the French Commander-in-Chief in December 1915 (a year later than Colonel Swinton put forward his plans to the War Office), with the result that in February 1916 the Department for Artillery and Munitions placed an order for four hundred armoured vehicles with the firm of Schneider. Two months later another order for four hundred was given to the St. Chamond works, for a different and heavier type of machine.

In June 1916 Colonel Estienne heard of the existence of the British tanks, and visited England to see them, and to ask for co-operation. Having decided that France should specialize in light tanks, he interviewed the Renault firm and the latter set to work to produce a light machine to meet his requirements.

In October, a month after our own tanks had been in action, the first batch of sixteen Schneider tanks was delivered. These machines were 6 metres long, weighed $13\frac{1}{2}$ tons, had a 60-h.p. engine and a crew of six, and were armed with one short 75 mm. gun and two machine guns.

The St. Chamond type weighed 24 tons, was 8 metres long, had a crew of nine, and carried one 75 mm. gun and four machine guns. It had an 80-h.p. engine with a petrol-electric drive.

Both of these types of *chars d'assaut* differed from the British heavy tank, for the track did not go right round the body, but only round the chassis, as in our whippet, so their climbing powers were limited.

They were used with varying success during 1917, and

sustained heavy losses. The St. Chamond tank generally failed to get into action.

Meanwhile Colonel Estienne, who had been promoted to General and made Commandant de l'Artillerie d'Assaut aux Armées, was trying hard to convince the French War Office of the utility of the light Renault tank, and after months of trials and delays 3,500 were ordered in June 1917—a striking contrast to the programme of 1,000 tanks approved by our War Office. The Battle of Cambrai dispelled all doubts from the French mind. It was decided to concentrate on building the light Renault; in January 1918 plans were passed to form thirty light battalions, each of seventy-five machines, and twenty-seven of these battalions were in the field at the time of the Armistice.

The handy little Renault, which was manufactured at a very rapid rate, was almost a toy tank used as an armoured skirmisher. The crew consisted of a driver who sat on the floor, and a gunner who fired a gun (either a Hotchkiss or a 37 mm.) from the revolving cupola which formed the top of the machine. It weighed only $6\frac{1}{2}$ tons, was 4 metres long, and had a peculiar skid tail of curved iron. It could travel at six to seven miles an hour, and could spin round like a top. These little machines were used in swarms, and contributed greatly to stemming the German advances in May and June 1918.

The Second Battle of the Marne, a terrific surprise blow at the Germans, was modelled on Cambrai; two hundred and twenty-five tanks attacked without preliminary bombardment, the Germans were hurled back in disorder, and their offensive power was finally destroyed. The only part of the front where the Germans beat off all attacks was opposite the XI. French Army Corps, where no tanks were used.

From that date until the Armistice French tanks,

especially the Renaults, were continually in action. General Foch had great faith in them, and issued a special order of the day : " Vous avez bien mérité de la Patrie."

The United States of America came into the war in April 1917. On September 23, 1917, plans were made to form a Tank Corps consisting of five heavy and twenty light battalions, and in May 1918 this was expanded to fifteen brigades, each brigade made up of one heavy and two light battalions. The heavy battalions were to be armed with what was known as the Mark VIII. tank and the light battalions with the Renault. The crest of the American Tank Corps was to be an angry cat, and its motto, " Treat 'em rough."

A big programme of construction was mapped out. At Neuvy-Pailloux, two hundred miles south of Paris, Great Britain and the United States were to build between them fifteen hundred Mark VIII. or Liberty tanks, so called because they were equipped with Liberty aero-engines. The armour, guns, and machine guns for these tanks were to be provided by Great Britain, and the engines and internal parts by the United States. At the same time fifteen hundred more were to be built in the United States, besides thousands of light Renault tanks and tractors.

In spite of this ambitious programme, only some twenty Renault tanks made in America had been landed in France at the time of the Armistice, but if the war had lasted into 1919 the Germans would have been absolutely swamped and overrun by masses of American, French, and British machines, for their vital importance was now so fully realized that all the factories were working at top speed, and British soldiers were released from the Army in the latter part of 1918 to work in the tank factories.

TANK WARFARE

In the Liberty tank the engine-room was separated from the fighting part of the landship by a strong bulkhead, and a conning tower was built in the centre of the fighting-room for better control. The machine was fitted with a 300-h.p. Liberty engine, weighed 37 tons, was 34½ feet long, had a speed of six miles per hour, and could easily cross a trench thirteen feet wide.

The first of these tanks was completed in the United States in November 1918, too late for the war; but meanwhile five hundred American volunteers were trained at the French depot of Bourg, and were eventually fitted out with Renault tanks, forming two battalions. They took part in the attack on the St. Mihiel salient on 12th September, where the difficult ground prevented them, for the most part, from catching up the infantry, and afterwards fought in several actions with the United States Army.

The 301st U.S.A. Heavy Battalion came to England in April 1918 to be trained under British instructors, left for France in August, and was attached to the 1st British Tank Brigade. They were equipped with the large Mark V. Star tanks, and fought with great keenness and determination in several battles. Every man was a trained mechanic, and although their discipline was of a much more free and easy nature than that prevailing in the British battalions, they were tremendously eager to learn, and very grateful for any assistance or advice.

Their fighting spirit is well displayed by an incident in the Argonne, on 4th October.

An officer, leading his tank on foot, fell into a trench and had the misfortune to be captured. Luckily he was rescued by another tank, and immediately set off in search of his own. He had not gone far when he was forced to put on his gas mask, then a shell exploded near him, knocked him out, and tore off his mask. The gas fumes seriously affected his lungs, but coming-to in about an hour, he staggered to his feet and went into action again, fighting for several hours. When at last he returned to report he was just able to gasp out: "Gee! I wouldn't have given two cents for my life out there." Then he completely collapsed.

The 301st Battalion first went into battle on 28th September, in an attack on the Hindenburg Line near Ronssoy, and during their reconnaissance on the night before the action their officers showed great zeal and efficiency in laying their tape under a continuous fire from the enemy outposts. A shell killed one officer and wounded two others, who helped each other back to the dressing station. After their wounds had been dressed, one of them, Lieutenant Neadale, was ordered to wait for the ambulance, but he quietly slipped away and returned to his job in no-man's-land, continuing to lay the tape under heavy shell-fire and gas. His work was done so thoroughly that next day some of the tanks actually had to start fighting before they reached the end of the tape, and for his determination and courage he was awarded the Military Cross.

The attack itself was marred by an unfortunate disaster. As the tanks of the 301st Battalion went forward they ran over an old minefield consisting of rows of buried two-inch trench-mortar bombs, each containing fifty pounds of ammonal. The bottoms of many of the machines were completely torn out by the terrific explosions, ten tanks being blown up and most of the crews killed. The remainder of the battalion, undeterred, went on into action and ran up against a very strong defence; only ten tanks out of the thirty-four returned to their rallying-point.

Lieutenant E. Kusener had his tank set on fire by a direct hit, four of the crew being killed. He dragged out the remaining three from the blazing tank, and, under heavy machine-gun fire, carried one who was seriously wounded back to the dressing station. He then returned and carried back a second badly wounded man, winning the Military Cross by his conspicuous bravery.

Another feat of endurance which displayed great coolness and courage was accomplished this day by Lieutenant Earl Dunning of the 301st Battalion. He was the only tank commander to reach his objective, and naturally his tank became a target for all the German artillery. After crossing the Escaut it was knocked out and set on fire by three direct hits. Although in the midst of the Germans, Lieutenant Dunning got his crew out of the burning tank, and they lay hidden in shell holes until dusk. Then he began to lead them back to our lines, crawling on all fours, flattening themselves beneath the wire, in the attempt to creep through the German machine-gun positions. Although he was badly burnt about the hands and face, Lieutenant Dunning managed to get through, accompanied by Sergeant C. Rosenhagen, and immediately they returned they insisted on reporting to their battalion headquarters, where they were able to give most valuable information concerning the German position. Lieutenant Earl Dunning was awarded the M.C., and Sergeant Rosenhagen the D.C.M. The remainder of the crew were not so lucky: they were taken prisoners.

The 301st Battalion took part in further battles, fighting with both British and American troops, and rendering great assistance to them, and many of the American commanders distinguished themselves.

Major Sasse of the 301st Battalion went into action on 8th October in a wireless tank. After driving the enemy out of Brancourt, he got out of his machine and climbed the church steeple to get a better view of the

MAJOR SASSE, D.S.O.

battlefield, and saw that the infantry were retiring under the heavy German bombardment. He therefore descended, and, finding no officer, took charge of the troops himself, stopped the retirement, and organized Lewis-gun positions on the outskirts.

A heavy German counter-attack was hurled against the village, but the infantry, heartened by the presence of Major Sasse, held their positions. The Germans came forward to the attack again, however, this time in much greater strength, and being almost surrounded, Major Sasse sent back a wireless S.O.S. for assistance. American reinforcements arrived a few hours later, in response to the call, and rescued the gallant party as they were making a last desperate stand. For his resource Major Sasse was awarded the D.S.O.

This was probably the only time in the war when troops in a tight corner were able to send back a wireless appeal for help which resulted in their rescue, and the whole incident was a striking example of the adaptability and bravery of the American troops.

CHAPTER 22

What the tanks accomplished—The infantry's battering-ram—
How they affected the Germans—A civilian force.

TANKS did not win the war, but they created conditions of warfare which made victory possible. They alone were capable of breaking through the most highly fortified trench-systems and crushing down all resistance. Tasks that would have taken the unprotected infantry week after week of tremendous effort and enormous casualties, were accomplished by tanks in a single day with but little loss of life. They also brought back the element of surprise to warfare, for attacks could be staged with them at a week's notice without preliminary artillery bombardment.

They could not, however, hold ground or continue to attack indefinitely. After three days in continuous action a heavy tank became unfit for further fighting, and its crew were on the verge of exhaustion. If we had possessed light, speedy tanks in large numbers, in the latter days of 1918, they could have continued the work of pursuing and rounding up the enemy and shortened the war by at least a couple of months; but this work had to be carried out by the foot-slogging infantry, who naturally could not advance fast enough to cut off the retreating Germans completely, and cavalry flung through the gaps made by the tanks were soon brought to a standstill by handfuls of determined machine gunners.

The tanks really acted as a vast battering-ram for the infantry, hammering away at the German line and

THE SOLDIERS' FRIEND

denting it heavily, until a final thrust broke it down altogether.

Moreover, by flattening a path through the barbed wire and crushing machine-gun nests they saved thousands of lives, and attracted to their steel sides the concentrated fire of the enemy's artillery and machine guns, so that millions of bullets and scores of thousands of shells, which otherwise would have decimated the ranks of the infantry, expended their wrath on the uncomplaining tanks.

The infantryman, seeing the hardest part of his task so easily performed for him by these comrades of iron, went into battle with renewed confidence. He knew that he would no longer be called upon to sacrifice himself blindly against uncut wire and death-dealing machine-guns. The bloody days of the Somme and Passchendaele were over; the day of the tank had arrived.

This same machine, which on its first appearance had been ridiculed, misused, and later scorned, had quietly revolutionized the art of warfare. By the autumn of 1918, in spite of rebuffs and threats of extinction, it had come into its own; the light had shone upon those in high places at last. Infantry clamoured for tanks. On one occasion the Canadians refused point-blank to attack unless their friends the tanks led the way. A weary brigade, withdrawn for a much-needed rest, was called back to the battlefield, and half-exhausted crews went into action once more in their battle-scarred machines. The creed of the tankmen was, " Never let the infantry down."

Even in the last few days of the war, when Jerry was falling back rapidly, tanks were continually in request. Crack divisions like the Guards insisted on tanks following up the advance, on account of the great moral effect the mere sight of them had on the men.

TANK WARFARE

That this effect was fully realized by the Germans, although they possessed only about fifty tanks in all, can be seen from a note issued by the XVII. German Army : " Our own tanks strengthen the *moral* of the infantry to a tremendous extent, even if employed only in small numbers, and experience has shown that they have a considerable demoralizing effect on the hostile infantry."

The Allied Commander-in-Chief, General Foch, was a great believer in tanks, and made them the basis of his brilliant surprise stroke at Soissons on July 18, 1918. The tactics employed were those used at the Battle of Cambrai. Without any artillery preparation the French X. Army, preceded by two hundred and twenty-five tanks, struck a lightning blow at the enemy's exposed flank. Completely surprised, the Germans were forced to withdraw and abandon all hopes of a further offensive. It was one of the turning points of the war, and indeed the motive power that everywhere turned the Allied plans from defence to offence was the invaluable tank.

A few days later, on 24th July, Foch made a vital suggestion in a note to the Allied armies : " Aviation and tanks should receive the greatest development possible."

That tanks were fully appreciated by some politicians is proved by the following extract from a letter to Mr. Lloyd George, the Prime Minister, which was written from France in September 1918 by Mr. Winston Churchill, and is quoted in the latter's *World Crisis* :

" Up to the present there have only been about 18,000 men in the Tank Corps, and they have only had 600 or 700 tanks to use in action. It is universally admitted out here that they have been a definite factor in changing the fortune of the field and in giving us that

THE TANKS' ACHIEVEMENTS

tactical superiority without which the best-laid schemes of strategists come to naught.

" It is no exaggeration to say that the lives they have saved and the prisoners they have taken have made these 18,000 men the most profit-bearing we have in the Army. . . .

" Every time new success is gained by their aid there is an immediate clamour for large numbers. The moment the impression of that success passes away the necessary men and material are grudged and stinted. I repeat that there ought to be 100,000 men in the Tank Corps. . . ."

Beside these expressions of faith we may set a quotation of cold facts from one of Sir Douglas Haig's dispatches, which will show what the British Commander-in-Chief thought of tanks at the end of the war. He is writing of the months August to November, 1918 :

" On the different battle-fronts 187,000 prisoners and 2,850 guns were captured by us; also over 29,000 machine guns. These results were achieved by fifty-nine fighting British divisions, which in the course of three months of battle engaged and defeated ninety-nine separate divisions.

" Since the opening of our offensive on 8th August tanks have been employed on every battlefield, and the importance of the part played by them in breaking up the resistance of the German infantry can scarcely be estimated. The whole scheme of the attack of 8th August was dependent upon tanks, and ever since that date on numberless occasions the success of our infantry has been powerfully assisted or confirmed by their timely arrival."

In the days of the Somme we attacked with double the strength of the enemy and failed to break him, yet

TANK WARFARE

in 1918 fifty-nine British divisions defeated ninety-nine German divisions, an achievement which would have been impossible without the aid of tanks. Truly the 10,000 fighting men of the Tank Corps were easily worth an extra dozen divisions to the British Army.

The Germans themselves were under no illusions in the matter. At first they pretended to ignore the tanks, but as one mighty blow after another was rained on them by the battering-ram of iron they grew afraid. The German official communiqués attributed the success of the Allied attack to the employment of " masses of tanks." The infantry, knowing that they could do nothing against them, developed " Tankschrecken " or " Tank fear " ; their bullets had no effect on the iron sides of these charging monsters, and they realized only too well that resistance was hopeless. The feeling that their attackers had the sole use of a powerful weapon, and the fact that their generals ascribed all their defeats to the use of that same weapon, gave them a sense of inferiority before a battle started—the kind of feeling that a knight in armour must have inspired in a bowman.

The German Staff feverishly devised anti-tank defences. A German Army Order, issued after the Battle of Amiens, was full of urgent instructions :

" The Enemy now relies chiefly upon tanks for the success of his attack. This weapon can only be overcome by the strictest attention to prescribed counter-measures. Specially selected look-out men are to be always in position day and night to give warning. Messages *re* attack by tanks are to be given *absolute priority*, and are to be sent immediately to the artillery, which is especially detailed to fire on tanks. An officer is to be appointed in each trench to have charge of light-signals for warning in case of tank attack."

GERMAN TRIBUTES

One would have thought that the British Army was composed entirely of tanks !

Anti-tank guns were greatly increased, but the brilliant bombing work of the air squadrons attached to the Tank Corps nullified their efforts.

In October 1918 the German Higher Command, realizing that defeat was inevitable, issued a long statement to the party leaders of the Reichstag, the German parliament. The following is an interesting extract :

"The Higher Command has been compelled to come to the enormously difficult decision that in all human probability there is no longer any prospect of forcing the enemy to sue for peace.

"Two factors have had a decisive influence on our decision, namely, tanks and our reserves.

"The enemy has made use of tanks in unexpectedly large numbers. In cases where they have suddenly emerged from smoke-clouds our men were completely unnerved. . . .

"Solely owing to the success of the tanks we have suffered enormous losses in prisoners. . . ."

To hearten their soldiers they pretended that large numbers of German tanks would soon be available; but it was a vain promise, for they had neither the time nor the material to construct machines in sufficient numbers.

Whilst the German Higher Command, which had previously despised tanks, had been obliged to embark on a tank-building programme, the British War Office, which had at first tried to abolish tanks altogether, had laid down plans for the construction of a huge fleet of no less than six thousand machines for 1919. The force of events had actually made the professional soldier change his rigid ideas, but the conversion had come too late, for

TANK WARFARE

in a month the war was ended. In 1921, when there had been time for reflection and investigation, General Von Zwehl returned his verdict: "It was not the genius of Marshal Foch that defeated us, but 'General Tank.'"

These achievements, so openly acknowledged by our opponents, were accomplished not by a highly disciplined professional army, but by a small body of men, not twenty thousand all told, who were practically all civilians, for not more than a little over two per cent. of the Tank Corps were regular soldiers, though fortunately that two per cent. included some of the finest brains in the British Army. The General Staff officers were nearly all regulars, but the Administrative and Engineering Staffs contained only one regular officer—a state of affairs which would have been tolerated nowhere else in the Army.

In the strict sense of the word the Tank Corps leaders were not fighters. They did not come from the infantry, cavalry, or artillery, but, luckily for the tanks, from that hard-working and unassuming body of men, the Royal Engineers. Woolwich gave its best to the Tank Corps. The idea of tanks sprang from the fertile brain of one sapper, General Swinton, who commanded the original Heavy Branch Machine-Gun Corps, and he passed on the torch to another young sapper, General Elles; whilst in the background, scheming, planning, and organizing was the far-sighted Colonel Fuller.

These officers had one quality in common: they were not afraid of new ideas. Moreover, they were young and not hampered by tradition; Field Service Regulations were not their only gospel, but merely a stepping-stone to a more advanced creed. They fought for that creed tooth and nail, and in the end their faith was justified. They saw the despised "Cinderella" of the Forces, who was given all the dirty work to do and received no thanks for it, gradually rise in fame and achievement until she became the favoured daughter of Whitehall and Downing Street.

The men of the Tank Corps were the most highly trained soldiers in the British Army, for every private had to be an expert in driving and mechanism. He learnt how to handle the 6-pounder, the Lewis and Hotchkiss guns, he went through signal, revolver, and compass courses, and had to be versed in the difficult art of reconnaissance—all these subjects in addition to the ordinary infantry training.

A tank man was not taught to do things by numbers; he was not a military automaton. When in action each member of a crew had to carry on with his own particular job in his own particular fashion. There was no time to wait for orders. The discipline of a Guards regiment would have been thoroughly out of place in a tank. I remember the remark made by a Brigadier-General of the Tank Corps after inspecting the 1st Battalion: " Your discipline is very poor, but your fighting record is the finest in the Tank Corps." There was a twinkle in his eye as he spoke.

The *moral* of the Tank Corps, in spite of periods of profound depression, was very high. They escaped the nerve-racking monotony of trench life, and when resting, their life was made pleasant by games and not overburdened with drill.

When they went into battle they always led the attack. They were used to fighting with the storm troops of the Allied Army—the Moroccans, the Australians, the Canadians, the Foreign Legion, and the Guards. Their steel walls gave them a sense of security, and their faith in their machines inspired them with great confidence. But they were not puffed up with pride, they often had insults hurled at them, they felt that the Tank Corps was perpetually on trial, and so, quietly and without any fuss, this " gang of greasy mechanics " fought and died. The tracks of their clumsy monsters of iron have stamped themselves indelibly on the history of the world.

CHAPTER 23

Post-war machines—Mechanized warfare—Cross-country lorries—
The amphibious tank—The pole-jumping tank—The four-track tank—The Halger-Ultra bullet—Tanks in the future—Destruction or peace ?

AFTER the war the Tank Corps was reduced to four battalions with Mark V. machines, and by 1920 these machines were becoming worn out, and the decisive part played by the tank in the war was rapidly becoming forgotten, so once more there was talk of dispersing the Corps.

The tank authorities decided to try for a reprieve by constructing a lighter and faster machine, which would attract the attention of the Press and the War Office by its speed. So the Vickers light tank was introduced. It weighed 12 tons, was 17½ feet long, and was fitted with a 90-h.p. eight-cylinder Armstrong-Siddeley engine. It consumed 1½ gallons petrol per mile, and attained a speed of 20 miles per hour. Its radius of action, without a refill, was 130 miles, as compared with 12 miles of the old Mark I.; it was armed with one 3-pounder gun and two machine guns, and it carried a crew of five. It spanned a gap of six feet as against the Mark V. ten feet, and its tracks were sprung. Improved patterns of this tank are in use to-day, for it saved the Corps from the sentence of death, and since then steady advances have been made in tank design and in the general mechanization of the Army.

In 1925 plans were made for one-man tanks which could act as scouts for the fleet of heavier tanks, and after much experiment it was decided to construct a tank for two men, one to drive and the other to act as a gunner.

From these proposals emerged the modern Carden-Loyd two-man tank or tankette, as it was first called when it appeared on the scene in 1927, a tiny machine weighing two tons, with a speed of twenty miles per hour, and costing only £500. A later pattern, now called the light tank, is fitted with a 21-h.p. motor, developing 60 h.p., and attains a speed of thirty miles per hour.

Some units are also equipped with the Carden-Loyd armoured machine-gun carrier, which runs on tracks but is not covered in on top, and this handy little machine has recently been adopted by the Canadian Army. In addition to the carrier there is a tracked trailer, to carry extra men and equipment, and a wheeled transporter. When long distances are to be covered the carrier is run on to the transporter, which is then hooked on to the back of a lorry.

The United States Army is equipped with a heavy tank of 23 tons, having a crew of four, a speed of 12 miles per hour, one 6-pounder and two machine guns; and with a light tank which has a radius of 80 miles, a speed of 18 miles per hour, and carries a crew of two.

The French, who were first in the field with the light tank, the famous Renault, have now twenty-five tank battalions, and during recent manœuvres their tanks distinguished themselves in an attack on a mountain fortress by climbing through pine forests and actually crossing a glacier before tackling the snow-clad slopes.

Germany's tanks were taken away from her after the Armistice in 1918 and handed to Poland, and by the Versailles Treaty she was forbidden to construct others, but she still manages to have tank manœuvres, using dummy tanks consisting of baby cars covered with tin and cardboard.

MECHANIZED WARFARE

In England, however, their original home, tanks have not been regarded too favourably since the war, and it is due largely to the efforts of one man that we still lead in tank construction. Major-General Fuller, the Tank Chief of Staff during the war, the man who was mainly responsible for the entirely new and brilliantly successful tank tactics at Cambrai, Hamel, and Amiens, has devoted his life to fostering the growth of the ideas he helped to bring into being, and he has been preaching the gospel of mechanization up and down the country for the past fourteen years.

Like so many men ahead of their time he has found great difficulty in getting a hearing, but within the last few years his work has begun to bear fruit. A Mechanical Warfare Establishment has been founded at Aldershot, where new ideas and improvements are constantly being tried out, and on General Fuller's recommendation light tanks have been introduced into India for use on the North-West Frontier, where they will be invaluable in breaking up the invasions of fierce tribesmen, operations which used to cost hundreds of lives.

Arising from the experience gained in the war with supply and gun-carrying tanks, great experiments have been made with cross-country tractors and lorries for transporting troops and supplies over rough country.

In 1927 an experimental mechanized brigade was formed consisting of Vickers tanks, armoured cars, light tanks, mechanized artillery, a mechanized machine-gun battalion, and mechanized Royal Engineers, including signals and wireless. This self-contained force has taken part in manœuvres on Salisbury Plain, much has been learned, and, as a result, four brigades of field artillery and all the first-line infantry transport of the British Army have been mechanized.

The artillery is being provided with the new Carden-

TANK WARFARE

Loyd light two-ton tractor, a remarkably powerful machine for its size, which can haul heavy guns and limbers over the roughest country with ease. It is similar to the chassis of the light tank, and whilst attaining a speed of over twenty-five miles per hour, can do nearly seven miles to the gallon. What few people realize is that the cost of a mechanized field brigade is much less than that of a horsed brigade.

The mechanized infantry are carried about in buses and lorries, whilst the horse-transport has now been converted into six-wheeler lorries, with independently sprung wheels which enable them to go across country, and detachable tracks for use over rough slopes and ditches.

A heavy lorry has also been recently produced by Vickers-Armstrong which can carry six and a half tons of goods and haul a trailer loaded with another three and a half tons over any kind of country. It represents the last word in cross-country transport, and is a direct descendant of the tank, for it moves on double half-tracks, can cross desert sands, go through swamps, climb rough slopes, and ford streams or ditches. To traverse very swampy ground it can be fitted with special swamp plates. Its engine is air-cooled, and its tracks have a life of from two thousand to three thousand miles.

Nothing has proved the remarkable strides made in British motor engineering more than a test made in Egypt and Africa between January and April 1932, by an experimental War Office convoy.

The vehicles included a 6-wheeler Crossley 30-cwt. lorry, a four-wheeler Commer 30-cwt. lorry, a Morris commercial 15-cwt. van, and a 9-h.p. Riley car. They were all overloaded, yet they covered a distance of 5,600 miles, mostly across desert sands, bush, rocky hills, and gullies and even greasy ground. In fifty-four days'

MOUNTAINEERING

running only four hours' delay was caused by breakdowns, and though the temperature was in some places over 100 degrees, no boiling occurred. It was indeed a great triumph of the motor industry.

More recently, rigid hill-climbing tests of tanks, machine-gun carriers, armoured cars and lorries have been carried out in the mountains of North Wales. All vehicles carried full loads, and had to tackle gradients of 1 in 3, stopping and starting again in the middle of steep slopes, but practically every machine passed the test without overheating or clutch trouble.

These tests have shown that the army can definitely base its mechanization, apart from fighting machines, on vehicles now being produced by British motor manufacturers for ordinary commercial purposes. It can thus make quite sure that large numbers of cross-country vehicles would be immediately available in the event of a war.

The progress of mechanization has had one very beneficial result for the infantryman, for as warfare is being speeded up he will naturally have to move at a quicker rate than formerly, and this necessitates reducing the weight he carries. During the war the foot-slogger was a regular beast of burden, trudging along with a load which was almost two-thirds of his own weight. In future the infantryman will wear lighter clothing, his water-bottle will be so designed that it can fit into his mess-tin, and his bayonet, instead of being carried in an awkward scabbard, will be smaller and be fixed to the rifle, folding back on a spring like the blade of a penknife. The greatest change of all will be in the iron ration which, from 1 lb. biscuit, 1 lb. preserved meat, and small quantities of tea and sugar, will be reduced to one small concentrated tablet.

When these changes take place he will be a real light

infantryman, and for his good fortune he will have to thank the first " Willie " that blundered over the shell craters of the Somme in 1916.

The Mechanical Warfare Establishment has lately made great strides, also, in devising new and highly efficient tanks.

The latest heavy tank with which the Royal Tank Corps is being equipped is a speedy 16-ton battle cruiser, with four machine-gun turrets and a central turret for a 3-pounder gun; but owing to the great cost—some £15,000—and the national need for economy, only about half a dozen of these tanks have been so far supplied. The construction of light tanks has also been curtailed, so that the present-day Tank Corps has many old machines and is sadly below strength, as the Corps was at the end of the war.

On the other hand, a wonderful new amphibious tank was introduced in October 1931. The idea was proposed by Major-General Fuller as far back as 1917, when it was highly ridiculed, and a tank which could float was actually constructed and tried out on Fleet Pond in 1922, but sprang leaks and sank. Now the idea has been more than realized, for the modern machine is not only able to swim across wide and deep rivers, but can climb up steep and marshy banks, penetrate the thickest undergrowth, and cross the roughest country.

This revolutionary landship is a Carden-Loyd machine made by Vickers-Armstrong. On land it reaches a speed of forty-five miles per hour, climbing slopes of 1 in 3 at six miles per hour, and in the water, by means of a special propeller, it travels at six knots, leaving a distinct wash in its wake. It looks much like an ordinary light tank, save for float-like mudguards made of special wood. It weighs 2 tons 15 cwt., is 13 feet long, 6 feet high, and can cross a ditch five feet wide. Its heavy armour, nine

THE AMPHIBIAN

millimetres of special plate in front, is proof against ordinary bullets at point-blank range, and armour-piercing bullets at one hundred and fifty yards, and it is rendered unsinkable by elastic water-tight joints. A special manhole in the roof enables the driver to emerge when all is clear and disappear inside when danger is at hand.

The Carden-Loyd amphibian tank coming ashore.

In its trial in the Thames at Chertsey it raced down the banks of the river and sailed up-stream against both wind and current, treating the river bank to doses of machine-gun bullets as it went. It then crawled ashore like some antediluvian reptile, and made off across country over hill and dale.

TANK WARFARE

Henceforth the great obstacle to tanks—a river—will be no obstacle at all. These swimming monsters could attack, from the water, infantry defending a river bank or engineers constructing a pontoon; or could defend our own bridging operations. They would be invaluable in the invasion of a country from the sea, for squadrons of them, carried on battleships, or, better still, in large submarines, could easily be launched off the enemy coast, and within six hours they could be over two hundred miles from their starting-points, creating havoc and destruction far in the interior. Keeping in touch with flights of aeroplanes by wireless telephony, they could be directed back to another part of the coast, where they could swim out again to the waiting ships. A series of such raids, rapidly delivered, would soon lower the *moral* of the enemy, who would never know where to expect a real invasion.

If these landships had been available for the "hush-hush" scheme of 1917, a landing on the Belgian coast would have been certain of success.

The next machine to be evolved should be a submarine tank, capable of swimming under water, crawling along river beds or the bottom of the sea, and then racing across country.

The weak spot in a tank was the track, for if only one plate were broken the whole machine was brought to an immediate standstill. To remedy this weakness many experiments have been carried out by the Mechanical Warfare Establishment, and at last a new and stronger type of track has been produced which will be fitted on all future tanks.

Another ingenious invention brought out recently is the "pole-jumping tank." A projecting arm has been added to the front of the tank, and hinged to this is a short pole, shaped like a spade, the whole thing making

THE POLE-JUMPING TANK

the tank appear to have grown a trunk. A similar contrivance is also fixed on the tank's tail. When a machine is crossing a gap and its nose is thrust out over the void, the pole in front engages the bank on the far side. Then with a sudden heave the tank vaults across, its tail being supported by the rear pole, which remains on the rear bank long enough to prevent the machine from falling into the gap.

By means of this pole-jumping the light tank, which formerly could span only four and a half feet, can now cross a gap of eight feet, and this greatly adds to its usefulness, for it is now capable of crossing ditches, streams, and trenches which formerly would have limited its range of action.

Yet another recent mechanical development is the four-track tank, which has been devised by Colonel Le Q. Martel, another clever sapper who was on the tank staff during the war, and has since been prolific in inventions. He was the originator of the "one-man tank," from which the present-day light tank was developed.

The four-track tank is long and low, looking like a dachshund, but it gets over obstacles in regular greyhound style.

With the single pair of tracks a tank can only turn by one track being stopped, so that it skids round. Moreover, when a large tank climbs over a bank or breasts a slope, its nose is tilted high in the air until the point of balance is reached, with the result that the gunners in the rear are "blind" until the tank reaches the level, while the machine itself presents a splendid target for field guns, especially against a sky-line.

In this, the very latest type of tank, the armoured fighting cab containing the crew is situated between the front pair of tracks, while the engine is at the rear. Being long, the machine can cross wider gaps than the ordinary light tank, and it runs more smoothly, because each pair of tracks can cross over a small obstacle in turn, and as the space between them absorbs the top of any larger obstacle, an easier motion is obtained which enables the gunners to get much steadier and better shooting. All four tracks are driven, and the steering is almost as easy as that of an ordinary motor-car. Altogether it is a formidable machine, for it has the speed of a light tank and the spanning power of a heavy tank, it is well armed and well armoured, and its flatness and resiliency make it a difficult target to hit.

Whilst all these new tank improvements have been going forward, Germany, forbidden to build tanks, has naturally concentrated on anti-tank defences. The result has been startling, for a few months ago she announced the invention of a super-bullet with a velocity of 5,800 feet per second, more than double that previously attained.

It is called the Halger-Ultra bullet, and was invented by Herr Gerlich of Kiel. At fifty yards' range it can penetrate five-eighths of an inch deep into thick armour plate. Fired against compound chromium nickel armourplate, half an inch thick, which resists ordinary steel-core armour-piercing bullets, this wonder bullet simply blasted its way clean through, making a circular hole about twice its own diameter. Moreover, it has a stream-line or boat-tail shape which is supposed to make it much more accurate in aim than any other existing bullet. Fired from the ordinary .303 rifle it could be used against tanks with deadly effect by infantrymen or machine gunners, apparently nullifying the tank's great advantage—protection from armour-piercing bullets.

Thus it would seem that all our brilliant tank improvements since the war have been rendered useless by one revolutionary invention, and that henceforward the

FUTURE DANGERS

tank's only protection will be its speed. But, strangely enough, the German is once again too late in the field. The new bullet will pierce armour plate of fifteen millimetres (five-eights of an inch), but some time ago a new armour was produced in England which provides forty per cent. greater resistance, so that a twelve-millimetre plate of this armour would stop a Halger-Ultra bullet at point-blank range. The latest light tanks are protected by this new armour plate, of sufficient thickness to make them absolutely secure against the Halger bullet.

With the gradual increase of mechanization in the armies of the world, there is no doubt that if any nations are stupid enough to commit again the folly of going to war, tanks will play a large part in deciding the result.

Fleets of tanks will then meet in action, and the tactics of naval warfare will reign on land. Light, speedy scouts (two-men tanks) will be sent forward to reconnoitre and skirmish, and then throw out a smoke-screen behind which the medium machines will endeavour to attack the enemy tanks in the flank, whilst the heavy battle cruisers, moving swiftly across the zone of battle, will deliver rapid broadsides against their heavy opponents.

These operations will be assisted by aeroplanes which will bomb the enemy squadrons. The whole battle will be controlled from the air by the Tank General in a hovering helicopter, who will guide his squadrons by wireless telephony. Victory will go to the side that has the best knowledge of the ground, the widest range of fire, and the highest co-operation.

On the other hand, a clever enemy might be able to render an attacking fleet of tanks entirely useless by means of powerful wireless waves. Already aeroplanes without pilots have been controlled in the air by means of wireless, and empty motor-boats sent twisting and swerv-

TANK WARFARE

ing across the sea. There is therefore every possibility that in time waves will be produced which will be strong enough to stop any engine in a given area.

Masses of swift and light tanks will also be used, not to fight the enemy's army but to attack his army and corps headquarters, and thus disorganize his entire fighting machine. This might be termed attacking the brains instead of the body, and if the brains are destroyed the body will cease to function.

Carried a step further still, attacks will be made on factories and cities. Armies cannot exist without food or shells, and mechanized armies are useless without petrol. Therefore the best way to defeat an army in the field is to cut off or destroy its source of supplies. This could easily be done by vast fleets of aeroplanes and hosts of speedy tanks making gigantic raids on army bases and civilian munition centres. Both tanks and aeroplanes could carry supplies of deadly gases which they could let loose in cities where shells, tanks, and guns were being manufactured, or food supplies stored. This would be a certain means of paralysing an enemy nation.

Perhaps in raids of this description swarms of light tanks would be carried by aeroplanes and dropped at selected points in the enemy's country; or a flying tank might be evolved which could land, fold its wings, and race across country, leaving behind it a trail of destruction before taking to the air once more.

It is most certain that in future wars the chief centres of slaughter and destruction will not be on the battlefield but in the big cities and bases which supply the sinews of war, and at the chief civilian and military headquarters from which the war is directed. The soldier himself, protected by a wall of steel and the great speed of his war chariot, will be comparatively safe.

As soon as the politicians and generals realize this

fact, as soon as they know that they themselves run the greatest risk, then war will become less likely and should finally disappear altogether as a method of settling quarrels. The only alternative is destruction, for soldiers, statesmen, and scientists agree that if all the unimaginable horrors of scientific mechanized warfare were loosed upon Europe our civilization would be wiped out of existence.

And even more appalling than the horror of war is the immense stupidity and futility of it all. The old and middle-aged declare war, but it is the young who go forth to fight and be slain.

Imagine a herd of elephants of which most of the young elephants are suddenly killed. What happens? The older beasts will sway that herd for years, because they will have no young rivals to contest their claims to leadership. Not only that, but not having to fight to retain their power they will grow fat and lazy; the herd will degenerate.

Europe is in that state to-day. The pre-war politicians with their pre-war ideas still rule in most countries. The old men have continued so long in power that they have lost the art of leadership. The younger men, who should be knocking at their doors, were exterminated by the Great War. Hence the reign of confusion, stupidity, and distress.

If, during the last war, the millions of men on both sides, who were endeavouring to massacre each other yet loathed the idea of it, had said one day to themselves, " Well, I have had just about enough of this, I am going home," who could have stopped them? The war would have ended abruptly. So if all the citizens of the world were to organize themselves now against war, refusing to take part in it, the very threat of their proposed action would prevent any future wars.

TANK WARFARE

In that anticipation tanks would naturally die a natural death, but they would not have died in vain, for even now the mechanization of the Army has produced marvellous vehicles, which should be of immense service in opening up the vast roadless spaces of our Empire, and bringing prosperity to the hitherto unapproachable wilderness.

Who knows, too, but that one day we shall all own a little runabout, a descendant of the tank, a machine that will take us wherever we want to go; one that will fly, swim, or go across country just as the fancy takes us. In that day we shall look back fondly on the old " Willie " of the Somme and say, " Even war has its uses."

THE END

GLOSSARY OF TANK TERMS

Approach March.—The journey from the point of assembly to the starting-point. (Illustration on page 1.)

Assembly Point.—The spot near a railhead where tanks gathered before going up the line.

Ball-socket.—The machine-gun mounting shaped like a sphere used in tanks. It could be swivelled in any direction, and when the guns were taken out it could be completely closed, leaving no gaps or crevices for bullets to penetrate.

Beam, Boom.—See "Unditching Beam," page 308.

Bellied.—When the belly of a tank was caught on a tree stump, or a similar obstacle, so that its tracks failed to grip the ground, it was bellied.

Bolo.—An officer who clung tightly to a job at the base. He generally suffered from battle-shyness.

Case-shot.—A collection of small projectiles, including particles of lead linked together by tiny chains, enclosed in a 6-pounder shell case with a flat end. Often fired at short range with great effect. Had the same results as buck-shot among birds.

Camouflage Net.—A net dyed various shades of green and brown, dotted with tags representing leaves, which was thrown over a tank to give it the appearance of a clump of foliage when seen from the air.

Comb-out.—To wade through machine-gun nests, wiping out a few *en route*.

Conning.—The steering of a tank, especially over difficult country.

Crib.—A strong hexagonal-shaped framework of timber braced with steel, weighing 12 cwt., carried on top of a tank and used for crossing wide trenches or shallow rivers.

Decamouflage.—To take the camouflage net off a tank.

Fascine.—A huge bundle of brushwood composed of seventy-five small bundles, 10 feet long, bound tightly together. Weight 30 cwt., diameter 4 feet 6 inches. Carried on top of tank and used

GLOSSARY OF TANK TERMS

for crossing the Hindenburg Line at Cambrai. Superseded by cribs.

Female.—A tank armed with machine guns only.

Flap.—The steel window in the front cab of a tank.

Hand Feeding.—Keeping an engine going when in action, after carburettor has collapsed, by supplying petrol straight from a tin through a rubber tube. A highly dangerous pastime.

Horn Covers.—Specially shaped tarpaulins placed over the horns or nose of a tank to disguise its shadow, and thus deceive enemy airmen.

Idle Wheel.—The wheel in the forward part which guided the track over the nose of the tank.

Jumping-off Point.—The point either immediately behind or in front of the line from which tanks went forward into battle. Also called the starting-point.

Male.—A tank armed with two 6-pounder guns and machine guns. It was wider than a female.

Mock-up.—A wooden model of a tank.

Mop up.—To destroy machine guns left behind by the first wave of attack.

Rallying point.—The spot where machines of one company assembled after an attack.

Ramp.—An incline constructed at a railhead from the ground to the level of a railway truck, so that tanks could drive straight on to the trucks.

Reconnaissance.—The art of spying out the enemy's land and planning the approach march before a battle.

Sighting Slit.—The small, narrow slit through which a tank gunner gazed over the gun-sights at his targets.

Splash.—Particles of lead from bullets which ricochetted through the sighting slits.

Splinters.—Fragments of steel knocked off the inner walls of a tank by machine-gun bullets beating on the outside. Looked like showers of sparks, and often blinded the crews.

Sponson.—A projection from the side of a tank containing a 6-pounder gun or machine guns, made to give a greater arc of fire.

Sprocket Wheel.—A wheel with cogs, or sprockets, which engaged with links on the caterpillar tracks. Situated in the tail of a tank.

Spuds.—Iron shoes fixed on the tracks for crossing muddy or greasy ground.

GLOSSARY OF TANK TERMS

Swing.—To make a full turn.

Tankodrome.—Parking place for tanks.

Torpedo-boom.—A cigar-shaped beam of wood and iron about 6 feet long clamped to tracks by chains; used for unditching tanks.

Trekking.—Taking tanks across country.

Unditching Beam.—A large beam, reinforced with iron, which was carried on top of a tank, and could be attached to tracks by chains. Used for getting tanks out of muddy shell-holes or when ditched in trenches. Replaced the torpedo-boom. (See pages 45 and 93.)

Whippet.—A small light tank. (See page 166.)

Willie.—The name familiarly given to a tank by tank men. Arose from the name of the first tank, "Little Willie"—the English nickname for the German Crown Prince.

INDEX

Aeroplane message, 234.
Aldershot, 293.
Allen, Pte., 120, 121–122.
American Infantry, 204.
American tanks, 277–281.
Amiens, Battle of, 231–262.
Anderson, Pte., 62.
Anti-Tank defences, 286.
— — rifle, 264.
Argonne, the, 278.
Armoured cars, 241–244, 271.
Arnold, Lieut., 239–241.
Arras, Battle of, 49–51.
Arthurs, Gnr., 116.
Australians, the, 56, 57, 58, 203–209, 231, 234–235, 238, 257.

Bapaume, Battle of, 262.
Batter, Mr., 2.
Battle cruiser, 296.
Battle History Sheet, 64.
Bayonvillers, 235.
Beaucourt, 222, 250.
Beaumont-Hamel, 41, 42.
Bentley, Gnr., 116.
Bermicourt, 46.
"Big Willie," 9, 11.
Bihucourt, 265.
Bion, Lieut., 146–147.
Bois de Blangy, 184.
— d'Aquenne, 185.
— l'Abbe, 184, 185.
Bourlon Wood, 134, 149.
Bovington Camp, 47, 76–85.
Boyson, Pte., 248–249.
Bray, 165.
Brown, Capt. J. C., 188–189, 236–238, 248, 249.
Budd, Gnr., 116.

Bullecourt, 55, 57, 60–61, 66.
Bussey, Pte., 265.
Byng, Gen. Sir Julian, 133.

Cachy, 188, 190, 194.
Cadet School tank, 68–75.
Cambrai, Battle of, 131–151.
Canadian Army, 292.
— Corps, 226, 231, 250, 283.
— Machine Gunners, 229, 238, 247, 252.
Canal du Nord, 268.
Carden-Loyd machine-gun carrier, 292.
— — tank, 292.
— — — amphibian, 296.
— — tractor, 293–294.
— — two-man tank (see "Tankette ").
Cassels, Lieut., 228, 254.
Chars d'assaut, 275–276.
Chinese Labour Coy., 51st, 135.
Chuignolles, 242.
Churchill, Rt. Hon. Winston, 5, 9, 150, 263, 284, 285.
Cockroft, the, 106, 108.
Colincamps, 182.
Cross-country lorries, 294.
Cugnot, M., 1.
Curlu, 181.

Debeney, Gen., 210.
Deutschlands Tod, 272.
D'Eyncourt, E. T., 6.
Divisions, 21st, 39–40, 178.
— 9th, 178.
Dodo Wood, 219.
Domart Bridge, 222.
Dummy tanks, 269.
Dunning, Lieut. Earl, 280.

309

INDEX

Edgeworth, R. L., 2.
Edward II., 146.
Elfriede, 197.
Elles, Gen. H. J., 10, 105, 133, 134, 140, 141, 202, 267, 288.
Elveden, 13.
Erin, 47, 184.

Flers, 33.
Flesquières, 146, 147.
Foch, Gen., 284.
Fontaine-Notre-Dame, 156.
Foucaucourt, 242.
Four-track tank, 299.
Framerville, 242.
Fray Bentos, 110–116.
French Infantry, 210, 231, 250.
— Moroccan Division, 197.
— tanks, 275–276, 292.
Fuller, Gen. J. F. C., 136, 204, 288, 293, 296.

Gaza, Battles of, 273–274.
Gentelles Wood, 222.
Gerlich, Herr, 300.
German tanks, 201–202, 292.
— — duel with, 184–197.
Goebel, Herr, 3.
Graincourt, 147, 148.
Grove, Capt., 238, 250.
Gueudecourt, 33, 40.

Haig, Gen. Sir Douglas, 38, 63, 285.
Halger-ultra bullet, 300.
Hamel, 205, 208, 209.
Harbonnières, 234, 235.
Havrincourt, 147, 149.
— Wood, 139.
Hayton, Gnr., 116.
Heavy Section Machine-Gun Corps, 12, 46, 93.
Hendecourt, 57.
Hetherington, Major, 6.
Hi-hi bird, the, 229–230, 254.
Hilda, the, 141, 143.
Hill, Lieut., 110, 116.
Hillock Farm, 107.

Hindenburg Line, 132–133, 143, 145, 243, 268, 279.
Hotblack, Capt., 42, 43.
Hotchkiss Machine Gun, 61, 89, 166.
Hoult, Gnr., 154, 155.
Houston, Lady, 244.
"Hush-Hush" Scheme, 94–98.

India, tanks in, 293.

Joye Farm, 91.

Keogh, Capt., 238, 251.
Knight, Lieut., 62.
Kusener, Lieut. E., 279.

Landrecies, 270.
Lateau Wood, 143.
Latham, Sergt., 54, 55.
Le Quesnel, 223, 247, 250, 254, 255.
Lewis Machine Gun, 61, 89.
Liberty Tank, 277, 278.
"Little Willie," 8.
Lloyd-George, Rt. Hon. D., 11, 47, 284.
Lorries, cross-country, 294.
Ludendorff, Gen., 244, 268.
Lulworth, 85.
Lusitania, The, 52–55.

"Man who won the war," 244.
Marcelcave, 235.
Marcoing, 144, 150.
Maricourt, 180.
Martel, Col. Le Q., 299.
Masnières, 144.
Mata Hari, 33.
Maxse, Gen. Sir Ivor, 107.
McElroy, Lieut., 149.
McKenzie, Sergt., 196.
Mechanical warfare establishment, 293, 296, 298.
Mechanized brigade, the, 293.
Merlimont, 95.
Messines, Battle of, 89.
Middelkerke, 94, 97.
Missen, Sergt., 112.

INDEX

Mœuvres, 161.
Moislains, 171.
Mole, L. E., 2.
Monchy-le-Preux, 58–60, 63.
Mont du Hibou, 106, 107.
Moreuil, 210.
Moroccan Division (see French).
Morrey, Gnr., 116.
Musical Box, 239–241.

NEADALE, Lieut., 279.
Neuvy-Pailloux, 277.

OLDHAM, Lieut., 181.
One-man tanks, 291.
Oosthoek Wood, 100.

PARSONS, Lieut., 152.
Passchendaele, 97, 99, 117, 127.
Percy-Eade, Lieut., 235.
Perry, Gnr., 266.
Pershing, Gen., 204.
Phillips, Sergt., 100–101.
Pill-boxes, 106–108.
Pirbright, 68–75.
Poelcapelle, 123–125.
"Pole-jumping tank," 298.
Post-war tanks, 291–300.
Proyart, 242.

RAWLINSON, Gen., 203, 231.
Renault tank, 276, 292.
Reutel, 120.
Richardson, Capt., 110–116.
Richardson, Pte., 146.
Riencourt, 58.
Robertson, Capt., 119–122.
Robertson, Sir W., 25.
Rolling, Lieut., 244.
Ronssay, 279.
Rosenhagen, Sergt., 280.

ST. JULIEN, 106, 118.
Salonika, 274.
Salvage Companies, Tank Field, at Ypres, 127–129.
— at Hamel, 208.
Sasse, Major, 280–281.
Savage, Pte., 66.
Selle, River, 268.

Smith, Pte. T., 161.
Smith, Sergt. W. E., 259–260.
Soissons, 284.
Somme, Battle of, 25–38.
Stern, Col. A., 7, 26, 126.
Storey, Lieut. C. E., 40.
Summers, Pte., 153.
Swinton, Gen. E. D., 4, 7, 12, 43, 48, 150, 273, 274, 288.
Sykes, Pte., 155–156.

TANK BRIGADE, 1st, 100.
— — headquarters, 138.
— — 5th, 210.
— building programme for 1919, 287.
— Cadet School, 68–75.
— Corps, 93, 291.
— — central workshops, 135.
— — colours, 141.
— — leaders, 288.
— — men, 289.
— Field Salvage Companies, 127–129, 208.
— fighting in the future, 301–302.
— hill-climbing tests, 295.
— log, 103.
Tankette, 292.
Tankschrecken, 286.
Tanks, types of:
— American, 277–281.
— "Big Willie," 9, 11.
— Carden-Loyd, 292.
— — amphibian, 296–298.
— *Chars d'assaut*, 275–276.
— dummy, 269.
— four-track, 299.
— French, 275–276, 292.
— German, 201–202, 292.
— Liberty, 277.
— "Little Willie," 8.
— Mark I., 18, 88.
— ,, II., 44, 56, 58, 273.
— ,, IV., 19, 88, 268.
— ,, V., 201, 233, 257.
— ,, V. Star, 214, 253–254, 264.
— ,, VIII., 277.

311

INDEX

Tanks, one-man, 291.
— " pole-jumping," 298.
— post-war, 291–300.
— Vickers light, 291.
— Whippet, 166, 182, 193–194, 196, 239, 264, 271.
— Willies, 8, 9, 11.
Tortille, the, 173.
Treport, 164.
Triangle Farm, 108.
Tritton, Mr., 8.
Tunnelling Coy. of R. E., 184th, 101.

" UNDITCHING BEAM," 93.
U.S. Army Tanks, 292.
U.S. Heavy Tank Batt., 301st, 278–281.

VAIRE WOOD, 205.
Vaux, 268.
Vernon, Pte., 262.
Vickers-Armstrong, 296.

Vickers-Armstrong lorry, 294.
Villers-Bretonneux, 184, 187, 194, 231, 237.
Vimy Ridge, 51.
Volckheim, Lieut., 197.
Von Zwehl, Gen., 288.

WAIN, Capt., 145.
Walsh, Lieut., 265, 266.
Wareham, 68, 75.
Warfusee-Abancourt, 241.
Wateridge, Lance-Corpl., 62.
Weber, Lieut., 52–55.
Wells, H. G., 2.
Wilson, Lieut., 8.
Wireless tanks, 140.
Wool, 47, 76.
Workshops, Tank Corps central, 135.

YPRES, Third Battle of, 94, 99, 133, 150.
Yvrench, 26.

www.ingramcontent.com/pod-product-compliance
Lightning Source LLC
Chambersburg PA
CBHW020808100426
42814CB00014B/373/J